The Gnostic Path of St. Thomas

About the Author

Tau Malachi is a Gnostic Apostle, or Gnostic Master, of a Magdala Tradition of Gnostic Christianity, one that has a rich oral tradition of Mirya Magdala (Mary Magdalene) as the Anointed Bride, or female spiritual counterpart of Yeshua Messiah (Jesus Christ), and that teaches mystical teachings of the Christian Kabbalah.

He was something of a spiritual prodigy, having a strong spiritual and mystical inclination from his early youth. In 1970, when he was eight years old, he met his spiritual master, Tau Elijah, who received him as a disciple and taught and initiated him into the Gnostic Path and Holy Kabbalah. In 1983, he founded The Fellowship, the beginning of a gnostic community, where he began teaching, initiating, and guiding spiritual seekers in the Gnostic Path as well as teaching the Kabbalah revealed to him. Today The Fellowship has evolved into Ecclesia Pistis Sophia (EPS), an international gnostic community, or Christian Gnostic "church." He and Tau Sarah are the "Sacred Tau" of the lineage and community, the living messengers and spiritual masters of the present generation.

Adding to the seven books he has written and published, along with many thousands of pages of teachings he has posted in the forums on the main website of the Fellowship/EPS, Malachi has just completed a masterwork of a gnostic transmission and revelation of Mirya Magdala that spans several volumes: *The Holy Gospel & Acts of Mirya Magdala: Teachings of Her Anointed Community*.

Engage with Tau Malachi through:

- Facebook: https://www.facebook.com/tau.malachi
- Ecclesia Pistis Sophia website: https://www.sophian.org/forum/
- YouTube: https://www.youtube.com/@ecclesiapistissophia9764
- His most recent writings online: https://www.sophian.org/index.html

The

Gnostic Path

of

St. Thomas

Exploring the Heart
of the Gospel

Tau Malachi

Llewellyn Publications • Woodbury, Minnesota

FIRST EDITION
First Printing, 2023

Cover design by Kevin R. Brown

Library of Congress Cataloging-in-Publication Data (Pending)
ISBN: 978-0-7387-7565-4

Llewellyn Publications
A Division of Llewellyn Worldwide Ltd.
2143 Wooddale Drive
Woodbury, MN 55125-2989
www.llewellyn.com

Printed in the United States of America

Other Books by Tau Malachi

The Gnostic Gospel of St. Thomas: Meditations on the Mystical Teachings
(Llewellyn, 2004)

Gnosis of the Cosmic Christ: A Gnostic Christian Kabbalah
(Llewellyn, 2005)

Living Gnosis: A Practical Guide to Gnostic Christianity
(Llewellyn, 2005)

St. Mary Magdalene: The Gnostic Tradition of the Holy Bride
(Llewellyn, 2006)

Gnostic Healing: Revealing the Hidden Power of God
(Llewellyn, 2010)

Gnosis of Guadalupe: A Mystic Path of the Mother
(EPS Press, 2017)

Dedication

To Tau Sarah, who has sojourned with me on the Gnostic Path as a most beloved companion and dear friend for decades and who is something like a "soul twin" to me. I have found her to be a very intelligent, holy, and wise woman with deep compassion who has a profoundly motherly way of teaching, initiating, and guiding people in the Gnostic Path. I feel especially blessed and delighted to have her as my spiritual sister and a best friend, and I rejoice she is present for those in anointed community with us today and those yet to be with us in the future generation of community.

Acknowledgments

It is from the Holy and Eternal One alone that Truth is revealed and known, and it is through the Holy One that the Messiah comes to be, who reveals the way to true knowledge of the Holy One, unity with the Eternal One. All praise and thanks belong to the Holy One; may all blessings and peace of the Holy One be upon Yeshua Messiah.

In the mercy and compassion of the Holy One and Messiah are the messengers and mystic saints who appear among us, who teach and initiate people in the way, who are true guides in the path to knowledge and unity—enlightenment. I was blessed as a boy to meet one of these holy and enlightened people, a gnostic apostle, gnostic master, my beloved tzaddik, Tau Elijah, who taught and initiated me into the gnostic path and Christian Kabbalah. He was as a star of heaven that shone in this world, and the grace and mercy of the Holy One and Messiah continues to shine through him to me, to the people of our gnostic community, and the world to this very day. Whatever revelation and realization I have experienced in my life, and whatever knowledge, understanding, and wisdom I may be able to share, it is because of him. May his name and memory be blessed and may the Holy One preserve his secret.

This book would not have come into being without the help and hard work of my close friend, Elder Gideon, who attended to the detailed editing of the original manuscript and follow-ups, as well as weaving a historical comment on the Gospel of Thomas. I hold deep gratitude and appreciation for all that he has done and for his spiritual companionship over the years. As he has been such a blessings to myself, our community, and the people in his life, I pray that he is blessed in the Holy One.

I also want to acknowledge all of the people of our gnostic community—The Fellowship, Ecclesia Pistis Sophia—all of my spiritual companions and friends, without whose support, encouragement, and fellowship neither this book nor any other spiritual works would be possible. Among them I am especially thankful for Tau Sarah, who has a peculiar gift of drawing out deeper teachings and revelations, powerful movements of the Spirit with me and the people of our community. Tau Sarah and the companions are a most precious and radiant constellation of souls, a truly luminous assembly in the Lord, the Spirit.

Finally, I want to thank Llewellyn Worldwide and all the people at Llewellyn who have helped bring this book to publication. The facilitation of many voices that might never reach a significant audience is a noble work and great service that seems especially important in these tumultuous and difficult times. I have deep appreciation for the place Llewellyn holds in publication and much gratitude.

Contents

Introduction

The Gospel of Thomas is very different from other gospels. It was written earlier than the four canonical gospels that appear in the Bible. Rather than presenting a narrative of the life of Jesus, Yeshua, it presents 114 verses of the Living Yeshua, something like essential heart teachings that are called *secret sayings*. Instead of focusing upon sin and the forgiveness of sin and constructing a religious doctrine around Christ as the Savior in that way, in this gospel he is the Gnostic Revealer, as it were, who comes to share the secret, the true knowledge of Christ and God, that leads to salvation: an experience of realization or enlightenment.

In this gospel, the issue isn't sin and the forgiveness of sin. Instead, it confronts the ignorance that leads to sin and death, sorrow and suffering, and points out how to dispel the ignorance and bring it to its end. This gospel teaches that the ignorance is an illusion of separation, a delusion of lack, that causes people to live in outwardness, in ego cherishing, attachment, and aversion: unaware of their inner being, unaware of Christ and God, or the Inner Light and Spirit, within themselves. From the perspective of this gospel, Christ, Messiah comes to reveal the secret, the knowledge that dispels the ignorance, the knowledge that enlightens and liberates people, souls, and that brings about their reintegration with their source: the Infinite Light and Eternal Spirit. He points us to us our innate unity with God—the Holy and Eternal One—who and what we are in God. He reveals the inner Christ, Messiah or Inner Light and Spirit within us all and teaches us how to realize and embody that Truth and Light of Christ, Messiah. It is revelation that brings true salvation, the actual realization of our soul, or our Divine Self.

As Christ, Messiah is with us, we need to learn how to go deep within to find and know Christ and God within us to experience an inward communion with Christ and God in our heart and soul. This knowledge begins as an experience of intimate nearness and then evolves into an experience of oneness—conscious union with Christ in God—Christ being realized and embodied in us, in our person and life. In gnostic teachings, in the gnostic path of Christ, the Christ, Messiah is not only incarnate, embodied, in the person of Jesus, Yeshua, but is to appear and be revealed through us as well, embodied and realized in us. We are to embody the fullness of the Holy Light and Spirit, just as Yeshua our Elder Brother, our Great Teacher and Guide did. This is the gnostic understanding of the true gospel—the good news of Christ, Messiah.

Therefore, in this holy gospel we are told that the kingdom of heaven is inside and outside of us, that Christ, Messiah is the light over all and is in all, even in a piece of wood or under a stone. We are told that whoever has intimate knowledge of Christ, Messiah and merges with the Inner Light and Spirit, Christ, Messiah will become that person. This is a very different teaching and understanding of Christ and God than what is presented in mainstream churches and the man-made religious doctrines presented throughout much of Christendom. In fact, according to Thomas, such religious doctrines, rites, and rituals will prevent true knowledge of Christ and God. They keep us outside and do not teach us how to be deep inward, to have direct spiritual, mystical knowledge of Christ and God, or to experience actual revelation and realization of Christ, Messiah within us. In one saying in this gospel, Yeshua goes so far as to say that to engage in devotions such as prayer, fasting, and charity in the way of speculative, man-made religious doctrines and formulas will actually cause psychic and spiritual harm to us and lead us into further bondage, a greater separation and lack.

You see, in most forms of mainstream religion and religious doctrines, people are taught to invoke and pray in twoness, in separation and lack, as though they are separate and apart from the Divine. However, in the Gospel of Thomas and the gnostic path—or what is also called the straight path—we are taught to be inward: Having faith in Christ, Messiah within us and more so awareness of that Inner Light and Spirit, we invoke, pray, meditate, and worship in oneness, in unity and fullness, no longer in twoness, separation, or lack. Receiving the Holy Light and Spirit—our initiation into the gnostic path—we are united and filled, unified with Christ in God, filled with the Holy Light and Spirit. We are to bring forth what is in us, we are to let our light shine. So we are taught how to be deep within and live from within, from Christ, Messiah: from the light and love that is in our inner being, our heart and soul.

This book is a journey through the sayings of the Gospel of Thomas, the commentaries being heart-essence teachings of the gnostic path, or a deeper mystical spirituality in Christ as it is presented in this gospel. In writing this book, my intention has been to share essential and straight-forward teachings of the gnostic path and Christian Kabbalah in a most simple and concise way, so that it may be easily understood by those new to the gnostic path while benefitting those who have already sojourned along the path for some time. It has been my intention to speak to you, the reader, from inwardness to inwardness, from my heart to your heart, from my soul to your soul, and for the Spirit to speak through me to you and perhaps to communicate something of the love and the light through what has been shared. What I am sharing are heart-essence teachings that have emerged from more than fifty years of travel in the gnostic path and Christian Kabbalah. It is my heart-wish and prayer that what is shared may bless and empower you in your own spiritual life and practice and be of some benefit to you in your spiritual journey.

Christian Kabbalah

Jesus, Yeshua, Yoshua—as his name is spoken in Greek, Aramaic, and Hebrew—was a Jewish man and a Jewish apostle and prophet. All of his close disciples and the majority of his followers during his life were Jewish people. As such, if he shared inner and secret teachings with his close disciples, it would have been those of the inner mystical tradition of Judaism, the prophetic tradition: merkavah mysticism, chariot mysticism, or the Holy Kabbalah. He would not have taught secret mysteries from Greek or Egyptian mystery schools, because there would be no need. The inner and mystical tradition within Judaism itself runs very deep. Jewish Kab-balah remains a vibrant and living mystical tradition to this very day and the Christian Kabbalah has strong roots in the Judaic Kabbalah. Naturally, Christian Kabbalah is an evolution of the Holy Kabbalah founded upon the knowledge of Christ, Messiah and the Holy Gospel: an ongoing revelation of the secrets of the Kabbalah in the Messiah and Holy One.

The teachings of the gnostic path in our lineage and community are a Christian Kabbalah. When we speak of Christian Gnosticism, we are speaking of Christian Kabbalah. There are a number of deeper, esoteric sayings in the Gospel of Thomas that directly express teachings of the Holy Kabbalah, which cannot be reasonably understood apart from knowledge of the Kabbalah. So this book is written from a knowledge of Kabbalah and shares essential teachings of our Christian Kabbalah.

The word *kabbalah* means "what is received," and it connotes direct and ongoing revelation and realization of the Divine: To have true knowledge and understanding of the Kabbalah, there needs to be an unveiling and self-disclosure of God within a person, revealing the secret mysteries of creation and redemption within a person's heart and soul. This knowledge, in truth, does not come from books, but from the Spirit of God and experiences of light transmission: movements of the Spirit when oral teachings of the Holy Kabbalah are being spoken by those who have the corresponding knowledge and realization.

With this in mind, you will find that we use Aramaic or Hebrew names of significant spiritual individuals in our teachings, holy and enlightened ones in the gospel who represent specific personifications of the Divine within our Christian Kabbalah: Yeshua Messiah, Mother Miriam, Mirya the Magdala, and Yohanan the Baptist. These names have deeper mystical and symbolic meanings in our Kabbalah.

Likewise, you will find that we honor the Divine and Sacred Feminine, as well as the Divine and Sacred Masculine, so we use both feminine and masculine terms when speaking of the Divine, often referring to God as Mother, for example.

A Historical Comment

The *Gospel of Thomas* existed only in fragments until found in Naj° Ḥammādī, (Nag Hammadi) Egypt, with other ancient writings in a sealed jar. The jar had been hidden in the opening of a boulder, perhaps by individual Christian Gnostics or a monastic community for safe keeping from local heresy-hunting. It was all but lost for some fifteen hundred years, until two peasant brothers dug around the base of a boulder for nitrates to fertilize their fields. Upon first discovering the jar, they stepped back in fear. There was a reason this jar was sealed and hidden—could it contain an evil spirit? The brothers had heard many stories growing up of the misfortune befalling those who opened such jars. Releasing a malevolent spirit could be as disastrous as an unearthed mine or bomb. The brothers surely pondered this while handling the jar. But what if there was gold?

Greater than all gold is the *Gospel of Thomas,* the crown jewel of a secret library named after the site of its discovery in 1945. Against the backdrop of the end of World War II, the timing of this discovery of *Thomas* is a message of hope: Here is proof for a smoldering world of the gnostic path of enlightenment and liberation. That *Thomas* and the larger part of the Nag Hammadi library later survived the fire of local superstition and the greed of those buying and selling it between Egypt and Belgium is a wonder. Like the Tibetan Buddhist tradition of *terma*—hidden teachings for future discovery at the destined time—*Thomas* is a hidden treasure without price that has come to light during modern humanity's evolutionary crisis.

The place of *Thomas* in the development of gospels as we know them is critical. Like another collection of sayings of Yeshua called *Q* (from the German *Quelle,* meaning "source"), *Thomas* was a vital source of written materials predating the canonized gospels. The first editions of *Thomas* and *Q* are believed to be from around 50 CE, making them contemporary with Paul and the circulation of his letters. The first version of gospels such as *Mark* (about 70 CE), *Matthew* (about 80 CE), and *Luke* (about 90 CE) quote and elaborate on material from *Q* and *Thomas*. If lines and ideas from

Thomas feel familiar, it's because they're the source of canonized gospels. Thomas is precious, for it's about a century older than the first emergence of the four "recognized" gospels around 150 CE. Because it predates the rise of Christian orthodoxy, it resists and repudiates everything that would come to be done in the name of Yeshua. For this reason, we can hear anew the teaching of the Living Yeshua as for the first time.

The Adaptive Translation of Thomas

I used an adaptive translation of the Gospel of Thomas from the *Gnostic Bible* edited by Willis Barnstone and Martin Meyer (Shambhala, 2003). Here and there I have chosen to change a word in a saying to clarify the spiritual meaning; I set these changes in brackets. While academic professors tend to think of disciples as being like their college students, I do not hold that view, having been the disciple of a gnostic apostle and master and serving as a gnostic apostle to my community today. Discipleship is a very different, sacred relationship than that of a mere student. It is far more intimate on a psychic and spiritual level and runs far deeper. There is a deep heart and soul connection in discipleship, a very special bond in the Spirit. So I refer to disciples as disciples, which to me is very special, holy, and sacred, unlike any other kind of human relationship. Likewise, I am inclined to capitalize words like God, Father, Mother, Son, Daughter, and so on, in direct reference to the Divine.

The words *gnostic, knower of God, gnosticism,* and the phrase *way of knowledge* I do not capitalize because there are what I would call gnostics and gnosticism within various faiths and wisdom traditions. To me, gnostics and gnosticism are universal. Those words are capitalized, however, when in reference to specific lineages and traditions, like Christian Gnostic, Sophian Gnosticism, Sufi Gnostic, and so on. For the most part, however, I have used the translation as it appears in the Gnostic Bible.

Aramaic names are preserved throughout this translation. Here is a guide to their English translations:

Yeshua: Jesus
Toma: Thomas
Mirya: Mary
Shimon Kafa: Simon Peter
Yaakov: James
Yohanan: John
Matai: Matthew

I define key terms of Kabbalah and gnosticism within the writing. For further study, please consult the glossary at the back.

Tau Malachi
Sophia Fellowship
Ecclesia Pistis Sophia
July 2022

Verse 1

"Whoever discovers what these sayings mean will not taste death."

The brief prologue introducing this gnostic gospel states that these are secret sayings that the Living Yeshua spoke to the apostle Thomas and refers to Thomas as the twin of Yeshua. In these few words, an essential key and teaching is given: how to discover and understand the spiritual meaning of these sayings.

First understand that in the gnostic path and Christian Kabbalah the name Living Yeshua, or Hayyah Yeshua, connotes the revelation of the risen and ascended Messiah, and the outpouring of the Holy Light and Spirit in the resurrection through which souls are saved—enlightened and liberated. More importantly, however, it denotes Yeshua living in us, the inner Christ, Messiah or Inner Light and Holy Spirit in us. As we will learn from this holy gospel, the Inner Light and Spirit is within all peoples, all creatures, all things in creation, even wood and stone. According to this gospel, it is through the revelation and realization of the Messiah within you, the Inner Light and Holy Spirit, that there is true salvation, the enlightenment and liberation of your soul. Indeed, in Christian Gnosticism, and the Christian Kabbalah, to have faith in Yeshua as the Messiah, the Anointed, the Son of God, is to have faith in Christ, Messiah within yourself, this Inner Light and Spirit within you. To embody faith is to seek and find and know the Lord, the Spirit, within you, then to live from and embody that Truth and Life, letting the Inner Light shine from within you, letting the Holy Spirit move with, in, and through you, taking up your person and life.

When you let this Inner Light shine, when the Spirit enlightens your mind, heart, and life and is embodied in you, manifest as you, and so is revealed through you, your person, and life, so Christ, Messiah appears in you as in Yeshua, and you are a twin resembling him, resembling the

Messiah, the Anointed of God. On a spiritual level, to resemble the Divine is to be near the Divine: the greater the resemblance, likeness, the more intimate the nearness. When there is a complete resemblance—image and likeness—there is oneness, unity with the Divine—the Infinite Light, the Eternal One. The experience of eternal life, the realization of born-less being—the enlightenment and liberation of the soul—is in conscious union with the Infinite Light, the Eternal One. In this spiritual and supernal realization when passing beyond at the end of life, souls do not fall uncon-scious or taste death, but unified with the inner Christ, Messiah, with the Eternal One, they experience reintegration with the Infinite Light—the Fullness of Light, Pleroma of Light.

The inner Christ, Messiah is the True Savior, True Teacher, and Guide, and it is through direct experience of this Inner Light and Spirit that true knowledge comes, true understanding and wisdom of the Gospel, the Messiah and Eternal One: the discovery, revelation, of what these secret sayings mean. They are secret because only the Lord, the Spirit, can give us this knowledge—gnosis, da'at—and enlighten our souls, hearts, and minds. It is God and God alone who reveals the secret of secrets to us.

Yet, in that Christ, Messiah appears through us in anointed commu-nity, and having received the Holy Light and Spirit, and awakened to the Holy Light and Spirit within us, this Holy Light shines from within us, the Holy Spirit moves with, in, and through us. There is a play of light trans-mission and the imparting of the Holy Spirit in gnostic community. The gnostic path is one of initiation, an experience of light transmission and passing of the Holy Spirit, as it was with the original followers of the Way. It is through receiving the Holy Light and Spirit—baptism of fire and the Spirit—that the inner Christ, Messiah is revealed and realized, and we are united and filled: filled with the Holy Light and Spirit, united with Christ, Messiah in the Supreme—the Infinite Light, Radiant Nothingness. Quite naturally, when we are united and filled, Christ, Messiah speaks and acts through us, manifesting as us, the Messiah being in us, and we being in the Messiah—the Holy Light and Spirit.

To experience the revelation of Christ, Messiah within you and so have knowledge of the Lord, the Spirit within you and true communion, you must believe, have faith, and you must go within, deep within, in prayer and meditation, and open to the Holy Light and Spirit, and wait upon the Spirit to reveal the Lord within you—the Messiah and Eternal One in you. You must learn how to be inward to live in an inward communion; when the Lord is revealed to you in you, so you must follow the teachings and guidance of the Lord and live according to the Truth and Light revealed to you, embodying that Truth and Light—Christ, Messiah. This is the gnostic path, this is Christian Gnosticism. It is a mystical spirituality of direct revelation, direct experience, of Christ and God, the Messiah and Eternal One; it is a path of actual self-realization, enlightenment, in Messiah. This is the salvation gnostics preach and that this holy gospel is teaching.

As we go on to the next saying and those following, seek to be inward. Open yourself to the Holy Light and Spirit, and invoke and pray before reading and contemplating what is shared. As much as you listen to and hear what is being revealed and shared, listen and hear inwardly and be open to the insights and illuminations that arise from the depths of your soul, from the Lord, the Spirit within you. Only in this way can the true meaning, wisdom, understanding, and knowledge of this, or any holy scripture, come to you: from the very same Holy Light and Spirit that inspired it, that speaks through it to you who are able to listen and hear the word of the Holy One, spoken in your heart and soul. Amen.

Verse 2

Yeshua said, "Seek and do not stop seeking until you find. When you find, you will be troubled. When you are troubled, you will marvel and rule over all."

In teachings of the gnostic path, or straight path, within our lineage and community it is said: Seek God, and God alone. Go straight to God, and cleave to God; do not turn to the right or to the left, and do not turn backward, but go to God and cleave to God. Be in God and know God within you. Seek to see, hear, and feel with God; seek to smell, taste, and touch with God. So invoke, pray, and meditate with God and in God, no longer in twoness, but in oneness—unity and fullness. Be inward, be in God, be with God: from God, to God, for God—the Holy One. Be One from One—an Anointed One.

Invoke often, pray and pray and pray, and meditate, contemplate deep, until God unveils and discloses Godself in your heart and soul, and gives Godself to you—the Messiah and Holy Spirit. In this way be faithful, and you will acquire knowledge of God—True Gnosis.

This is the Way of the gnostic path, the straight path: Going within, going straight to God, and more than seeking a place within the seven heavens or communion with angels and lesser divinities, seek direct communion with God, the Messiah and Eternal One.

Your Lord is within you and is nearer to you than you are to yourself. Why do you seek the Lord outside and separate from you? If you have faith, and you indeed seek the Lord, go within, go deeper still and search within until you find, until the Lord within you is revealed, until God reveals Godself in your heart and soul, and the Spirit enlightens you. When you know the Lord, the Spirit within you, then you will know the Lord, the Spirit in others and all things, the Lord being within you and surrounding you on all sides.

First you need to go within and in faith invoke, pray, and meditate; open to the Holy Light and Spirit, then wait upon the Spirit to reveal the Lord in you, the inner Christ, Messiah. When you receive the Holy Light and Spirit, being inward, the Spirit will ingather you and show you a deeper place within your soul where the Lord is, where your inner being is inseparable from the Messiah in the Eternal One. The Spirit will bring you into a true holy communion, not dependent upon anything outward, like bread, wine, or oil, but dependent upon the supernal grace of the Eternal One, the living presence and power of the Eternal One within you, the Messiah. When the Spirit moves, when the Spirit ingathers you, this is finding: really it is more like you have been found and returned to yourself in God. Finding is a delight: It is awesome and wonderful to experience the overwhelming presence and power of the All-Powerful One within you, the immeasurable Light and Love of Christ, Messiah within your heart. There is peace and joy in it, and there is rejoicing in the soul, praise and thanksgiving from deep within.

Yet at the outset there is also a troubling, an agitation, a deep disturbance. We begin in darkness, in ignorance, and then come into the light and knowledge. When we come into the Inner Light, our thoughts, words, and deeds are exposed. We become aware of what is good and true, and in harmony with the Light and Love of Messiah, and so in the Holy One; we become aware of what is not good and not true, and not in harmony with the inner Messiah, and so not in God, the True Light. This is troubling, naturally so, for we all begin in ignorance, the illusion of separation and lack. Before faith dawns, before we come into the light of awareness and knowledge, in the ignorance we sin, we err, we follow unconscious, habitual karmic patterns of thought, speech, and action. These can be very strong in us and are reinforced in the psychic atmosphere of unenlightened society and this world.

While we have been ingathered, united, and filled by the Holy Light and Spirit, there is a very strong downward and backward pull in this world, a negative psychic gravity, as it were, that tends to pull us back into outwardness and feelings of separation and lack, of self-grasping, desire, and fear—the ignorance. As we receive the Holy Light and Spirit and are ingathered—aware of the inner Christ, Messiah—and we begin to receive insights, illuminations, and various leadings of the Holy Spirit, we'll come to the awareness of troubling changes we'll need to make: transformations of things in our person and life, our thoughts and emotions, words and deeds, letting go of some activities and company we keep. While some needed changes may be easy for us, other changes may be a great struggle wherein part of us is willing to be transformed but another is unwilling to change, to transform. Once direct awareness of the Inner Light and Holy Spirit dawns and the Truth and Light is revealed to us, this resistance can naturally be very frustrating and troubling.

When we receive the Holy Light and Spirit and are ingathered, there is a need for a progressive, active, and dynamic surrender to the inner Christ, Messiah—the Inner Light and Spirit—and a co-labor with the Spirit for our salvation, a full spiritual and supernal realization in Christ, Messiah: a need to follow the word, the teachings of the Lord within us and follow the leadings, the guidance of the Spirit in all things, sacred and mundane, spiritual and material. We need to continue to strive with the Spirit to be inward, deep within, and to live from within, from the Lord, and let the Holy Spirit take up her full divine action with, in, and through us, to take up our person and life, and transform it into a true image and likeness of Christ and God—the Messiah and Holy One. So while we need to seek until we find, when we find we need to strive, co-labor, with the Spirit until the Truth and Light revealed to us is lived and embodied. In the Lord and with the Lord, we need to strive always for a greater spiritual and supernal realization: to be and become divine and enlightened being, to be and become Christ, Messiah—one anointed of God, the True Light.

If we do, through grace—the Holy Spirit—we will be inward more and more. Our communion in and with the Lord will deepen. There will be a greater and greater manifestation of the knowledge and power of heaven and God with us, the Divine Presence of the Messiah and Holy One—the Holy Shekinah. We will indeed marvel and be astonished as greater powers of the Holy Spirit become manifest with, in, and through us, and a greater radiance of the Inner Light shines from within us. Through the Spirit, with the Spirit, we will come to master the force of will-desire in us, and master our mind, heart, and life—thoughts, words, and actions. So we will rule over all, the entirety, and be victorious in the Lord, the Spirit, the Holy Spirit accomplishing the Great Work in us—the revelation and realization of God. Amen.

Verse 3

Yeshua said, "If your leaders tell you, 'Look the kingdom is in heaven,' then the birds of heaven will precede you. If they say to you, 'It is in the sea,' then fish will precede you. But the kingdom of heaven is [within and all around] you. When you know yourselves, then you will be known, and you will understand that you are sons and daughters of the Living Father. But if you do not know yourselves, then you dwell in poverty, and you are poverty."

This echoes a passage in Deuteronomy where Moses taught the people that they did not need someone else—angel or human—to bring to them the law or knowledge of God, but that the word of God was written on their hearts (30:14). So true knowledge of God comes from within. Here, though, it is the kingdom of heaven that is said to be within.

Contemplating the kingdom within, we may recall what Yohanan the Baptist and Yeshua preached to the people in the Gospel of Matthew when announcing the appearance of the Messiah: "Repent, for the kingdom of heaven has comes near" (3:2). The true kingdom of heaven—Pleroma of Light—is neither some ideal earthly paradise nor a gated community in the sky as some ignorant, religious faithful imagine it to be. The true kingdom of heaven is the Messiah and the Eternal One—Living Father. The experience and delight of the kingdom of heaven is an intimate communion, growing into conscious union, with the Messiah in the Eternal One: the experience of an endless expansion into and merging with the Infinite and Eternal One. Indeed, it is for this reason that in the Book of Revelation, concerning New Jerusalem, we are told there is no temple, but that the Eternal God and the Lamb are the temple. In this you may understand that the kingdom of heaven inside you is, in fact, the inner Christ, Messiah—the Inner Light and Spirit.

Now, there is a common admonition among gnostic traditions: know yourself. If you do not know yourself, how shall you come to know God, the Infinite and Eternal? But more so, understand that the life and light in you is a direct manifestation of God—the True Light and Life. Your soul, your being and consciousness, is an emanation of the Supernal Light and Spirit of the Infinite and Eternal. The essence and nature of your soul, consciousness, mind, is Christ, Messiah. Therefore, to know yourself—your inner being, your true self—is to know Christ and God—the Messiah and Holy One. The revelation of Christ and God to you, the Holy Gospel, is as your Divine Self, Christ Self: who and what you are in the Eternal One, your innate perfection and unity in the Eternal One—the Living Father.

Truly, in going within and going to God, you are going to yourself, returning to yourself as you are in God and inseparable from the Infinite Light. In speaking of self, we are not speaking of the outer being, the little self, the ego, to which people cleave in the ignorance, but an inner and higher self, the Divine I Am in you.

Unless we are inward and receive the Holy Light and Spirit and the inner Christ, Messiah is revealed to us—our Divine Self, Divine I Am—and realize our innate unity and fullness in the Eternal One, we will remain in separation and lack, dwelling in poverty and being poverty. We will continue to be bound up in the gilgulim—the potentially endless rounds of birth, life, aging, illness, and death, and all that goes with its immeasurable sorrow and suffering. From a gnostic perspective, there is neither eternal damnation as taught in the outer and unspiritual churches, nor do we live a single lifetime and get it right or wrong and go to heaven or hell forever. Rather, it is known and understood that spirits and souls pass through many lives, many incarnations, and so through afterlife states again and again. They remain bound in transmigrations until they awaken and are saved—enlightened and liberated, fully reintegrated with the Infinite Light. There are experiences of relative realities of heavens and hells, and various in-betweens in afterlife experiences, but souls are driven to reincarnate, until eventually they awaken and are self-realized. In this regard, people, souls, and all sentient beings are in need of salvation, redemption, certainly so!

In this you will understand that Christian Gnosticism is a path of self-realization or enlightenment in the West, comparable and equivalent to those in the East. Unfortunately, with the emergence of religious leaders in the Christian faith who had not received the Holy Light and Spirit and so were unrealized and unenlightened, theological speculation, man-made doctrines, rites, and rituals replaced the spirituality of direct experience and ongoing revelation of God that was the foundation of the original church. False churches were conceived, devoid of light transmission—the revelation of something of the reality of Christ, Messiah—and the true passing of the Holy Spirit. The True Gnosis of Christ was lost in much of Christendom, as is very obvious in many churches today.

However, we are also living in a time of a gnostic revival, a restoration of True Gnosis—true knowledge of Christ and God. The second coming of Christ, Messiah in glory is underway, a great outpouring of the Holy Light and Spirit upon all flesh, so that as Christ, Messiah is revealed and realized in us, so Christ, Messiah is appearing again. Yeshua is living in us. The second coming among gnostics is not thought to be the man Jesus, Yeshua appearing in the sky and magically floating down to earth but as the Christ Presence, Christ Spirit—Holy Light and Spirit—embodied and made manifest in many faithful and spiritual people. The first coming was in Adonai Yeshua, Lord Jesus, and the second coming is in us.

The divine play of light transmission and the passing of the Holy Spirit has been restored among us. Hallelu Yah! Praise the Lord! Amen.

Verse 4

Yeshua said, "A person old in days will not hesitate to ask a little child seven days old about the Place of Life, and that person will live. For many of the first will be last, and become a single one."

First, the suggestion that an infant holds knowledge of the kingdom of heaven emphasizes the teaching of the kingdom of heaven—the inner Christ, Messiah—within all people, whether realized or unrealized. Moreover, it suggests that generally speaking, souls are aware of the kingdom of heaven and God and the true purpose of life and why they have come at the outset of their incarnation. However, they swiftly forget and fall into the ignorance, the illusion of separation and lack that is so predominant in the flesh and material world. Indeed, as souls enter into incarnation, they have an awareness of previous lives and the corresponding afterlife experiences. They are aware of the Pleroma of Light and have knowledge of specific intentions that bring them into incarnation in their desire to fulfill their purpose and destiny. They know, all in a great mystery, it is through physical incarnation that the realization of souls occurs, not in the afterlife, or realities of the inner dimensions. If we are to become realized and enlightened, it is here in the material life and world where it happens. Only when the realization of divinity, enlightenment is embodied here do we ascend and reintegrate with the Infinite Light, free from the gilgulim, or the necessity of physical, material incarnation.

When faith dawns in people and they begin to seek enlightenment or God, in part this corresponds with this knowledge and memory deep within their soul, being, and consciousness from the inner Christ, Messiah in them. As many can testify who have had true near-death experiences that brought about a real change in their lives, the true purpose and meaning of life is very different than the vainglory of worldly wealth, power, idle entertainments and gross consumerism and materialism chased by unenlightened culture and society. They can bear witness that life is very brief and a very precious opportunity to fulfill our soul's true purpose and desire, and that there is no time to waste, lest when one dies they will have many painful regrets in retrospect.

It is, of course, most auspicious if very early in life we come to faith and seek enlightenment or God and find, awaken, and tend to the messianic works and mission of the soul, thus fulfilling our destiny in this life. However, at any time and as long as we live, even near the end of life, if we come to faith, turn to the Lord, open to the Holy Light and Spirit, and live the Life Divine, living with the Lord, and in the Lord—Christ, Messiah— we may fulfill something of our divine destiny. If a woman or man old in days inquires of an infant, that person will live, for they have lived truly, in accordance with the Truth and Light revealed to them. That person will have been redeemed and enlightened by the Holy Spirit.

The verse goes on to say: "For many who are first will be last, and become a single one." This makes clear that whether in youth or old age, if a person comes to faith and awakens in the supernal grace of the Eternal One in Christ, Messiah they are ingathered just the same. This is parallel with Yeshua's parable of laborers in canonical gospels. Some were hired in the morning, some in the afternoon, and some very late in the day; the one who hired them paid them the very same wage, regardless of when they began working. Such is the power of the grace of the Eternal One through the reception of the Holy Spirit: the realization of the inner Christ, Messiah and the Divine I Am in the Infinite and Eternal.

There is, however, another way of reading this saying, one interconnected and parallel with what has been shared. As is known, in canonical gospels Adonai Yeshua teaches his disciples that unless they become like little children, they cannot enter into the kingdom of heaven, and later something similar is taught in Thomas. Likewise, the phrase in this saying is echoed in canonical gospels, wherein Yeshua teaches that the first will be the last and the last will be the first. "The first being last" is often understood among gnostics to be about souls that are realized and reach full enlightenment and liberation but in the love and compassion of

Christ, Messiah choose to continue to reincarnate for the sake of the salvation, enlightenment, and liberation of others. These are realized souls appearing as messengers—gnostic apostles, prophets, tzaddikim—bearing the light transmission and the capacity to impart the fullness of the Holy Light and Spirit. Likewise, to inquire of a little child may connote disciples, anointed community from which the Holy Light of the Messiah radiates and through whom the Spirit of the Messiah moves and transmits light; the passing of the Spirit flows for those who have faith and love with inward cleaving.

Here we may recall that anointed community is called the body of Christ, Messiah for in true anointed community, gnostic community, Christ, Messiah—the Holy Light and Spirit—continues to appear and live and move in this world. There is true initiation, a play of light transmission and passing of the Holy Spirit; those who receive the Holy Light and Spirit, who awaken to the inner Christ, Messiah are ingathered and joined to that Holy Body as a single one. As the holy scriptures teach, Christ, Messiah is the head of that body, the messengers are as the heart, and each sister or brother is an integral part of that Holy Body corresponding with their messianic works and mission, embodying who they are in Christ and God—the Messiah and Holy One.

This saying may be understood to speak of seeking out a messenger of the Pleroma of Light and anointed community and initiation: baptism with living water, and more so baptism with fire and the Spirit—the anointing with the Holy Light and Spirit of the Messiah. The gnostic path and gnostic community are founded upon initiation and actual discipleship—companionship in spiritual community. This was the Way of the original Christian movement. The same is true of actual anointed communities today as a greater outpouring of the Holy Light and Spirit are flowing in these end times. Many are being ingathered into the Pleroma of Light—Messiah—the Anointed One. Amen.

Verse 5

Yeshua said, "Know what is in front of your face and what is hidden from you will be disclosed. There is nothing hidden that will not be revealed."

There is a teaching in the Holy Kabbalah: "As above, so below; as below, so above." It is taught that what appears in creation and the world is founded upon supernal patterns above, within. Through contemplating nature, creatures, and what appears and transpires in the world, one can know and discern those supernal patterns and spiritual forces within and behind what appears and transpires. In this regard, we may consider the teachings of Adonai Yeshua and the many rich images of creatures, things in nature, and ordinary life used metaphorically and poetically to communicate and illustrate teachings and revelations. He clearly observed and contemplated in great detail what was before his face, what happened in life around him, and beheld deeper mysteries of creation and God as well as of himself and others as they were in God.

This saying alludes to a common practice among the prophets of ancient Israel of contemplating the glory of God, the presence and power of God, in nature and what was happening around them, and meditating upon what was seen, heard, and felt in the Spirit. The practice is called *hitbonenut* in the Kabbalah, which essentially means "contemplation." While there are many forms of spiritual and mystical contemplation taught in the gnostic path and Kabbalah, the contemplation of the glory of God in creation was likely engaged the most because it is so simple, straightforward, and accessible to all.

Who has not marveled at all the various wondrous plants, animals, and vistas in the wilderness, or been struck deeply by beautiful sunrises or sunsets or awed by the force and fury of great storms, or delighted in a starry night sky? It is an innate human quality to take notice and appreciate such things in life. But if done from inwardness, aware of the presence and power of God within oneself and in all things, appreciation and contemplation of the glory of God in nature and what is happening takes on whole new dimensions. Just as we abide in an inward communion with Christ, Messiah, so are we also in communion with the Inner Light and Spirit within all things, the living presence and power of God within and behind all that appears and transpires.

If you are deep inward with the Spirit, you can see, hear, and feel people, creatures, things, in their inwardness as they are in God, and God in them, and truly be aware of the kingdom of heaven inside and outside, within and all around you. And when the Spirit uplifts your soul into higher stations and states, spiritual and supernal, there is nothing hidden that will not be revealed on earth or in heavens.

This is an essential devotion, spiritual practice, of the gnostic path, or straight path.

Know and understand that the word of God is spoken in your heart and the Lord, the Spirit, is within you. So you need to abide in an inward communion and listen to the voice of the Lord—Adonai, Hayyah Yeshua—speaking from the depths of your soul, your inner being. Yet also know and understand that the Lord is speaking to you through others you encounter in life, not just in nature or the wilderness and such. God is speaking to you through all of the situations, circumstances, and events of life. If you are inward, you will be able to listen, hear, and discern what God is speaking to you and be well guided in your life, both interior and exterior. Contemplating the glory of God, the presence and power of God in nature, will open you to the awareness of the presence and power of God moving within and behind all that happens around you. This is how you'll discern spiritual forces moving within and behind people and things, whether those powers are divine, archonic, or demonic, or of some other kind.

Now, *there is nothing hidden that will not be revealed* also has another implication. This is the reality of souls passing beyond and arising in the afterlife experience, for therein, all that was held in mind and heart in secret, along with things said and done in life, arises and is seen, heard, felt, and relived. All that arises shapes the soul's experience in the afterlife, whether heavenly or hellish, or something in between. All that arises also shapes the circumstances of the next life, the next incarnation for souls that neither pass into the Pleroma of Light, nor reintegrate with the Infinite Light to enter the rest of the Eternal One—Yahweh. Being inward, knowing the Lord within you, following the guidance of the Spirit in your life, communing with the living presence and power of God within you and around you, and becoming aware of the kingdom of heaven within you and surrounding you on all sides in this life—this will transform your experience of death and the afterlife. Experiencing a most intimate communion in life, being united and filled, so you will experience a most intimate communion in the afterlife. Through grace you will be ingathered, unified with Christ in God, with the Messiah in the Eternal One. Amen.

Verse 6

His disciples asked him and said to him, "Do you want us to fast? How should we pray? Should we give charity?" Yeshua said, "Do not lie, and do not do what you hate. All things are disclosed before heaven. There is nothing hidden that will not be revealed, nothing covered that will not be undisclosed."

This verse extends upon what was discussed regarding the experience of souls in the afterlife, making it clear that how we live this life will determine our experience of death, the hereafter, and the incarnation to follow for those who are not resurrected and ascended, or ingathered into the Pleroma of Light. There is something very interesting and important about this saying, however; while his disciples inquire about devotions, spiritual practices, Yeshua does not answer their questions or give them any direct instruction about devotions or worship.

Understand that if you engage in devotions, invoke often and pray and pray and pray, meditate, and contemplate deep, fast and give charitably in religious obligation but do not strive to be loving, compassionate, and forgiving, your devotions are not bearing good fruit and are in vain. If you have mystical and visionary experiences, have acquired knowledge of all manner of secret mysteries and psychic or magical powers but have neither changed in your person and life nor generated love and compassion, then all that knowledge and power is as nothing and will not bear good fruit or serve to facilitate the salvation or realization of others in your life.

True mystical experience is one of the overwhelming presence and power of God within us, the immeasurable light and love of Christ, Messiah. True experience will progressively change us, the way we live, and more and more inwardly compel us to live according to the Truth and Light revealed to us. Mystical experience will incline us to love others as we love ourselves and do no harm. Unless the Truth and Light is lived in thought, word, and deed and so embodied, it remains unrealized. Quite naturally, true spiritual and mystical experience leads to active compassion, active engagement for social, environmental, and economic justice: living love, living compassion.

In the intensity of afterlife experience is an infinite, spacious radiance that souls enter, within which an amplified awareness of everything a soul has done, has realized, or left unrealized is all seen, heard, and felt by that soul in a state of extreme openness and sensitivity. Things so often considered important in this world turn out not to be important at all. What is important is the knowledge of the Messiah and Holy One that has been acquired, the progress made in the realization of the soul, how they have related with and loved others, and what they have done to uplift humanity. Needless to say, for some souls that may be a very joyful, blissful experience; for others, there may be great sorrow and pain. For most, this experience will be some combination of both. Know and understand in this radiance of the Infinite and Eternal One, there is no judgment; if judgment is present, it comes from within souls themselves and the complete awareness of what they have done and how they have lived that arises in this Infinite Light.

My beloved tzaddik, Tau Elijah, used to say that if you wish to know the experience that will arise for you in the afterlife and your next incarnation, look into how you are living today, your thoughts and emotions, words and actions. Your experience in the future is being woven and created here and now, today. When we read a scripture and teaching like this saying of Yeshua in Thomas, it is an invitation to go within and look at how we are living our life, where we are today in our spiritual journey, and to inquire of the Lord, the Spirit for guidance to refine ourselves, to progress in our spiritual and supernal realization, and deepen our inward communion.

Understand that the Inner Light and Spirit in us is the very same spacious radiance we encounter in the afterlife. If we go within, go deeper still and abide in that Holy Light and Spirit, we can see, hear, and feel what is to be done, what is good and true in our lives, what needs to be changed, and what is not good or true in our lives. Here and now is the time to make changes, work out our salvation, progress in our spiritual and supernal realization, live according to the Truth and Light revealed to us, practice the teachings of the Lord, accept the guidance of the Spirit, and so realize and embody the fullness of the Holy Light and Spirit. Quite naturally, if we realize our unity and fullness in this life, then unity and fullness will be our experience in the afterlife: In the Light of the Infinite One in our afterlife experience, there will be perfect peace and joy; rest in the Eternal One. Amen.

Perhaps take a few moments right now to be inward and pray to see, hear, and feel in the Inner Light how your life is going. Inquire of the Christ Spirit, Holy Spirit what changes might be good at this time in your life or where you might strive for progress in the Christ Life or living the Life Divine. Amen.

Verse 7

"Blessing on a lion if a human eats it, making the lion human.
[Cursed] is the human if the lion eats it, making the lion human."

The Holy Kabbalah teaches that there are five aspects or levels of our soul, our being and consciousness. The inmost is our divine spark, *yechidah*, from which emanates our life force, light power, *hayyah*. From this emanates our heavenly and supernal soul, our divine nature, *neshamah*. Then there is our spirit, our human and divine intelligence, *ruach*, and the outermost aspect of our soul, the vital soul, *nefesh*. The divine spark, light power, and divine nature corresponds with who and what we are in the Messiah and Eternal One, while our intelligence and vital soul corresponds with who we are in ourselves. For the most part when incarnate, our vital soul, intelligence, and divine nature are the principle aspects of our soul that we labor to actualize, realize, and embody. In our divine nature we are inseparable from the Messiah and Eternal One—the Infinite Light—and receiving the Holy Light and Spirit, which is a fiery divine intelligence, the Holy Spirit merges with our human intelligence, enlightening us. Our vital soul is regenerated, transformed through our enlightened intelligence. Who we are in God is joined with who we are in ourselves, our incarnation, and so embodied.

Just as the Holy Gospel speaks of the Incarnation of the Divine within Yeshua—the Spirit and Soul of the Messiah—so it is given for us to incarnate, embody our divine nature, our true and divine intelligence, unified with the inner Messiah and Holy Spirit, united with the Eternal One—the Infinite Light. This is what it means to be a human being, to be in the image and likeness of God. From a gnostic perspective, as expressed in this saying, until we receive the Holy Light and Spirit, until Christ, Messiah is revealed in us and through the Spirit we realize and embody our true intelligence, our divine genius and nature, we who appear in human form are not a true human being as yet. Rather, we resemble a beast of the field, or something like the king of beasts, a lion.

There is the Inner Light and Spirit, the Christ, Messiah within all people. All have a divine nature and divine intelligence in them. But living in outwardness, in separation and lack, living from the little self, the ego-grasping, and its play of desire and fear—people do not realize their divine nature and intelligence. Their experience Christ, Messiah is neither in them, nor are they in Christ, Messiah. Their *nefesh*—their person and life—is manifest in a bestial state—*nefesh behamit*—not a godly and divine-human state—*nefesh elokit*. People who live in outwardness, not inwardness, who do not come to faith, who neither seek nor find enlightenment or God—this is the lion eating the human, making the lion human. However, when people come to believe, have faith, and they go within to seek and find God in themselves—the Inner Light and Spirit—when they bring that Holy Light forward and the Spirit takes up their person and life, when their *nefesh* is regenerated, transformed, into a godly, human-divine state—this is the human eating the lion, making the lion human.

If you wish to ponder living in outwardness and the bestial state as being cursed, just look around you in these end times. See how many souls are being broken and shattered by the severity of these times. Look at how many people among the masses are being driven into extreme narcissism, selfishness. From fear, anger, hatred, and violence to believing in insane, delusional falsehoods and bizarre conspiracy theories, people succumb to great darkness, wickedness, and evil. Do understand that the extreme right and left are the same: One form of the ignorance becoming the justification of the other form of the ignorance in something of a death spiral of mutual self-destruction. It is indeed cursed, a state that brings great harm to others, the world, and to oneself.

In this, perhaps, you may recall the teaching of Adonai Yeshua in John: "My kingdom is not of this world," not of unenlightened culture, society, neither its politics nor its ways. Indeed, the kingdom is not experienced in outwardness but inwardness, corresponding with a true spiritual conversion, a self-transformation, a radical change in being and consciousness through which we have a true and direct communion with Enlightened or Divine Being—God.

This saying is a call to be inward, deep within, to strive with the Spirit for a full spiritual conversion in Christ, Messiah in an ongoing self-transformation and self-realization in the Inner Light and Spirit: to let that radiance of heaven and the Eternal One shine from within you, to let the Eternal Spirit take up your person and life so that you are an incarnation, embodiment, of the True Divine—a son or daughter of God, the True Light.

Here we may also recall another saying of Yeshua, in John 10:34: "Do you not know that you are sons and daughters of God?" To realize and know you are, and live as such, is to be a true, spiritual Christian, and more so a gnostic: a knower of God, your Father, your Mother, your All-In-All. Amen.

Verse 8

Yeshua said, "Humankind is like a wise fisherman who cast his net into the sea and drew it up from the sea full of little fish. Among them he found a fine large fish. He threw all of the little fish back into the sea and easily choose the large fish. Whoever has ears to hear should hear."

This saying plays upon and is an extension of the teaching in the previous one. There is an open secret taught in the Kabbalah that will clarify its meaning. In Hebrew each letter can be spelled out and is composed of other letters and so forms a word. The shapes of the letters are also often composed of various letters; from the spelling of the letters and their shapes and forms, teachings are drawn, including esoteric secrets of creation, redemption, and God.

There is a letter that is called the soul bird in the Kabbalah, the letter *Nun*, that spelled out is *Nun-Vav-Nun*. *Nun* and *Vav* mean "fish." The Kabbalah teaches that these three letters correspond with the three principle aspects of souls that may be actualized, realized, and embodied in incarnation: *neshamah*, *ruach*, and *nefesh*—our divine nature, intelligence, and vital soul.

There is another open secret to be shared that will illuminate the meaning of this saying. In the Kabbalah, the word for "sea"—*yam*—is a cognomen of Malkut-Kingdom, the outermost emanation of the Infinite Light. Malkut-Kingdom is also the Divine Presence, the exterior Shekinah—the Indweller. As we know from an earlier teaching, the kingdom of heaven is within us. The presence and power of the Eternal One—Shekinah—is within us, indwelling us. So to go fishing in the sea is to go within, deep within, to seek and find the living presence of the Eternal One, the Eternal Messiah within us: to realize and embody the fullness of our soul, which is inseparable from the fullness of that Inner Light and Spirit.

The fullness of our holy soul, our vital soul, intelligence, and divine nature, unified with the Messiah in the Eternal One—the Inner Light and Spirit—is the big fish. It is this Inner Light and Spirit to which we cleave and identify, not to name, form, and personal history. We let go of the little fish thrown back into the sea—all of the various inane thoughts and emotions of the ordinary mind, the surface consciousness, and the perpetual arisings of the little self, the ego in it.

This speaks of an integral self-realization in Christ, Messiah; an ingathering, as it were, of sparks of our soul bound up in various unenlightened mentalities and a plurality of little selves arising from them which are often in conflict, striving against one another to get their way and have dominion.

How often do we resolve ourselves to do something good and true or make a change for the better in our lives but then later, as though an entirely different person with an entirely different mindset and agenda, not carry out the intention?

A simple example we have all likely experienced is setting an alarm. When have we gone to bed to wake up on time to do something we have agreed or need to do, only to disregard the alarm in the morning? Quite clearly, there was a self who wanted to wake up and another self who did not want to wake up in direct contradiction to one another. Oversleeping, the self who did not want to wake up early won out. In the unenlightened condition, which is a relatively unconscious and fragmented state of consciousness, this isn't happening only with small, trivial things as waking up on time. It is happening on various levels in all manner of things in our lives, including crucial, critical things: getting a good education and livelihood; being true, honest, and loving in our relationships; keeping our commitments; and being kind to others. Most important of all is the resolve of our faith and devotion, our spiritual life and practice, growing true zeal for a spiritual and supernal realization, for daily devotions—invocation, prayer, meditation—and for remembering and keeping Shabbat while active in anointed community. Without this, we will make little if any progress in an actual realization.

There is a need for an integral self-realization in Christ, Messiah; a focus of the force of our will-desire inward, upward, and Godward, living in an inward communion with the Lord, the Spirit in us, and following the teachings and guidance received from the Lord, the Spirit: living from God, to God, and for God, and being who we are in God, the True Light.

There is, of course, another teaching in this saying, one that will be drawn out further in the saying that follows. Perhaps you may recall that when Adonai Yeshua called his close disciples, those destined to be messengers—apostles and prophets—he said to them, "I will make you fishers of humans, fishers of souls" (Mark 1:17, Matthew 4:19). There is a harvest of souls here that is plentiful today, just as Yeshua said of his time. In every generation, messengers—apostles, prophets, tzaddikim—appear to fish, engage in the harvest of souls, and ingather them into the Pleroma of Light. In each generation are souls that are big fish, mature for catching, while those in their spiritual evolution and realization are little fish, immature, not ready for catching. Quite naturally, the messengers are sent for the big fish who are to be ingathered. The little fish are to be cut loose, left alone to continue in their journey until they grow, mature, and are in season for harvesting, ingathering into the Messiah and Eternal One.

This is especially true of gnostic apostles, gnostic masters, and individuals being ingathered into gnostic community.

Understand that mystics, gnostics, and their spiritual communities tend to be more focused and passionate in their spirituality, faith, and devotions than the faithful in mainstream churches and exoteric religion. It is not about a conceptual change in creed or agreement with doctrine that brings a person into gnostic community; rather it is taking up a more passionate spirituality and lifestyle. Being in a gnostic community is not a side affair or hobby as in new ageism but a priority and central focus in one's life. So there is indeed fishing for big fish, more evolved or progressed souls among gnostics.

Know and understand that anyone who desires to receive light transmission and the passing of the Holy Spirit, who is willing to be inward, who is willing to surrender to the leadings of the Spirit, and willing to change and be transformed can indeed be received and ingathered. Being among the chosen, the spiritual elect, is about choosing what we do with our life, what we love and cleave to, and embody. We are choosing! And so Adonai Yeshua said, many are called but few are chosen. Amen.

Verse 9

Yeshua said, "Look, a sower went out, took a handful of seeds, and scattered them. Some fell on the road and the birds came and pecked them up. Others fell on rock and they did not take root in soil and did not produce heads of grain. Others fell on thorns and they choked the seeds and worms devoured them. And others fell upon good soil and brought forth a good crop, yielding sixty per measure and one hundred per measure."

This is a version of a well-known parable that also appears in canonical gospels. Although slightly different in wording, the teaching and meaning are the same. The seeds sown are the word of the Eternal One spoken with power, an imparting of something of the Holy Light and Spirit, and so are seeds of light. These seeds are sown in hearts and minds of people; the various places in which the seeds fall correspond with various states of souls, various conditions in consciousness and life. The word of the Eternal One is spoken to all, directly into the hearts of all and through apostles and prophets, messengers, and those in anointed community in whom the word has taken root and borne fruit: the Christ Spirit, the Holy Spirit speaks through them. When the word of the Eternal One is spoken with power, it is not a person speaking but the Spirit speaking through them: The Spirit is the power of God in what is spoken and heard. As with the parable of the fisherman and fish, the same is true of this Parable of the Sower. But in this parable, clarification is given regarding various karmic conditions and various negative states of the soul that pose an obstruction to the reception of the word, to the Holy Light and Spirit, preventing us from being ingathered and realized in the Messiah.

Listen and hear and understand! Seed falling on the road and being eaten by birds is the word spoken to those whose hearts are hard and whose minds are closed, those deeply immersed in the bestial nature, and in self-will, self-cherishing, desire, and fear, bound up in great darkness and wickedness—evil. The birds eating the seed sown is the satan—the adversary—as it were, who snatches it away before the word has been heard and received, such that a mean-spirited person might be inclined to hostility and persecution of those who speak the word.

The seeds falling on rock or shallow soil that do not take root are those who initially hear the word and may have felt something of the Holy Light and Spirit in it and been uplifted and excited in the moment but afterward do nothing. They neither take up further teachings and initiation in the spiritual life and practice in Christ, Messiah nor turn to the Lord inward to know and commune with the inner Christ, Messiah and Holy Spirit.

The seeds that fall among thorns that grow but are later choked out and devoured by worms are those who hear the word, receive the Holy Light and Spirit, receive further teachings and initiation, and for some time may take up the Divine Life and entertain an inward communion in the Inner Light and Spirit but then are carried away or led astray by desires, distractions, or doubts because of the world. In self-will and self-cherishing, they fall into outwardness, turning away from the Lord, the Christ, Messiah within them, separating themselves from anointed community—the Body of Christ, Messiah. Unlike those in the former unreceptive conditions, these poor souls among the thorns are haunted by what they have seen, heard, felt, and known. If they have progressed in a spiritual realization to some extent, there is self-judgment and much suffering being devoured by worms: devoured by their own awareness of what they have done, unwilling to mend what has been done, unwilling to be regathered.

In all of these various conditions, people are not ingathered. They are not in Christ, and in a manner of speaking, Christ is not in them, not in their own experience. Little if any progress is made in an actual spiritual realization, let alone supernal realization.

Now those seeds that fall on good soil and bring forth a good crop, who yield sixty per measure and one hundred per measure are those with true faith and love and inward cleaving, who receive the word of the Eternal One—the Holy Light and Spirit—and who remain faithful throughout their lives. They are sisters and brothers of anointed community who strive with the Spirit for a greater revelation and realization of Christ, Messiah within and through themselves. They not only strive to be Christ-like and truly Christian but to be and become Christ, Messiah—gnostic—who, through the Spirit, bring their initiation to fruition in an actual spiritual or supernal realization in the Messiah. "Sixty per measure" is spiritual realization, an inward communion in various grades of nearness to intimate nearness. These advance with the knowledge of the Messiah and Eternal One in higher states of mental being and consciousness, the peak of which is experiences of cosmic consciousness and the overmined. "One hundred per measure" is supernal realization, an inward communion in oneness, the realization of unity and fullness, and the knowledge of the Messiah and Eternal One in states of supramental, supernal being and consciousness—fully Christ or God Consciousness.

To give some hint of this distinction in spiritual realization or higher states of mental consciousness and nearness, we experience seeing, hearing, and feeling with God, the Spirit more or less. But in supernal realization or in states of supramental, supernal consciousness, and oneness, there is the experience of God being the seeing, hearing, and feeling, God being the smelling, tasting, and touching, and so the full embodiment of Enlightened or Divine Being: conscious union with the Messiah in the Eternal One. So, it is in supernal realization the fullness of the Holy Light and Spirit is incarnate, embodied more or less, as it was in Yeshua Messiah and Mirya the Magdala but in a unique and different revelation and divine action than that of Yeshua and Mirya with another messianic mission and work to be accomplished. Such holy and enlightened ones would not claim to be the Christ, Messiah just as Mirya, who embodied the same realization as Yeshua, did not claim to be the Christ, Messiah. For Yeshua was and is the Messiah, the Firstborn Sun of God: There is no other in this world who is, or will be, the Savior and Gnostic Revealer in that way. Yet as with Mirya the Magdala, we are to be co-redeemers with him.

Here we may recall a teaching of Messiah Yeshua to his disciples in his final discourse in the Gospel of John: "You will do greater works—other works—than you have seen me do" (14:12). As the Living Yeshua teaches in the *Secret Book of James*, we are not saved or realized for the sake of ourselves alone, but so that others might be saved, realized, with us. So the bearing of a good crop, whether in spiritual or supernal realization, is helping to facilitate the realization of others along with ourselves. All who are in anointed community, who gather and tend the messianic continuum together, who worship in spirit and truth together in an ingathered communion, nurture and nourish one another in the Divine Life as the presence and power of God moves among them. They serve to facilitate one another's progressive realization in Christ, Messiah. Amen.

Verse 10

Yeshua said, "I have thrown fire upon the world, and look, I am [tending] it until it blazes."

This follows up on the Parable of the Sower in a very insightful and beautiful way, for the seeds now become fire cast upon the world. As we know, when Yohanan the Baptist proclaimed the arrival of the Messiah to the people, he told them that while he baptized with water, one greater than he was coming after him who would baptize with fire and the Spirit. In the Gospel of John we are told that the risen Messiah appeared to the disciples who had gathered in the upper room, greeted them with a blessing of peace twice, then laid hands and breathed upon them, saying to them, "Receive the Holy Spirit." When they had received the Spirit, he told them that the power of mercy and judgment was in them, as were all divine attributes, powers, actions. Then, according to Acts, sometime after the disciples witnessed Yeshua Messiah's ascension, his dissolution into pure glory, light, spirit, the disciples were gathered in the upper room in prayer and meditation on the day of Pentecost. A great whirling wind stormed into that space. Tongues of fire came upon each of them, and they went out to preach the word of God with power to followers who were gathered outside. To those who desired to receive it, they imparted the Holy Light and Spirit. Through the resurrection and ascension of Messiah Yeshua, Holy Light, Holy Fire, and the Eternal Spirit were poured upon the world. The first generation of anointed community came into being and was made manifest in the world.

In this same way, manifestations of anointed community continue to come into being.

The outpouring of the Holy Light and Spirit continues to this very day. Influxes of the Holy Light and Spirit come into messengers—apostles and prophets—and through them new generations of anointed community come into being and are made manifest in the world, that same Light and Spirit passing through them to those gathered with them. Once there is a generation of anointed community, the Holy Light radiates into the world: The Holy Spirit moves with, in, and through that Body of Christ, Messiah; every woman and man of the anointed community becomes a dwelling place of that Holy Light and Spirit.

Truly, Living Yeshua continues an outpouring of the Holy Light upon the world—Supernal Light and the Eternal Spirit—and is tending it until it blazes, until all who receive the Holy Light and Spirit are ingathered into the Pleroma of Light, reintegrated with the Infinite Light

It is taught in the scriptures that the Eternal One—Yahweh—is like a fire consuming fire, making all like unto itself. So it is with the Holy Light of the Messiah, the Sun of the Eternal One: a supernal, nuclear fire that transforms everything into itself—a true image and likeness of God Most High, the Absolute Light.

When we receive this Holy Light and Spirit, the Sun of God is ignited in us, the inner Christ, Messiah is being revealed to us: If we abide in an inward communion and follow the teachings and leadings of our Lord and Savior within us, the Holy Spirit will transform our soul and our body into a true dwelling place and vehicle of the presence and power of God in this world and beyond.

As Yeshua teaches in this passage, the Holy Light and Spirit is poured out upon the world, all people, all flesh. Whoever believes, has faith, and is inward, invoking and praying, inviting and welcoming that Holy light and Spirit into their person and life, they will receive that Holy Light and Spirit and be united and filled. This Holy Light and Spirit is present for all people and in truth is in all people, though in many, it is as yet unrealized. In effect, in the relative reality of experience, some do not have the Holy Light and Spirit and remain in ignorance, separation, and lack apart from God.

In gnostic community are messengers—gnostic apostles, gnostic masters—who understand that all who receive the Holy Light and Spirit, as taught in First Peter, are ordained in a royal priesthood—the Order of

Melchizedek. Women and men alike are anointed, ordained, and conse-crated so that all in anointed community may engage in the divine actions of a sacred and holy priest of God Most High—*El Elyon*. As the Gospel of Philip teaches, if a priest can bless bread, wine, oil, or pass light power or the Spirit into things with intention, then along with their soul, their body is also holy. As such, having the Holy Light and Spirit in them, wherever they dwell, and wherever they go is a holy place—reality of the true Holy Land in Christ, Messiah.

Regarding the soul and body as holy, as a true dwelling and vehicle of the presence and power of the Eternal One, we may recall the faith-ful woman who was healed merely by touching the very edge of Yeshua's outer garment, power going from him into her, healing her. More so, we are told in Acts that people were healed when holy apostles passed by, merely by being touched by the shadow of the apostle. When we receive this Holy Light and Spirit and the inner Christ, Messiah tends and makes it blaze, the fullness of the Holy Light and Spirit is made manifest in us: any and all powers of the Spirit—divine attributes and actions—can be made manifest by the Spirit through us.

Here we may recall what Adonai Yeshua said to his disciples in his final discourse to them, as recounted in the Gospel of John: "You will do greater things—other works—than you have seen me do" (14:12). Know and understand that whoever receives this Holy Light and Spirit, the inner Christ, Messiah revealed and realized in and through them will be a unique and individual emanation and manifestation of the Divine Presence of Christ—the Shekinah of Messiah. They will have all of the gifts and the powers of the Holy Spirit necessary to accomplish their messianic works and mission. Having been consecrated, sanctified, and made sacred and holy—transformed by the Holy Fire, Holy Light of the Sun of God—so the Spirit will take up her full divine action in them, and move with, in, and through them and manifest as them.

Christ, Messiah is indeed tending this Holy Fire in us until it blazes forth and we are radiant with supernal glory in the Lord, the Spirit.

You will find that when the Spirit moves in a gathering of anointed community and moving with, in, and through yourself, there often tends to be an experience of intense inner heat and radiance, such that it may be accurately said that we are lit up or set on fire with the Spirit. When one or more in a gathering are set on fire with the Spirit, it tends to blaze forth, passing to others who are present, becoming in the gathering like a wild-fire. When this happens in a gathering of anointed community, it breaks out and radiates into the world, so that others may also be touched and taken up by this Holy Light and Spirit, setting the world on fire. Hallelu Yah! Amen.

Verse 11

Yeshua said, "This heaven will pass away, and the one above it will pass away. The dead are not alive and the living will not die. During the days when you ate what was dead you made it alive. When you are in the light what will you do? On the day when you were one, you became two. But when you become two what will you do?"

In the Book of Revelation, the vision of New Jerusalem dawns after the first heaven and earth pass away, followed by the revelation of a new heaven and new earth, all in the Pleroma of Light. There are seven heavens: the exterior, astral heavens and interior, spiritual heavens. But the true kingdom of heaven, the eighth heaven—Pleroma of Light—is within and behind them, beyond them. The seven heavens are impermanent; like this world, they will eventually pass away. While there is respite for faithful and righteous souls in those heavens in the afterlife, they are neither the eternal realm nor the reintegration with the Infinite Light. From heavens, souls return to material incarnation to complete their realization.

Unlike the religious faithful in the outer and unspiritual churches, when the gnostic path teaches us to seek God and God alone, gnostic initiates do not seek the rewards of the seven heavens, but they seek the true kingdom of heaven which is Christ and God—the Messiah and Holy One. They seek conscious union with the Eternal One, reintegration with the Infinite Light, Radiant Nothingness. Their inmost desire is to return to be One—unified with Christ in God, the True Light.

Until we receive the Holy Spirit and True Light and Life, we are like corpses: We cannot see, hear, or feel with the Spirit or smell, taste, or touch with the Spirit. We are unable to move or speak with the Spirit or have true knowledge of God. On a spiritual level, apart from the Holy Spirit, people are dead. In receiving the Spirit, however, we are alive—resurrected and ascended—able to see, hear, and feel with the Spirit, to smell, taste, and touch with the Spirit. Moving and speaking with the Spirit, we acquire knowledge of God, along with understanding and wisdom. Through the Spirit we are united with Christ in God, filled with the Light of Christ—supernal radiance of the Sun of the Eternal One.

As taught in a previous passage, receiving the Holy Light and Spirit, the kingdom of heaven is within and all around us here in this world, and we will be ingathered into it when we pass beyond to abide in the eternal realm, the Pleroma of Light—reintegrated with the Endless Light, the enlightenment and liberation of souls in Christ, Messiah.

If the Holy Light and Spirit is in us here in this world and we are eating and drinking in mindfulness, inwardness, what we eat and drink is absorbed into our holy flesh; its energy is used in service to heaven and God and so is uplifted, alive. Likewise, being in the Holy Light and Spirit, the Holy Light and Spirit being in us, so can we speak the word of God with power, not only to human beings but to all creatures visible and invisible, engaging light transmission, passing the Living Spirit, uplifting them in the resurrection and ascension, ingathering them into the kingdom of heaven—the Messiah and Holy One.

In our origin we were one, inseparable from the Eternal One, though unrealized, in an unconscious union. Having become two and fallen into the ignorance, the illusion of separation and lack, arising in self-will, self-cherishing, desire, and fear in outwardness makes us divorced, as it were, from our inner being, the inner aspects of our soul. What are we to do? We need to go within and live within, receive the Holy Light and Spirit, realize the truth, the inner reality of and our innate unity with Christ, Messiah in the Eternal One—the Infinite Light. We need to return to be One.

Our inside and outside need to be joined as one, aligned and in harmony with one another, the outside—our person and life—resembling the Sun of God within us. We need to unite who we are in ourselves with who we are in Christ and God—the Messiah and Holy One.

In truth, in reality, there is no true existence—True Light and Life—other than the Holy One. There is the Holy One and the Holy One alone. There is no other; there is nothing else, and there never has been. The inmost being of all things is inseparable from the Holy One, is a pure emanation of the Eternal One—the Infinite Light.

We live and move and have our being in the Holy One and have never been separate and apart from the Holy One. From a gnostic perspective, this is what Christ, Messiah came to reveal to us. In Christ, Messiah, we might realize our innate unity with the Eternal One and receive our salvation—our enlightenment and liberation. Amen.

Verse 12

The disciples said to Yeshua, "We know you will leave us. Who will be our leader?" Yeshua said to them, "Wherever you are, seek out James the Just. For his sake heaven and earth came into being."

While canonical gospels cite Peter as the leader of the early church, here James is cited as the leader. Given what is said of Thomas at the outset of this gospel and what is said about an exchange between him and Yeshua in a later passage, one might expect Yeshua to have pointed to Thomas. However, according to tradition, Thomas was sent on an apostolic mission to India as recounted in the Acts of Thomas, far away from the churches of the original anointed community. That James is cited as the leading apostle in this gospel is very interesting, very telling.

The truth is that the assertion of Peter as the leading apostle of the early church in canonical gospels is very curious, given the many times he struggled during the earthly ministry of Yeshua and afterward, to receive and understand the Holy Gospel, the word of God, and revelations of Christ, Messiah given to him. John or James would seem to be the more understandable and wise choice. That this gospel cites James and not Peter speaks of a split that was occurring fairly early in the original anointed community, one between the religious faithful of the outer, unspiritual church who taught orthodox doctrines and priestcraft and those who preserved and taught a mystical spirituality taught by Adonai Yeshua of the direct spiritual and mystical experience of God. Those who taught an actual, ongoing revelation and realization of Christ and God and who held true knowledge of God were gnostics of the inner and spiritual church.

Essentially, within just a few generations, leaders began to rise in the early church who did not receive the Holy Light and Spirit, had not experienced revelation and realization of Christ and God, and so did not have true knowledge of Christ and God in a true understanding of the Holy

Gospel. Never having received the Holy Light and Spirit and thus bringing their realization to fruition, they could not engage light transmission and impart the Holy Spirit. Without the experience of actual revelation of Christ and God in their hearts and souls or true knowledge of God—gnosis, *da'at*—what they had instead was theological concepts and speculation as outsiders, not insiders; in outwardness, not inwardness. These deceivers, these false teachers, false apostles, and false prophets strove for worldly power through religious authority and to take over and rule the church for their own self-interests and self-ambitions, neither for the sake of serving heaven and God, nor the true salvation of souls.

Coming into rulership and power, they initiated a great persecution of Christians who were spiritual and mystical—the gnostics—calling them heretics for teaching the gnostic path, the straight path, and seeking to eradicate them. They did to those Spirit-filled Christians what Jewish religious authorities did to Yeshua Messiah before them. Such is the plight of most organized religion or larger religious institutions in the world. Most of the leaders or religious authorities lack actual revelation and realization or any anointing from God, the True Light, but are, as Yeshua taught, the blind leading the blind—teachers of theory, speculation, not the knowledge, understanding, and wisdom of God, not the true enlightenment and liberation. This is very obvious in many mainstream churches of various denominations today. Whether leaning right or left in the political spectrum, there is a lack of light transmission and passing of the Holy Spirit: There is neither an actual revelation of direct knowledge of Christ and God nor actual spiritual and supernal realization. The true knowledge and way of the Gospel—Christ, Messiah—has been lost.

This division between an exterior, unspiritual church oriented to the world and the interior, spiritual church oriented to heaven and God began long ago in the spiritual movement Adonai Yeshua initiated. The division continues to this very day. In the early movement, light transmission and actual reception of the Holy Spirit was common among those who professed to be Christian; they were Spirit-filled people. Today among many

Christian communities, gnosis is relatively uncommon and unknown except in speculation and conceptual theologies.

In this gnostic gospel, Peter, the head of the exterior church, is not acknowledged; James, the head of the interior church, is acknowledged. John is the other among the twelve originals often viewed as the head of the interior church, which is why the gospel written in his name by those in his lineage after him belittles Thomas, whose lineage would cite James as the leader of the inner and spiritual church. Regardless, to this day there is the exterior church and interior church: one that is man-made and bears an anointing and ordination from men, another that is made by Christ and God that bears an anointing and ordination from Christ and God Most High in the Way of Melchizedek. This latter is often called *gnostic* to indicate the knowledge of Christ and God born of the experience of actual revelation and realization of God.

When Yeshua says that heaven and earth came into being for the sake of James, the same is said in Judaism and Judaic Kabbalah of Abraham and Sarah, the first great prophets and holy tzaddikim—righteous ones, holy and enlightened ones—after the flood. According to the Holy Kabbalah, Jewish or Christian, heaven and earth—creation—comes into being for the generation of holy tzaddikim, realized souls, holy and enlightened ones. You see, the original intention of God in creation is that God be revealed and known, realized, and embodied. It is with, in, and through faithful and spiritual humanity that this happens. In this regard, it may be said that heaven and earth came into being for gnostics—knowers of God. Understand that by "gnostic," we do not just mean Christian gnostics but include the mystics and gnostics of all authentic wisdom traditions of the world, among all peoples of the world, those having knowledge of the Truth and Light that is above all, in all, and to which all shall attain, as will be clearly stated in a later saying of this gospel.

Here it may be said that the name Christian is one thing and that the name gnostic is another, but the name gnostic is beyond the outward names of Christian, Muslim, Jewish, Buddhist, Hindu, Taoist, and so on. It corresponds with the realization of the Absolute Truth and Light that is the source and foundation of all true revelations realized through the various ways taught by the inner and mystical traditions of all the world's great religions, not in their outer and unspiritual forms but their inner and spiritual manifestations.

Indeed, heaven and earth have come into being for gnostics—knowers of God—for the sake of the spiritual and supernal realization of souls. Amen.

Verse 13

Yeshua said to his disciples, "Compare me to something and tell me what I am like." Shimon Kefa said to him: "You are like a righteous prophet." Matai said to him, "You are like a wise philosopher." Toma said to him, "Rabbi, my mouth is utterly unable to say what you are like." Yeshua said, "I am not your rabbi. Because you have drunk, you are intoxicated by the bubbling spring I tended." He then took Toma and withdrew and spoke three sayings to him. When Toma came back to his friends, they asked him, "What did Yeshua say to you?" Toma said to them, "If I tell you one of the sayings he spoke to me, you will pick up rocks and stone me, and fire will come out of the rocks and consume you."

This is one of the wilder sayings of the Gospel of Thomas, one that reflects a very close spiritual relationship between Yeshua and Thomas. A moment like this is echoed in canonical gospels written after Thomas, but in those versions it is Peter whom Adonai Yeshua praises.

Whether in this version of the event or another, we may take note that Yeshua does not tell them who or what he is but inquires of them who or what they think or believe he is. This is significant because it suggests that true knowledge of Christ and God must come from within. Even if Christ, Messiah was embodied and manifest through a person standing before us, unless there is recognition and realization within ourselves from the Inner Light and Spirit, they would in effect appear to be another ordinary person among the throng of unenlightened humans. This of course is true of all messengers, all apostles and prophets of God: Unless we have faith and through the Inner Light and Spirit recognize and know who and what they are in God, that God has sent them, then we will neither be able to receive the full blessing nor the word of God spoken with power that they bring, only a measured blessing, only a partial word.

To recognize an apostle as an apostle, a prophet as a prophet, the Spirit of God must reveal it to us. Even if an apostle or prophet were to tell us who and what they were, if we believe them and have faith, it is through the Spirit that we believe. Secrets of creation, redemption, and God are revealed by God and God alone—the Holy Spirit. When through a holy woman or holy man, it is not the woman or man speaking, revealing, but is the Holy Shekinah, Holy Spirit.

In the Kabbalah, the Shekinah, the Spirit, is often called bubbling spring, well, river, or sea. It is the Holy Spirit whom the Living Yeshua waits upon and tends, who measures out as he blesses, heals, and enlightens those around him.

As those who have known a living apostle and prophet can bear witness, when moments of light transmission and powerful movements of the Holy Spirit are not in intimate nearness or in twoness or separation, it can be very intoxicating and overwhelming, so much so that it is not uncommon for one to pass out, fall unconscious, or slip into mindless bliss, unable to see, hear, and feel clearly, thus unable to speak clearly in the Spirit. When Thomas calls Yeshua his rabbi—spiritual teacher and guide—but then is unable to speak clearly in the Spirit, in effect he did not know Christ, Messiah in Yeshua or in himself. Thomas did not have the True Teacher and Guide leading him in the Way. He was not yet a full and true disciple, having realized the Inner Light and Spirit in himself, able to see, hear, and feel clearly with and in the Spirit. This is true of us all who are early on the path, early in sacred friendship, discipleship—a true and close sacred friendship only happens over time.

Nevertheless, this passage tells us that Yeshua took Thomas aside and spoke three sayings or words to him in private, in secret. This suggests that Yeshua acted with the presence and power of God in himself to sober up Thomas and uplift him into a higher station and state of soul—a higher, more expanded state of consciousness—so that Thomas could see, hear, and feel what was being revealed with greater clarity, knowledge, and understanding. This is very common with messengers of God—apostles, prophets, tzaddikim—in key moments of initiation and revelation with their disciples and spiritual companions. Concerning the secret teachings of riding the chariot of God, or engaging in mystical ascensions of the soul, it is said in the Holy Kabbalah that those teachings can only be spoken to one who knows already and then only one-to-one, in private. This passage alludes to such a transmission of deep, secret mysteries between Yeshua and Thomas of Christ, Messiah and the salvation of souls.

In receiving such inner and secret teachings and revelations, one cannot go speak of such holy things to others, not even others who themselves are close disciples and have progressed in their realization. Such things can be spoken only in the power of the moment, when the Spirit moves, and when the Spirit is the one speaking and revealing the deep secrets of God. That Thomas told his friends they would want to stone him to death if he told them just one of the sayings implies that they would have taken those sayings or words of the Lord as blasphemy at that time, a sin punishable by death. Thomas told his friends if they were to hear what he was told, fire would come from the stones and consume them, implying that the secret of secrets was revealed to him by the Lord. It was in this exchange between Thomas and Yeshua that he came into being as the twin of Yeshua, inwardly resembling him and sharing in something of the supernal realization.

Of course, what Yeshua said to Thomas is known to no one but God and the two of them. You and I cannot say what was spoken between them. But know that if you go deep within and invoke and pray, abiding in an inward communion and waiting upon the Spirit of the Lord, willing to completely pass away in the Inner Light and Spirit, those three words may be spoken in your heart; the Lord may reveal the secrets of secrets to you. Amen.

Verse 14

Yeshua said, "If you fast you will bring sin upon yourselves, and if you pray you will be condemned, and if you give charity you will harm your spirits. When you go into any region and walk through the countryside, and people receive you, eat what they serve you and heal the sick among them. What goes into your mouth will not defile you, but what comes out of your mouth will defile you."

Some of this saying can be found repeated in verses of canonical gospels, but what is said of fasting, prayer, and charity does not appear and is very specifically a teaching of the gnostic path, the straight path, one that is very important to us.

Generally speaking, the religious faithful in the outer and unspiritual churches pray to Christ and God as though separate and apart from them, unaware or in disbelief that Christ, Messiah is within them, denying that God, the Holy One is in as well as ever beyond them. They pray and enact devotions in separation and lack. To fast or pray or give charity in this way further binds the soul to the darkness and ignorance, the illusion of separation and lack which is the cause of sin and death, all sorrow and suffering. Devotions offered in this way do indeed bring sin upon them, condemn them, and harm their spirits—impairing their intelligence, their *ruach*. In the same way, to invoke, pray, and meditate with vital demand and lust for results, seeking realization or enlightenment as though our very nature is not divine or enlightened, or the Inner Light and Spirit is not in us or is something other than our inner being only serves to perpetuate ignorance, separation, and lack. Devotions remain in self-will, self-cherishing, and the play of desire and fear in it. This only serves to bind the mind, heart, and life to the unenlightened condition, reenforcing separation.

When we are initiated and set upon the gnostic path, we are taught to no longer worship the Divine in outwardness or twoness, but in inwardness and oneness—unity and fullness. So with the dawn of faith and more so the dawn of the mystical inclination, we go within to engage devotions in faith, love, and inward cleaving. Receiving influxes of the Holy Light and Spirit, the Christ, Messiah being revealed in us, we are united and filled. Being united and filled, we must no longer pray in ignorance, separation, and lack, but in the faith and knowledge of our being filled with the Holy Light and Spirit, our innate unity with Christ in God—the Messiah in the Holy One.

If in the moment of our devotions—whatever form they may assume—we are not aware of our unity and fullness on an experiential level and so are able to pray in knowledge, then we will pray in faith, and in remembrance, of our innate unity and fullness. We will refrain from praying in outwardness and twoness but always seek to be inward, ingathered in our devotions and communion. If we are not able to be inward, it may be better for us to go take a walk in mindfulness or take up some other practical activity in mindfulness, simply seeking to be in what is happening and be with whomever we encounter until remembrance or awareness is restored. Then, we will be able to shift inward and become re-centered inwardly, remembering the truth of all in the One and the One in all—the Reality of the Holy One.

Listen! There is in truth, in reality, God and God alone—the Holy One. There is no other, there is nothing else. All in its inwardness and its outwardness emanate from the Holy One. There is no other than the One—One from One. The very existence of all, the light and life of all—all the intelligence, attributes, and powers—are from the One and are the manifestation of the One. The Holy One of Being manifests in countless emanations and infinite diversity of people, creatures, and events visible to those invisible, on earth and in the heavens of the great matrix of creation. This is the meaning of the Name of the Holy One in Hebrew used in the story of creation—Elohim, God. *Elohim* is a feminine noun with a masculine plural, indicating female and male: One manifest as Many, the Many being One, and no other. In the Holy Kabbalah, Elohim is often translated to mean "the All-Powerful One" in English, which is to say the presence and power from which all comes, manifest as all: the All-In-All.

This is the truth and reality of the Eternal One. Yahweh is That Which Was, Is, and Forever Shall Be within and behind all that arises, appears, and transpires in creation, in heaven and on earth. Elohim is all that has, is, or shall arise, appear, and transpire. Yahweh Elohim is the Complete Name that appears in the second story of the creation of Adam, the Human One, in the garden of Eden. Yahweh Elohim is the Eternal God.

It is said in the scriptures that a river flowed out of Eden to water the garden. Among Christian Gnostics, this is called the River of Truth, for it waters the Tree of Knowledge and Tree of Life and in it there is salvation. The River of Truth is the remembrance and awareness of oneness, unity, and fullness. You must learn to bathe daily in this holy river of the waters of true knowledge and life, continually remembering the truth, reality of the Absolute Oneness of the Eternal God—Yahweh Elohim—the truth, reality of the Inner Light and Spirit, the Lord, the Christ, Messiah within you.

Invoke often, pray and pray and pray, and meditate, and contemplate deep, and abide in an inward communion, in intimate nearness, and unity and fullness. Invoke, pray, meditate, and be kind, loving, compassionate, and forgiving. Do this not to acquire something you lack or in the delusion of separation of self and other; do it to express who and what you are, the unique and individual emanation, manifestation of the Holy One that you are, being One from One, and no other: be light, be the divine attributes, and realize and embody the presence and power of the Holy One—the Holy Shekinah.

If you are inward in intimate nearness and more so oneness, not you, but the Lord, the Spirit in you will invoke, pray, and meditate. God will invoke God, God will pray to God, God will meditate upon God, and the presence and power of God will move through the invocations, prayers, and meditations. They will not be in vain, but great things will come to pass through them. It will come to pass that you will see with the eyes of God, hear with the ears of God, and feel with the heart of God, and God will delight in God. God in you will know God in all, and know God ever beyond, God knowing God, being God—the All-Present, All-Powerful, All-Knowing One. This is True Gnosis—true knowledge of God, with all understanding and wisdom—knowledge of the secret of secrets that God and God alone reveals to souls.

You, me, we do not invoke, pray, meditate, or deliver, heal, and enlighten, or perform good works. It is the Holy One, Holy Shekinah, who does all these things, that accomplishes all divine actions, all good works with, in, and through us. Being in Christ, Messiah and Christ, Messiah being in us, you, I, we are no longer the doer. The Holy One, Holy Shekinah is the doer in all things. There is no difference whether sacred and mundane, spiritual or material. It is all in the Holy One, Holy Shekinah. There is no other, there is nothing else.

If the Holy One, Holy Shekinah—the Messiah—is walking with you anywhere, in the countryside or in the city, and people receive radiance and Spirit of the Holy One and nourish it in themselves, they will be delivered and healed, realizing their innate unity and divine nature—enlightenment. They will surely be blessed and empowered!

As for what comes out of your mouth, when the Spirit of Truth speaks and is spoken and is nothing but the Truth—from the Lord, to the Lord, and for the Lord—there is no defilement, no sin, no karma. It is the pure, perfect, and complete word of God. It is nothing other than the word of God. When spoken with power, the word delivers, heals, and enlightens, and may prophesy and bring about all manner of great wonders.

Do you understand? I pray that you do! Amen.

Verse 15

Yeshua said, "When you see one not born of woman, fall on your face and worship. That is your father."

Your flesh, your body, is born of woman, from a conception between a man and a woman. They are called your father and mother in this world, and here they are that. But know and understand that you, your soul, are not born of a woman, and are not conceived between a man and woman, but you are born of the Eternal One, you are conceived in the Eternal One, without beginning, without end. As Adonai Yeshua teaches in the Gospel of John, we must be born from water and the Spirit, reborn from above. What is born of the flesh is flesh and is mortal, temporal, impermanent, with a beginning and an end. But what is born of Spirit is Spirit and is immortal, eternal, bornless—without beginning, without end.

As we know, there is a very mysterious character in the scriptures that appeared to Abram and Sarai after the battle with the kings of Edom who is called Melchizedek, King of Righteousness, also called the King of Salem—King of Peace. Melchizedek was not only a king but also priest of God Most High, of El Elyon. Appearing to them, Melchizedek blessed them and blessed God Most High. Having brought out bread and wine, they communed with him in the presence and power of the Infinite and Eternal One. Melchizedek appeared in such radiant beauty and holiness of the Divine Presence—Shekinah—that afterward Abraham tithed to him as to the Most High, giving to Melchizedek one-tenth of all that he had.

According to gnostic teachings and our Christian Kabbalah, Melchizedek was neither from this world nor incarnate in it but from the Pleroma of Light, a pure emanation of the Light of the Infinite One who spontaneously appeared to Abram and Sarai and disappeared in the same way. When Yeshua Messiah says to the religious authorities in the Gospel of John, "Before Abraham was, I Am" (8:58), gnostics understand him to mean that Melchizedek was an appearance of the Eternal Messiah to Abram and Sarai, initiating the messianic process, the messianic continuum in the world after the great flood. Understand that from the perspective of the eternal realm, the Pleroma of Light, there is no time—no past or future in eternity. The Messiah appearing as Melchizedek, Yeshua, or anyone else past, present, or future is a simultaneous event, all in the Eternal One, the Eternal Now.

The precise meaning of this saying in Hebrews is elucidated with perfect clarity, where it is said of Melchizedek: "Without father, without mother, without genealogy, having neither beginning of days nor end of life, but resembling the Son of God, he remains a priest forever" (7:3).

Now if this sounds wild, crazy, or fanciful to you, or too lofty, too remote, or removed from you, remember that while your flesh comes from flesh, you, your soul, comes from the One Soul—Soul of Christ, Messiah—and its true essence and nature is a pure emanation of the Light of the Infinite One, the Eternal One—Bornless Divine or Enlightened Being: the Holy One of Being. What is spoken of Melchizedek in this verse from Hebrews, and in this saying from Thomas, is the truth of your inmost being, the inmost aspects of your soul: who and what you are in the Eternal Messiah and Eternal One—the Pleroma of Light.

As Adonai Yeshua taught, we must be born again of water and the Spirit, reborn from above, from the Eternal Messiah, the Pleroma of Light. Understand that when we receive the Holy Light and Spirit, when the inner Christ, Messiah is revealed to us, so does the fullness of our holy soul come into us. Who and what we are in the Eternal One is united with who we are in ourselves, our soul and flesh uplifted with Christ, Messiah. In truth we are united and filled, resurrected and ascended. We are ordained in a sacred and holy priesthood—the Order of Melchizedek.

According to Hebrews, Yeshua Messiah is the high priest of that Most Holy Order to this world: being in Christ, Messiah and Christ, Messiah being in us, revealed and realized through us, so that all of us in true anointed community—Body of Christ, Messiah—are priest sovereigns of that Holy Order of God Most High, the Absolute Light.

To see one not born of woman is to see the true image of God in you, to see who and what you are in God—your true essence and nature inseparable from the Eternal Messiah, Eternal One, Yeshua, Yahweh. To fall on your face and worship that pure emanation of Truth and Light is to strive with the Spirit to realize and embody that enlightened being, that divine and supernal being—your Divine Self, Divine I Am. Amen.

Verse 16

Yeshua said, "People think that I have come to impose peace upon the world. They do not know that I have come to bring conflicts upon earth: fire, sword, war. For there will be five in a house, and there will be three against two and two against three, father against son, son against father, and they will stand alone."

We must first remember the second saying of this gospel: When we find and receive the Holy Light and Spirit and Christ, Messiah is revealed in us, we will be agitated, troubled, disturbed—an inner conflict already underway will be greatly amplified and accelerated. But if we then abide in inward communion, following the Lord, the Spirit within us, with the Lord, the Spirit we will be victorious and will rule over all.

Understand that the house, the dwelling is you and your life, and the five who are in it correspond with the five aspects of your soul: three inner aspects—divine spark, light power, and divine nature, or *yechidah*, *hayyah*, and *neshamah*—and two outer aspects—human intelligence and vital soul, or *ruach* and *nefesh*. The inner aspects of our soul may rightly be called father or mother and the outer aspects son or daughter. The inner conflict and discord early on between the inner and outer aspects of our soul or our inner and outer being is indeed something like that of a parent striving with an unruly teenage child who is as yet ignorant of themselves and inexperienced in life, striving to individuate and find themselves often in the wrong ways, often making very poor decisions.

Our initiation, the experience of light transmission and the imparting of the Spirit, brings mystical experiences of the presence and power of God in us, the light and love of Christ, Messiah in us. At first it is only natural that there will be ways of thought, speech, and action in addition to various aspects in our lives that are not aligned and in harmony with the inner Christ, Messiah. Many aspects may even be in complete contradiction and conflict with our inner being in Christ, Messiah. After all, we begin in ignorance and generally speaking, a bestial state, having strong self-will, self-grasping, desire, and fear. Much will likely need to be changed, transformed, and integrated over time. Likewise, as the Living Presence, Living Spirit initiates her divine action with, in, and through us, it is not uncommon that some tumult might ensue in our lives; some powerful temptations and distractions may arise in something of a test of our faith, love, and devotion and commitment to the Divine Life. It is also common that when we experience a spiritual conversion, some people in our lives might have an adverse reaction; changes in our relationships and friendships may occur. However, all of this is the Spirit revealing to us things that need to be changed and barriers that need to be overcome in order to fulfill our true hearts' desires, the true will of our inner being, our holy soul, which is the will of the Eternal One for us.

As the Parable of the Sower of seeds teaches, there are many who, upon hearing the word of God spoken with power, do not become rooted in the Christ Life. When troubles arise, they become discouraged and lose faith; when temptations and distractions appear, they succumb to them. Many spiritual seekers have misconceptions at the outset about the spiritual life and its rewards, thinking that through being spiritual, the desires of the ego, the little self will be fulfilled, that things will go their way; they will have good fortune and avoid troubles as though God is on their side. But God is not on anyone's side, or rather is on *everyone's* side, within all people and all things. God does intend the fulfillment of our true hearts' desires and dreams, the true will of our holy soul, our inner being. God does indeed provide for those who have faith. Troubles in our interior and exterior life are a natural part of life. If we remain faithful, inward, and cleave to Christ, Messiah, the Lord, the Spirit will see us through them. From whatever suffering arises, through the Lord, the Spirit we will experience great blessings and often leaps in spiritual and supernal realization. From a gnostic perspective, the spiritual life is not about rewards in this life, nor in the seven heavens for that matter. It is about the fulfillment of the holy soul's purpose and mission, not the superficial desires of the vital soul and ego: It is about the realization, enlightenment of our soul, being who and what we are in God, the desire for God, the love of God, the desire for nearness, and ultimately oneness with God. It is for God we strive, for the true kingdom of heaven—the realization of the Pleroma of Light, reintegration with the Infinite Light.

Rather than things always going our way or a desire to avoid troubles, in faith and the spiritual life we seek the fulfillment of God's will, which is our very own true will and true desire. Our trials and tribulations are understood to be vehicles for our realization. Just as with more pleasurable times, our sufferings hold blessings from God, often even greater blessings. Our challenges in life serve to mature our faith, love, and inward cleaving, all of which refine our soul and bring significant progressions in the realization of our soul in Christ, Messiah. In this regard, we might remember the example of Adonai Yeshua in the garden of Gethsemane before the suffering of the passion and cross: He prayed to God that if it were possible or there was another way for full revelation of Messiah and the manifestation of salvation not that the cup of suffering be taken from him but that God's will—not his own—be done.

There is another truth of the coming of Christ, Messiah in this world and the baptism of fire and the Spirit: Whether in the first coming or the second coming in glory in these end times, Christ brings great influxes of the Supernal Light and Spirit. As a previous saying taught us, this fire is cast upon the entire world, upon all people, and the Christ, Messiah is tending it until it blazes and all is consumed by it.

To some it will be light; to others, fire. Fire accelerates consciousness in faithful and spiritual people and in unfaithful and unspiritual people alike. Whether good and true, evil and false, righteous or wicked, there is an amplification and intensification of what is held in hearts and minds. There is an inner conflict within all people, all souls that must be resolved. If it is not resolved inwardly, the conflict becomes externalized; great conflict, great violence, breaks out in unenlightened cultures, societies, the world. Very severe conflict erupts even between family members and friends. What is present within people and the collective consciousness is revealed, exposed, and comes forward in powerful ways—good and evil, great righteousness and great wickedness. As we are witnessing in the end times, this second coming in glory with a greater force of influx, conflict becomes more extreme than ever before because of the culmination of ignorance, darkness, wickedness, and evil: It is a self-destruction of humankind and the world. It is not the judgment of God upon us, but our own self-judgment, severities, great sufferings, we bring upon ourselves.

Do know and understand, however, that while there is a greater and greater darkness being manifest, so also a greater and greater influx of light, the light and darkness being the manifestation of one and the same Supernal Force, or presence and power of God, manifesting through people. For those who are inward and who abide in an inward communion, for whom the inner conflict is resolved, who are in Christ, Messiah—the Holy Light and Spirit—being so united and filled, salvation, realization, and enlightenment transpires. But for those who are outward and for whom there is no resolution of the inner conflict, nor knowledge of the inner Christ, the Messiah within themselves, having no faith, communion, or peace, who are in separation and lack, the ignorance and darkness will consume them. They will fall into great sorrow and suffering with no salvation or deliverance at hand.

You see, this supernal force amplifies, intensifies, and makes manifest whatever is held within hearts, minds, and souls, generating the corresponding realities of experience in this life and the afterlife. Through their own thoughts, words, and actions, desires and fears, individuals are the creators of these relative realities. The realities of their experience are a radiant, magical display of their own energy, their own being and consciousness in whatever state they may be: godly or ungodly, righteous or wicked, or some admixture in between.

In Christ, Messiah—the Holy Light and Spirit—and true anointed community—the Body of Christ, Messiah—is refuge, true sanctuary, for those who desire it. Regardless of what transpires outwardly, there will be an inner peace and joy. They will be established in the true kingdom of heaven, the Pleroma of Light. Amen.

Verse 17

Yeshua said, "I shall give you what no eye has seen, what no ear has heard, what no hand has touched, what has not arisen in the human heart."

The messianic expectation among the Jewish people in ancient Palestine was very different from the coming of the Messiah as intended in the Eternal One. Though great prophets had spoken mysteries of the Messiah with clarity, and Daniel beheld in a vision the Spirit and Soul of the Messiah emanating from the Ancient of Days—Atik Yomin—the Israelites conceived of the coming of the Messiah in the context of previous revelations of the Holy One that were familiar to them: a messiah who would arise like the fabled kings of Israel, a great warrior-king like David.

When they heard of God's Anointed One, they envisioned a warrior-king who would lead them in battle with God on their side to vanquish every enemy of Israel and establish a new, earthly kingdom of God, something like what was lost long ago but greater and more powerful. They expected the Messiah to be a warrior-king, not a priest-king according to the Order of Melchizedek, let alone a divine human unified with the Eternal One, embodying the fullness of the Supernal Light and Eternal Spirit.

While prophets before the coming of the Messiah communed with the Holy One in states of nearness and some even a most intimate nearness, all remained in separation, more or less, such that among the people, oneness or conscious union with the Eternal One was inconceivable, unimaginable. So, the appearance of the Messiah as high priest and divine sovereign of the Order of Melchizedek, a divine-human being in conscious union with the Holy One, who embodied the fullness of the Holy Light and Spirit, had never been envisioned or conceived in their hearts, not in the least.

Curiously enough, the true mystery of the coming of the Messiah and true teaching of the Holy Gospel would soon fade away and be lost in a relatively short period of time after Yeshua, the original apostles, and original followers of the Way. It would be preserved only by a few people in secret. Apart from actual revelation and realization, or knowledge of the Messiah and Holy One, in the dawn of orthodoxy and its speculative, man-made doctrines, rites, rituals, and priestcraft devoid of the Holy Light and Spirit, God was once again conceived as far removed from human beings, and Christ, or the reality of the divine-human, was isolated to Yeshua, so that no other could be and become a divine-human, or Christ, Messiah. Basically speaking, the Father was conceived as something like the Greek Zeus, and the Son something like the Greek Apollo, removed from and lording over humankind, rather than as a Living Presence, Living Spirit in all people being called to realize the state of a divine-human, or the inner Christ, Messiah within themselves.

Consequently, just as a majority among the Jewish people misconceived the first coming of the Messiah and could not recognize or accept Adonai Yeshua as the Messiah, so now in the second coming of the Messiah in glory many Christians are not able to recognize or accept how Christ, Messiah appears again. They have misconceived of the second coming as the literal reappearance of the historical Jesus, Yeshua coming back to earth from heaven. The second coming, however, is not occurring through a single individual, but many individuals, all who receive the Holy Light and Spirit, and are ingathered into true anointed community. The glory is a greater influx of the Supernal Light and Spirit in the end times as Christ, Messiah is appearing again through many more people than in the first coming, many more people realizing the state of a divine human, or Christ, Messiah within themselves.

As with the first coming, and the revelation of Christ, Messiah risen and ascended, so now in the second coming of Christ, Messiah in glory with a cloud of witnesses of a greater outpouring, realization, and embodiment of the Holy Light and Spirit. This saying in Thomas remains true: "What has not been seen, heard, felt, or conceived in human hearts, is being given to us." Certainly so!

As Yeshua taught in his final discourse in the Gospel of John, those who saw him saw God, and those who received the Spirit and were filled with the Holy Light and Spirit are indwelt by Christ and God—the Eternal Messiah and Eternal One. Like him, they are divine and supernal human beings, a new humanity of a new heaven and earth, all in the Pleroma of Light, the Messiah and Holy One.

Understand that all people, creatures, and things are unique and individual. No two are alike. As in creation, so in revelation. God never repeats Godself; every revelation is new and is an evolution and progression from what was revealed before. So it is with the coming of Christ, Messiah. Just as with the first coming of Christ, Messiah in Yeshua and those with him, so now in the second coming through us, within and through all who open to the Holy Light and Spirit, within whom the inner Christ, Messiah is revealed and realized in unity with Christ, Messiah in the Eternal One.

This is the word of the Eternal Messiah and Holy One being spoken in and among us today. Amen.

Verse 18

The disciples said to Yeshua, "Tell us how our end will be." Yeshua said, "Have you discovered the beginning and now are seeking the end? Where the beginning is, the end will be. Blessed are you who stand at the beginning. You will know the end and will not taste death."

There is an open secret of the eternal realm: There is no time in eternity—no past and no future, only the Eternal One, Eternal Now without beginning or end. In the eternal realm, all arises from Radiant Nothingness, Endless Light from the One-Without-End. Our heavenly and supernal soul—*neshamah*—and the interiors of that holy soul, our divine spark and life force—*yechidah* and *hayyah*—are emanations of that Endless Light and so are eternal, without beginning, without end: They are immortal, bornless.

Although incarnate in this world, your soul reaches into the eternal realm from the depths of your soul, in the heart of your soul. Your supernal and heavenly soul is without beginning, without end: birthless and therefore deathless. The inmost aspects of your soul, the divine spark, life force, and divine nature are inseparable from the Radiant Nothingness, Infinite Light, the Eternal One. The inmost aspect of your holy soul is so holy that only God and God alone can enter it, even the most holy of supernal angels cannot enter that holy of holies; only the Eternal God— Yahweh Elohim—may do so. God and Godhead indwell that inmost aspect of your soul that is inseparable from the Infinite and Eternal One. The very essence and nature of your soul, your being and consciousness, is eternal, birthless, and Infinite Light, Radiant Nothingness—the glory and radiance of the Infinite and Eternal One.

The Eternal One, Infinite One is called Nothingness—Ain—because God, as God is in Godself, is nameless, unknowable, unspeakable, without beginning, without end, without any attribute or quality whatsoever. This Nothingness, however, is Everythingness. Nothingness is Fullness—Pleroma—for everything emanates and arises from it, exists in it, and returns to it, and is the very essence and nature of all that arises, appears, and transpires.

Although the Infinite One—Ain Sof—is without attributes, all in a great and supreme mystery, attributes emanate from the Infinite One, the supernal glory and radiance of the One-Without-End. Those attributes are called Sefirot or Aeons in some gnostic scriptures. It is through these supernal attributes that creation comes into being, by which the Infinite and Eternal One interacts with and is revealed in creation: attributes such as will, wisdom, understanding, knowledge, mercy, severity, beauty, eternity, glory, holiness, sovereignty, and the many qualities, attributes within them. Of all the literally countless attributes, we contemplate one hundred, each of which are immeasurable, endless depths, all the radiance of the Infinite and Eternal One—all Infinite Light, Radiant Nothingness. From this, souls emanate and are woven of these attributes and come into being through them, just as the entire matrix of creation—spiritual, astral, and material—emanates from this primordial and supernal Reality of the Eternal One, the eternal realm—the Pleroma of Light.

The Spirit and Soul of Christ, Messiah is this Pleroma of Light: the fullness of the Supernal Light and Eternal Spirit of human souls share in this enlightened, supernal, and divine nature. This is the intrinsic nature of the soul, consciousness, mind in all people, creatures, and sentient beings. Within that primordial and supernal nature—the bornless nature—are all of the attributes, powers, actions of the Eternal One, this presence and power of the Eternal God—Holy Shekinah, Holy Spirit.

Going within, going deeper still, and being ingathered by the Spirit, with the Spirit, it is the Spirit that reveals the Messiah and Holy One to you—within you and beyond you. Likewise, the Spirit reveals your holy soul, yourself, that you might know your true self—the Divine Self, Divine I Am—that you might have what is yours in the Eternal Messiah, the Eternal One: the full array of divine attributes, powers, actions, of the Living

Presence, Living Spirit of the Eternal God, the Almighty—Yahweh Elohim, Shaddai.

To discover the beginning is to go deep within, into the endless depths of you, your soul to rest and abide in the intrinsic nature of your soul, consciousness, mind, resting in the Messiah and Holy One. Resting in your intrinsic nature, abiding in an inward communion in and with the Spirit, you will see, hear, feel, and know the beginning: Bornless, Primordial, Supernal Being, the Holy One, without beginning, without end, from which your soul, consciousness, mind, in its essence and nature, is a pure emanation. There is none other than the Holy One—One from One.

Standing in the beginning in this way, indeed we are immeasurably blessed, knowing that in the Eternal Messiah, Eternal One, we are without end, from eternal life. Amen.

Verse 19

Yeshua said, "Blessed are you who came into being before coming into being. If you become my disciples and hear my sayings, these stones will serve you. For there are five trees in paradise for you. Summer or winter they do not change and their leaves do not fall. Whoever knows them will not taste death."

This is a very beautiful, very esoteric saying, as are many in this gospel. There are many layers of meaning and interpretations speaking deep truths, secret mysteries. What I can share with you here is just a hint of one or two interpretations. But know that is true of all holy scriptures; there is much more within it than any single comment or brief commentary can possibly draw out. If we learn to look and see, listen and hear, and feel with the Spirit, studying and contemplating scriptures in the very same Spirit that inspired them, we will find that they are endless depths of divine wisdom and revelation. In the Spirit, there is no end to the insights and illuminations that may come through them.

"Blessed are you who came into being before coming into being" corresponds with your bornless nature, your heavenly and supernal soul—neshamah—that, realized or not, is within and behind all incarnations, all the while holding true knowledge, understanding, and wisdom of the Eternal One and Pleroma of Light. Even when realized and embodied, that divine or enlightened nature abides in the Pleroma of Light and is pure from the very beginning, without taint, trace, stain, mark, impurity, or corruption of sin, error, karma. It remains ever pure and pristine—virgin. The bornless nature abides greatly blessed in the supernal beauty, holiness, and glory of the Eternal One. This holy soul shares in the divine nature of the Soul of the Eternal Messiah, being parallel and corresponding with the inner Christ, Messiah, the Divine Self, Christ Self. Those who become true disciples of Yeshua Messiah, who hear the word of the Eternal One spoken with power, who receive the Holy Light and Spirit, the inner Christ, Messiah—Divine I Am—will be revealed, realized, and embodied in them. To walk with the power, to spiritualize and transform the flesh and even matter itself is to be served by stones.

As we know, there are five aspects of the soul, and our divine nature, intelligence, and vital soul are the primary aspects realized in this world. Souls pass through many incarnations before coming into being and becoming realized or embodying their divine or enlightened nature, their heavenly and supernal soul. In each incarnation are new emanations of intelligence and vital soul through which the divine nature or supernal soul is incarnated and embodied. If unrealized in this life, those outer aspects of soul pass away in the afterlife, dissolving into their root. Only the karmic continuum of the soul is retained in the exteriors of the supernal soul. But when spiritual or supernal realization occurs, the intelligence and vital soul are ingathered into the interiors of the supernal soul, continuing immortally and remaining forever in the Pleroma of Light and Eternal One.

Quite naturally, when ingathered in this way, in the World-That-Is-Coming—the Pleroma of Light—the divine spark, the light power of the soul is realized and unified with the supernal soul, manifest as the enlightened intelligence and vital soul. These five unified aspects of the soul point to the five trees in paradise that do not change. Speaking of their leaves, know and understand that they correspond with the realization of all divine attributes, powers, actions: all stations and states of soul.

Another interpretation I am inclined to share with you is this: In the inmost secret teachings of the Christian Kabbalah are what are called Melchizedek teachings, which are parallel with essential teachings of the straight path, which describe the Great Vision of Melchizedek. In those teachings, the Infinite Light is called the Perfect Light, the Clear Light Nature, and the Great Natural Perfection, terms that speak of the intrinsic nature of the soul, consciousness, and mind. With these teachings and their corresponding devotions—primordial meditation, primordial contemplation—practitioners learn to rest in the intrinsic nature of mind and experience a complete passing away, dissolution, union with the Clear

Light Nature: a state of spacious, radiant awareness, or nondual gnostic awareness. For those who are able to abide in this Clear Light Union, there may arise the Great Vision.

At the outset of this divine and supernal vision arises a primordial sound-vibration—Word—that parallels the secret utterance of the Great Name of the Eternal One—Yahweh—but that no mortal or angelic voice, tongue, or mouth can intone. This sound-vibration stirs a generation of five essential, supernal lights, the arising of the five primordial elements of the soul, consciousness, mind in their innate purity and perfection: space, air, fire, water, and earth. Streams, rays, and lines of light emanate from these five points of essential light in something like a brilliant, translucent, glorious rainbow, forming geometrical patterns from which in turn light entities, images, and realms are generated in the appearance of countless holy and enlightened ones, supernal elders, supernal princes, and angels of the Messiah. It is a vision of the emanation of the Supernal Reality of the Holy One from the Primordial Reality of the Holy One, or the full array of the Pleroma of Light arising from the Radiant Nothingness. In this Great Vision, the Holy One is the seeing, hearing, and feeling.

Once arising in purity, generating the Pleroma, there is a shift of the sound-vibration that in the same way gives rise to the reality of the spiritual dimension-universe of creation, corresponding with the five elements arising in a most subtle and sublime impurity—duality or separation. Then another shift in vibration follows, generating the reality of the astral dimension-universe of creation, an arising of those essential lights in greater impurity—duality and separation. Finally is yet another shift or lowering of vibration that gives rise to the reality of the material dimension-universe, an arising of those essential lights in extreme impurity, a virtually complete apparent dualism and separation, such that they are as false, glowing lights compared with the Clear Light—the True Light—and the original arising of the five essential lights within it.

As this Great Vision dawns and this revelation, realization unfolds, parallel with it is a generation of what is called the Threefold Body of Melchizedek: truth body, glory body, and manifestation body. The truth body corresponds with the soul unified, reintegrated, with the Clear Light—Infinite Light; the glory body is the arising of the appearance of that holy and enlightened one in the Pleroma of Light and in the spiritual and astral dimensions; the manifestation body is their appearance in the material world, their flesh transformed by the power of this supernal realization in the Eternal Messiah, or Reality of Melchizedek—the Most Holy Order of primordial enlightenment, supernal realization. This corresponds with the full reaching, realization of the station and state of a gnostic apostle, gnostic Master. Within it, like a wave rolling forward, backward, and then further forward, there is a reaching, not reaching, and then a final reaching into the station and state of the Messiah. On an inmost secret level, this saying is speaking of this full supernal realization, the coming into being of messengers of the Pleroma of Light, or gnostic apostles, gnostic masters.

"Blessed are you who came into being before coming into being" connotes that those who are messengers were predestined to be messengers, having entered into supernal realization in Christ, Messiah in previous lives and returned to incarnate in love and compassion, having the desire for the enlightenment and liberation of all living spirits and souls. This reality of previously realized souls predestined to be messengers of the Pleroma is taught in a gnostic gospel called *Pistis Sophia*—"Faith-Wisdom." It opens with the revelation of the risen and ascended Messiah to close disciples, appearing to them as Messiah Yeshua again, telling them that he put their souls into their mothers' wombs, along with the twelve powers of the twelve saviors, and that coming into being as holy apostles, they are co-redeemers with him, the Christ, Messiah being revealed through them, as through Yeshua. Quite naturally, in such a realization of the Eternal Messiah, the Eternal One, a soul will not taste death, but will experience a continuum of bornless being, pure radiant awareness, passing beyond, going beyond. Amen.

Verse 20

The disciples said to Yeshua, "Tell us what the kingdom of heaven is like." He said to them, "It is like a mustard seed, the tiniest of seeds, but when it falls on prepared soil, it produces a great plant and becomes a shelter for birds of heaven."

This is a well-known parable that is echoed in canonical gospels. We need to first acknowledge that mustard is like a weed that can swiftly take over land. Once present, it is neither easy nor always possible to completely eradicate. So it is with the kingdom of heaven and the seeds of light sown in the hearts of people in each generation: Having been established in the consciousness of humanity and in the world, the kingdom of heaven continues to endure and will endure in the world until the end of days. If and when the light transmission and imparting of the Holy Spirit passes from a lineage and community after a time as it eventually does through the supernal grace of the Eternal One in Christ, Messiah, it will break out elsewhere in other places, and among other people from which new anointed lineages and communities will come into being. As much as the outer and unspiritual churches and unenlightened societies have sought to persecute and destroy true apostles and prophets and oppress mystics and gnostics, nevertheless, through the grace and mercy of the Holy One, Holy Shekinah, they continue to appear among us and continue to thrive. Hallelu Yah! Praise the Lord!

At the outset, when we first hear the word of God with power and experience light transmission and the passing of the Holy Spirit, it is very much like a seed of light planted in our hearts. When we are first reborn from above, just as being born below, we are like infants. There is a need to nurture and nourish that Holy Light and tend that Holy Fire until that light becomes brilliant and blazes like fire within us, such that others around us might also be ignited. This is why we need to abide in an inward communion and have a daily continuum of devotions. We need to invoke often, and pray and pray and pray, meditate, and contemplate deep, just as we need to gather with anointed community in invocation, prayer, and meditation. We must also remember and keep the Holy Shabbat. Joined with this, we must seek to be very, very kind and cultivate, generate, true human and divine attributes, and be willing to change and change and change, striving always with the Holy Spirit for a better resurrection, a greater realization in Christ, Messiah.

For those who are in the Lord, the Spirit, such devotions are a delight to them. As they progress in a spiritual and supernal realization, more and more they will experience the inspiration of the Spirit in their devotions as the Lord, the Spirit takes up their devotions, invoking, praying, meditating through them. So, a greater and greater presence and power of the Holy One will be in their invocations and prayers. They will find that they have the ear of heaven, that powers of heaven will move with them when they invoke and pray, taking action and fulfilling prayers swiftly, at times even before they are spoken, while still just a stirring in the heart of the devotee.

Quite naturally, abiding in an inward communion with the Messiah and Holy Spirit, being filled with the Holy Light and Spirit, as we resemble the Messiah, we also resemble the angels, the powers of heaven, whose souls are light and who manifest in bodies of light. As we have a communion with the Messiah and Holy One, so we also have a communion with angels, as well as with the spirits of apostles, prophets, tzaddikim of the past and present: a communion with saints and angels. For those who can see, hear, and feel with the Spirit around messengers and in gatherings of anointed community for Spirit-filled worship and sacred ceremony, the presence and awareness of angels coming and going from that space is very common. But then this is true of all faithful and spiritual people as they mature in faith, love, and inward cleaving. They progress in their spiritual or supernal realization, having the presence and power of the Holy One within and all around them. So they abide in the good company of heaven, of angels. Amen.

Verse 21

Mirya [the Magdala] said to Yeshua, "What are your disciples like?" He said, "They are like children living in a field that is not theirs. When the owners of the field come, they will say, 'Give our field back to us.' The children will take off their clothes in front of them and give it back, and they will return the field to them. So I say, if the owner of a house knows a thief is coming, he will be on his guard before the thief arrives and will not let the thief break into the house of his estate and steal the possessions. As for you, be on guard against the world, arm yourselves with great strength, or robbers will find a way to reach you, for the trouble you expect will come. Let someone among you understand. When the crop ripened, the reaper came quickly with sickle in hand and harvested it. Whoever has ears should hear."

This world and the unenlightened society ruling it are not our own. But for a time we are here in this world and we live in it. When we pass away and our soul departs our body, in effect for us, the entire world and all that is in it passes away. Our soul, consciousness, mind, arises in the afterlife states in a subtle body of astral, spiritual, or supernal light. It is something like awakening from your dreams in the morning. When you awaken, where does your appearance in the dream, its world, and all the people and things appearing in the dream reality go? They return to the source from which they arose, never having had any independent, substantial existence separate and apart from the intrinsic nature of the soul, consciousness, mind in which they were conceived and appeared. As it turns out, passing beyond, we discover that the reality of this world is in fact, dreamlike; arising in the afterlife states, we encounter the True Reality within and behind all that arises and appears, whether in incarnation and waking consciousness, sleep and dream, or death and the afterlife: the Eternal Messiah, Eternal One—Infinite Light, Radiant Nothingness.

The Holy Kabbalah teaches that every night in sleep and dream, the soul departs the body to wander in the realities, worlds, realms, of inner dimensions: astral, spiritual, and supernal. For those who abide in a deep inward communion, seeking God and God alone, they ascend and go to God to experience and delight in the presence, power, and knowledge of God in the realities of the supernal dimension—the Pleroma of Light. Along the way, however, souls encounter all manner of spiritual forces and influences—angelic, archonic, and demonic. If in self-grasping, desire, and fear, the soul clings to them, gets caught up in them, and is unable to ascend into the Supernal Reality of the Holy One, Holy Shekinah. Instead, it is bound up more or less in impure lights and realities of the astral and spiritual dimensions in dualism, separation.

According to gnostic scriptures as well as the Kabbalah, when people die and their soul arises in the afterlife states, something similar happens, but in realities far more powerful and intense on an experiential level: the possible experience of a prolonged wandering in the astral earth parallel with this world, or experiences of heavens and hells, and all manner of other astral and spiritual realities in between. If there is any turning right or left, or looking back, rather than going to God and straight to God, the True Light, souls get caught up in impure and false astral and spiritual lights, as it were, and eventually return to physical, material incarnation. In this regard, souls ascend who are able and willing to take off their clothes—their bodies—free from self-cherishing, attachment, and aversion, leaving the world behind. Not looking back but instead going straight to God, the True Light, is essential.

The Gospel of Philip teaches that we need to be resurrected and ascended before we die so that we can enter into the rest, repose of the Eternal Messiah in the Eternal One in complete reintegration with the Infinite Light. Understand that to go within and go deeper still into the depths of your soul, to merge with the Inner Light and Spirit—Christ, Messiah within you—is to pass away, to die before you die, and so be resurrected and ascended in Christ, Messiah before you die. As we mature in our inward communion and progress in our spiritual and supernal realization, we die to the world and are reborn from above, established in the kingdom of heaven. Self-grasping, desire, and fear—the cause of all sorrow and suffering—are progressively diminished and even brought to cessation. We experience resurrection and ascension—enlightenment and liberation—while as yet in this world.

When we abide in deep inward communion, the gnostic experience that arises is threefold: (1) it is the experience of higher, more expanded mental and supramental states of consciousness, the peak of which is supramental, supernal; (2) it is the opening of consciousness to new, inner, and metaphysical dimensions, and the entities and realities within them—realms within realms, worlds within worlds, astral, spiritual, and supernal; (3) it is true mystical experience, knowledge of Christ and God—the Messiah and Holy One—in states of nearness, intimate nearness, and ultimately oneness, conscious union with Christ in God, the True Light.

In this way, perhaps you may understand that there can indeed be direct spiritual and mystical experience of the resurrection and ascension before we die, all as is given to us in the Christ Spirit, the Holy Spirit. As we go within, deeper and deeper within, there is a greater and greater experience of consciousness beyond the body, a presence of awareness as we shift between states of consciousness, as from waking consciousness into sleep and dream, or from this life into death and the afterlife. We remain awake and do not fall unconscious. With this greater experience of consciousness beyond the body and an increasing presence of awareness, consciousness expands our body and life: The fullness of our soul in the Holy Light and Spirit are being realized and embodied in us.

Quite naturally, we do need to arm ourselves with great strength. We must arm ourselves with faith, hope, love, and passionate, inward cleaving and devotion, invoking often, praying and praying and praying, and meditating, contemplating deep. And while we are in this world, we need to be willing to change and change and change, always striving with the Spirit toward a better resurrection, a greater realization in Christ, Messiah. Our spiritual life and practice need to be the essential priority of our lives, not a hobby or side affair. We must not let any resistances or distractions in the world deter us from seeking God and God alone or abiding in direct communion with God. We must go straight to God and God alone.

All of these secret mysteries are possible for you in Christ and God— the Messiah and Holy One. Know and believe that they are! Amen.

Verse 22

Yeshua saw some nursing babies. He said to his disciples, "These nursing babies are like those who enter the kingdom." They said to him, "Then shall we enter the kingdom as babies?" Yeshua said to them, "When you make the two into one, and when you make the inner like the outer and the outer like the inner, and the upper like the lower, and when you make the male and female into a single one, when you make an eye in place of an eye, a hand in place of a hand, a foot in place of a foot, an image in place of an image, then you will enter the kingdom."

The first part of this saying is echoed in later gospels that were canonized, though in those versions it is little children, not nursing babies of whom Yeshua spoke. However, those gospels lack a teaching on what "being as little children" means, a teaching which Thomas offers that is a direct expression of the gnostic path or straight path.

Let me share an open secret with you as we contemplate the secret interpretation of this saying: The mystery of seeing the Eternal One face to face is not what most religious faithful people think, as though one stands before God enthroned, separate and apart from God, where you and God are seeing one another's faces in an apparent self and other—not in the least! Rather, it is God putting God's face *in* you; your face is a face of God, and so seeing God face to face is one holy face, your face *and* God's face. Do you see? I pray that you do!

When you make two into one, aware that there has never been two but only one, the Holy One, all the while realizing there has never been a self other than the Holy One and that there is no other than the Holy One—you then see your true self is the Holy One, Holy Shekinah. The apparent self, separate and apart from the Holy One, is empty of any independent and substantial self-existence. Such a self is illusory, unreal, like an image in a mirror, a mirage in the open desert.

When you are awake and recognize and realize this Truth of the Holy One, you will see God face to face. You will know and understand that the Holy One is the seeing, hearing, and feeling, the smelling, tasting, and touching, the sleeping and waking up. Sitting and standing, walking and running, eating and drinking, having sex—all that happens through you, through the Holy One, in this life and beyond—is all the Holy One, all in the Holy One, from the One, to the One and for the One.

Understand that the inner space and outer space are one space, the Holy One, the Place—Makom. The Holy One is the space or place of all. As all is in the Holy One, the Holy One is in all and is all—the All-In-All. There is no other; there is nothing else. There never has been anything else. In truth, there is no inside or outside, just one infinite radiant spaciousness, the Holy One of Being. What else is there? Nothing! What more can I say?

I will tell you that receiving the Holy Light and Spirit is awakening to the Inner Light and Spirit in you, that you and your soul are. You have received nothing other than yourself and what is your own from the very beginning. You have received yourself, which is the Messiah and Holy One: Yourself has been revealed to you, remembered, recognized, if but for a moment, so that you can be and become what you are, Christ, Messiah— One from One, an Anointed One.

If you abide in an inward communion and are deep inward, reaching into the depth of your soul, into the heart of your soul, therein you will know yourself, you will know the Messiah and Holy One. You will remember that in truth and reality, there is the Holy One and Holy One alone— no other, nothing else.

In this awakening, this revelation and realization, it is as though God puts God's face in you, God's eye, God's hand, God's foot, and well, God's everything in you—the mind, heart, and soul of God, all of the attributes, powers, actions of God—so that you are a true image and likeness of God, the Eternal One.

This is what is the inner Christ, Messiah is: God giving Godself to you, giving yourself to you, as it were, so God may be revealed, realized, and embodied in you, incarnate as you.

Man or woman, there is no difference, the Truth is the same, the true self of all is the Holy One—Infinite Light, Radiant Nothingness. There is no difference, none whatsoever!

It is in this way that we enter the kingdom of heaven, the kingdom of God, because that is what we are and so it is our own.

Quite naturally, a vital, sentimental belief or an intellectual, conceptual belief in this will neither accomplish nor attain anything. The Truth needs to be experienced and known, revealed and realized in the Spirit, through the Spirit. Once revealed, the Truth must be lived and so embodied. Amen.

Verse 23

Yeshua said, "I shall choose you as one from a thousand and as two from ten thousand, and they will stand as a single one."

There is indeed a harvest of souls underway, an ingathering of those who are ripe and mature for harvest, who desire to seek and find God, who desire actual enlightenment, realization, whether spiritual or supernal. While one from a thousand or two from ten thousand seems like very few —and relatively speaking, it is—if you consider the vast number of people in the world today, it is many people; if you consider the far greater number of people throughout the generation of humankind in this world, it is countless many more souls that are ingathered.

If it is troubling to you to hear that so few will be saved, realized, or enlightened from among the masses, consider and contemplate how many sea turtles hatch in a given year and how few survive and come full circle to conceive a new generation of their kind. Or consider salmon: How many hatch, and how few are able to reach the spawning ground in due season, to complete their life cycle and the continuation of their kind? It is the same with the realization or enlightenment of living spirits and souls in the worlds of creation. Among the throng of the masses, relatively few enter into enlightenment and are liberated or return to God, return to be One.

Yet it requires the masses of living things to fulfill the ultimate purpose of life, the Divine Intention of creation. It may rightly be said that realized or unrealized, all people and creatures are integral to the fulfillment of the Divine Intention. As souls are realized, enlightened, so all are uplifted and progressed with them toward their fruition, their realization or enlightenment. As we know, holy and enlightened ones—realized souls—return to incarnate for the harvest of souls, to facilitate the realization, enlightenment, to ingather all willing spirits and souls into the Pleroma of Light. There are messengers—apostles, prophets, tzaddikim—appearing among us in every generation; so it shall be until the end of days and fruition of the second coming of Christ, Messiah.

Salvation is universal. All living spirits and souls will eventually be realized, enlightened, reintegrated with the Infinite Light, if not in this world, then in another; if not in this universe, then another. However many countless lifetimes in such a distant future, eventually all will be realized, enlightened, and reintegrated with the Infinite Light.

"One from a thousand" refers to those faithful who enter into a spiritual realization in mental consciousness, those who experience inward communion in various states of nearness, even intimate nearness. The height of spiritual realization is the experiences of cosmic consciousness and the overmind, within which a most subtle and sublime dualism, separation remains. Two from ten thousand, this corresponds with spiritual people who experience the dawn of supernal realization, states of supramental consciousness, and an inward communion in states of oneness, conscious union—true Christ or God Consciousness.

These two groups of chosen ones or spiritual elect are also understood among gnostics to be those souls harvested and ingathered in a generation, by those who harvest and ingather—the messengers of the Pleroma of Light.

Yeshua teaches that they will stand as a single one: All will be uplifted. If living according to their faith and knowledge—the Truth and Light revealed to them—through the supernal grace in the Eternal Messiah, those in a spiritual realization may be brought into a supernal realization in Messiah in the Great Resurrection and Ascension. There is indeed salvation through grace in Messiah Yeshua for those who have faith, love, and inward cleaving. The inner Christ, the Messiah will bring their realization to fruition.

Such is the presence and power of the Messiah and Holy One in true anointed community—the true Body of Christ, Messiah. All become as a single one. Through grace, the Holy Spirit, all are united and filled, resurrected and ascended. Hallelu Yah! Praise the Lord! Amen.

Verse 24

His disciples said, "Show us the place where you are. We must seek it." He said to them, "Whoever has ears should hear. There is light within a person of light and [that light] shines on the whole world. If it does not shine [they are darkness]."

This is a very essential and beautiful teaching. Something similar is taught in the Sermon on the Mount in the Gospel of Matthew at the conclusion of the Beatitudes: "You are the light of the world; let your light shine" (5:16). Here, however, it is clearly stated what that light is: the inner Christ, Messiah, the Sun of God that shines from within us when we are inward and live from inwardness, from the Inner Light and Spirit.

There is something to be said of Adonai Yeshua—Lord Jesus—that many of the religious faithful do not understand. Quite literally, Christ, Messiah appeared in him to reveal our true self to us, to show us who and what we are in God, the True Light—a human one of light, a son or daughter of God, with the presence and power of God within us, surrounding us on all sides. Essentially, he is like a clear mirror within which the true image of ourselves, our image of God is reflected before us so that we might remember, awaken, be, and become that Divine Self, the Divine I Am. The same is true of the messengers who appear among us—apostles, prophets, tzaddikim. They are like mirrors reflecting the Inner Light and Spirit in us, the play of light transmission and imparting of the Holy Spirit, being an active reflection and expression of the Inner Light and Spirit in us.

In the same way, we are called to let our light shine, so that others might be illuminated through us and we might reflect to them Christ, Messiah within themselves, the Inner Light and Spirit in them. That is their true self, true being as they are in the Eternal One—Yahweh.

There is something to be said of this Inner Light: It is the radiance of the Eternal One in us, an emanation of the Light of the Infinite One. As we know, all of the divine attributes, powers, actions—Sefirot—are emanations and manifestations of that Infinite Light. Therefore, being a human of light, being light, is being and doing the divine attributes, manifesting the full array of the presence and power of the Holy One, Holy Shekinah. Letting our light shine is using all of our faculties, abilities, all we are and have in active compassion and service to the kingdom of heaven, letting the Holy Spirt take up her full divine action with, in, and through us, manifesting the glory and power of God through us for the deliverance, healing, and enlightenment of souls.

I will share an open secret with you. In the Gospel of Matthew, Yeshua teaches us to let our light shine, and in the Gospel of John he teaches us to "love one another as I have loved you" (13:34). These two teachings are one and the same, for the most essential expression of this light is love. Love is the spiritual essence of all of the commandments, fulfilling them all. If you have love, then all the divine attributes will be in you, the Spirit will naturally and spontaneously manifest any and all of the powers, actions, of the Messiah and Holy One with, in, and through you, all as there is need, all as the Holy One wills and ordains. More so, it is through love that intimate nearness exists. The perfection of love, the fruition of love, complete unity, is conscious union with the Messiah in the Eternal One.

If unconditional love and boundless compassion seem too lofty, begin with other stations and states of the soul that appear more accessible to you. Seek to be kind—very, very kind—and be polite to people, be hospitable and charitable. Seek to be patient, tolerant, understanding, and forgiving. In this way, let your faith, love, and inward cleaving deepen and bloom. Let your light shine and your faith and love manifest through various other human and divine attributes: self-restraint, surrender, acceptance, gratitude, thanksgiving, gentleness, openness, honesty, empathy, courage, endurance, vigilance, fortitude, and so on.

As you do, continue in your inward communion, invoke and pray that the Holy Spirit opens your heart and fills it with the light and love of Christ, Messiah. In truth, it is neither you nor me as we are in ourselves, nor in our vital soul that can generate unconditional love, boundless compassion: only the inner Christ, Messiah who has complete and perfect love and compassion. In active and dynamic surrender to the Lord, the Spirit within us, we need to actively strive and co-labor with the Spirit to generate love and compassion, and all the attributes of the Messiah and Holy One.

If this light does not shine from within us and we do not manifest true human qualities and divine attributes, we manifest something else and become darkness: As yet, we are not true human beings. As has been said, when Christ, Messiah is revealed in us, we must be willing to change and continue to change, willing to cultivate the qualities of Christ, Messiah until we resemble Christ, Messiah, the Anointed One appearing in us and through us. Amen.

Verse 25

Yeshua said, "Love your brother like your soul. Protect that person like the pupil of your eye."

This saying flows directly from the previous one: The light of Christ, Messiah shining from within us and illuminating others and our environment is love and compassion. In fact, the true sign of Christ in us, a spiritual or supernal realization in Christ, Messiah is love and compassion, self-offering, and tending to the spiritual and material needs of others around us. If we say that we have faith but do not have love and compassion, our faith as yet is weak, partial, imperfect, and incomplete. We do not have true knowledge of God—*da'at*, gnosis.

We have spoken about love and the need to strive with the Spirit for the full generation of the love and compassion of Christ, Messiah in our hearts. But here, as Yeshua speaks about love, he says something more: Love your brother or sister like your soul. Protect that person like the pupil of your eye.

Listen and hear and understand! As Christ, Messiah is within you, so also Christ, Messiah is within your brother or sister. As your soul is inseparable from Christ, Messiah, the same is true of your brothers, sisters, and all people. In Christ, in Messiah you are unified with your brothers and sisters; very truly, as Yeshua lives in you and in them, so you live in them and they in you. In the innermost parts of your soul and the inner Christ, Messiah, you are completely interconnected, interdependent, and inseparable from one another. Spiritually and materially, your good is their good, their good is your good.

This idea runs deeper still. As has been taught, the depths of your soul emanate from the One Soul and Holy One—the Infinite Light. You are an emanation of the Holy One, your brothers and sisters are emanations of the Holy One: Your true self is the Holy One, their true self is the Holy

One, none other than the Holy One. So to love them is to love yourself and loving yourself is loving them: Loving yourself and loving them, you are loving the Holy One—the Infinite and Eternal.

Loving one another fully and truly in this way, there is true inward cleaving to the Messiah and Eternal One.

As for protecting a person "like the pupil of your eye," the statement is powerful. As we know, if our eye is in threat of harm, we blink without thinking about it; it is an instantaneous response. The same should follow with spiritual love and self-offering in response to the needs of others, both spiritual and material. We wish it to be instantaneous, second nature, without thought or debate. Our aim is to respond to another's pressing need as swiftly as if it were our own. For in reality, in the Holy One, it is just that: our own need is God's own need. Amen.

Verse 26

Yeshua said. "You see the speck in your brother's eye but you do not see the beam in your own eye. When you take the beam out of your own eye, then you will see clearly to take the speck out of your brother's eye."

This saying also appears in canonical gospels and has a very straightforward, obvious meaning. Essentially, instead of paying attention to the faults, weaknesses, and errors of others or otherwise focusing on how they need to change to advance in the Divine Life or progress in their realization in Christ, Messiah, you need to pay attention to where *you* need to grow and change, identifying the barriers in yourself that prevent your own progress in realization or obstruct your own ability to see, hear, feel, and know yourself and God. Co-laboring with the Spirit, you need to focus first and foremost on working out your own salvation, continuing to progress in your own realization and living the Life Divine.

While in spiritual community, we are our brothers' and sisters' keeper. We are to guard and guide one another and help keep one another on the straight path so that they do not go far astray or cause harm to themselves or others. If there is something that truly needs reflection and correction, support and guidance, to overcome and heal, we first need to make sure we ourselves are clear and free of it. Likewise, we need to be inward, guided by the Inner Light and Spirit as we share reflection or feedback: We need to be in love, compassion, and forgiveness, not judgment and condemnation. Truth be told, though, such reflections to others in spiritual community should be infrequent, only when there is a true need to change, mend, heal, sooner rather than later. Of necessity, correction needs to be from a leading of the Spirit to prevent further harm to the person and others in the community. Before a reflection is given, it is good to remember the Inner Light and Spirit within others—the True Teacher and True Guide. When given time, others may self-correct and not require reflection from us.

This notion is expressed in a teaching of the Holy Kabbalah regarding messengers—apostles, prophets, tzaddikim—who have a word from God of reflection, correction, for their community. First, they will take it to heart themselves and go inward, in the Spirit; with the Spirit, they will bring about that very correction in themselves. Only then they will go to give a teaching, delivering the word of God reflecting and correcting their community, their disciples. Always they will begin with themselves; only thereafter will they then extend the reflection and give guidance for returning, mending, healing to any individual or the community for whom a word of the Lord is to be spoken.

Whenever we are speaking with others, we want to be inside, in the Inner Light and Spirit, and speak from that place in our heart and soul. We want to speak inside to inside, from inwardness to inwardness, even with those who may be speaking from the outside, in outwardness. Unless there is no other choice, we do not wish to speak outside to outside as is the way of unenlightened society. We do not want to use angry and harsh words unless truly there is no other way.

From inwardness, truth will be spoken in love, compassion, and tenderness. It will be the Spirit that speaks to the Spirit in others, the heart of one soul speaking to the heart of another soul. Seeing, hearing, and feeling with them, loving them, and truly desiring good for them, the Spirit will lavish upon them blessing and empowerments for a transformation and progression. Theirs will be happiness and peace. We want to speak inside to inside, from the inner being to inner being, not from little self to little self or ego to ego. We want to speak as the great messengers, apostles, and prophets do, from the Lord, the Spirit—the Inner Light and Spirit in us. In this our speaking will be good and true—righteous and loving.

We want to be the light, the love, the compassion, and the power and action of delivering, healing, and illuminating, letting the Holy Light shine from within us: Letting the Holy Spirit engage in her full divine action with, in, and through us, bringing grace, mercy, compassion, and forgiveness from God, the True Light.

It is inwardness speaking to inwardness where truth is spoken, seen, heard, felt, and received.

It is very skillful that Adonai Yeshua speaks of the impairment of an eye, for on a spiritual level, eyes correspond with desire and its energy. A blockage in an eye indicates an obstruction or barrier to the fulfillment of our true heart's desire or the true will of our holy soul—our true purpose in life. It indicates misdirected desire energy or false desires and fears held by attachments and aversions that prevent the fulfillment of our true intention, the true knowledge of ourselves in the Divine. These same barriers prevent us from enacting our true will, which is the will of Christ and God—the Messiah and Holy One.

Generally speaking, the reflections and corrections of messengers disrupt negative patterns by challenging the mentalities that keep us bound in self-will, self-grasping, attachment, and aversion: in outwardness, separation, and lack. It is all about remembering, awakening, and mending—healing, being, and becoming who and what we truly are in the Holy One, Holy Shekinah, is returning to be One. Amen.

Verse 27

Yeshua said, "If you do not fast from the world, you will not find the kingdom. If you do not observe Shabbat as Shabbat, you will not see the Father."

The very nature of turning to God, going within, deep within, is turning away from creatures and creation—the world—and instead turning toward the source and foundation of all, the life and light of all, the Holy One of Being. On a most basic level, "fasting from the world" means being inward in deep prayer and meditation, a most intimate communion in the Holy One, with the Holy One, just being in the Holy One—One from One. Among those who are on the gnostic path, this is a daily affair, often repeated multiple times each day, for the inward communion is their delight; it is everything, the height of the Life Divine. It is from this inward communion with the inner Christ, Messiah that True Light and Life flows: the resurrection and ascension, all blessings, and all good things. To abide in an inward communion is to find and enter the kingdom of heaven, kingdom of God, in this world. That kingdom, that garden of God, is the heart of your soul, where the Messiah and Holy One abides.

Joined with the meaning of inward abiding, "fasting of the world" also implies a natural wisdom that arises from inwardness, inward communion. Being inward, united and filled, no longer in separation and lack, we will no longer need or desire so much from the world. We are no longer so driven by unenlightened society's busyness and hyperactivity or its materialism and consumerism. Being inward and abiding in the Inner Light and Spirit, we are whole and complete. There is happiness and peace. We have enough. We are not always needing more, not always feeling that we lack. There is a natural clarification and simplification of life that develops when we focus on what is essential, truly good, and enjoyable when we focus on quality rather than quantity in our lives. We have a more spacious life with more time to be and be present with others in our lives in the Holy One. More than accumulating possessions, vain entertainments, and having worldly glory and power, we're being love, giving of ourselves to people in our lives, and valuing our relationships with God and people. Not needing so much from the world is the natural wisdom of fasting from the world, certainly so!

Keeping Shabbat as Shabbat is great wisdom for our times and is essential if we are going to progress in an actual spiritual realization, let alone supernal realization in Christ, Messiah. Quite naturally, even if our life is clarified and simplified and more space is made for daily prayer, meditation, study, and contemplation, our workdays are full and there is indeed much to do to earn a living, tend a family, and various necessities of life. Generally speaking, gnostics do not withdraw from life and the world to live in spiritual retreat but instead integrate their spiritual life and practice into daily living. While passionate about our spirituality and a progressive spiritual realization, they tend to live life fully. In wisdom and in Messiah is the Holy Shabbat, a day of rest for a deeper, inward communion, gathering with brothers and sisters in anointed community for invocation, prayer, spirit-filled worship and sacred discourse—teachings and revelations from the messengers in community—and for spiritual fellowship and conversation.

Given how full life can be, even when simplified and focused upon essential and real priorities, most people can have as much time to just be inward, to invoke, pray, and meditate, and to study and contemplate spiritual teachings, sacred writings, and scripture. The first day of the Christian week is Sunday, when we deepen our inward communion with Christ, Messiah in us. Remembering and keeping Shabbat holy, we have a day to turn away from the world. This practice is crucial if we wish to progress in an actual Self-realization in Christ, Messiah, the Anointing. In fact, the keeping of Shabbat as Shabbat is the cornerstone of our devotions, our spiritual life and practice in the gnostic path. The gathering of anointed community holds sacred space for all people and lets the Holy Light and Spirit shine through us into this world to bless the people and land in which we live. It is not only for us alone that we remember and keep the Holy Shabbat, but for the sake of all people, all creatures. We invoke, pray, and engage in self-offering on behalf of those unable and unwilling, desiring the good of all, the happiness and peace of all, the ingathering of all into God, the True Light.

In gatherings of gnostic community on Shabbat, there is often powerful, energetic transmissions of light in the Holy Spirit during invocation, prayer, and the sharing of teachings and revelations of secret mysteries of creation, redemption, and Christ and God—the Messiah and Holy One. As we abide together, ingathered in the Living Presence of the Eternal Messiah, the Eternal One—the Eternal Now—the Spirit moves, blessings flow, prophecies stir, and healing, illumination, and wonders manifest.

We may even glimpse or taste something of the Eternal Shabbat and the Lord of Shabbat—the World-That-Is-Coming. In the Kabbalah, the Living Presence, the Holy Shekinah is called the Queen of Shabbat, so we abide in her, resting in her as she rests upon and in us. The Kabbalah also teaches that on Shabbat, we receive a double portion of soul, something of the One Soul, or Soul of God, coming into us, through us, merging with our holy soul, intelligence, and vital being. As we learn how to truly remember and keep the Holy Shabbat, we find this to be true, profoundly so! And we find that blessings flow from Shabbat into the days of the week, that God does, indeed, provide for us all that we need to live the Life Divine—the Christ Life.

In Jewish faith, as a matter of law and returning to God, Shabbat is celebrated on the last day of the week. In Christian faith, in the grace of God, in the resurrection and ascension, being reborn from above—from heaven and God, the Pleroma of Light—Shabbat is celebrated on the first day of the week. On Shabbat among Gnostic Christians is a profound remembrance of our unity and fullness with the Messiah in the Holy One, the remembrance of who and what we are in the Eternal One—the Divine Self, Divine I Am. Amen.

Verse 28

"I took my stand in the midst of the world, and I appeared to them in the flesh. I found them all drunk yet none of them thirsty. My soul ached for the human children because they were blind in their hearts and do not see. They came into the world empty and seek to depart from the world empty. But now they are drunk. When they shake off their wine, they will repent."

This verse speaks of the vision of sorrow well-known to anointed messengers—gnostic apostles and prophets—who have reached lofty supernal stations and states of apostleship or prophethood, and are able to reach into the most holy station of the Messiah, or Messianic Consciousness. When the Holy Spirit elevates them into those inmost stations and states of soul, in the midst of the full and direct influx of the Supernal Light and Spirit, when in that pure joy and immeasurable bliss of passing away in the Infinity of Light and the arising of the Great Vision, it feels as though everyone will hear the word of the Eternal One spoken in them. For the gnostic apostle or prophet, it feels as though many, many people will desire to receive the light transmission and imparting of the Holy Spirit, to realize and embody the fullness of the Holy Light and Spirit: a full supernal realization or enlightenment. But then going out to ingather souls, speaking the word of the Eternal One to people, and engaging in light transmission and the passing of the Spirit—powerful movements of the Spirit—they soon find that few, if any, people in this world have ears to hear, eyes to see, or a desire for the Holy Light and Spirit.

Quite literally the anointed messengers find people intoxicated with themselves, their egos, and their desires for worldly things that bring no lasting happiness or satisfaction. They find most people have little or no faith in enlightenment or God, let alone any desire for the enlightenment experience or seeking and finding God. Many may dabble with religion, go to synagogues, churches, mosques, temples, and such but remain in the ignorance, unchanged. Some may even dabble with mystical spirituality, venturing into new ageism, esotericism, and occultism in various forms but go nowhere with it. Relatively few have true faith and are neither willing and able to receive influxes of the Holy Light and Spirit and be changed by it, nor have true passion for mystical spirituality—the gnostic path. As a previous saying of Thomas taught, with each casting out of their net they will find it filled with little fish, and then here or they that will find one or two big fish—souls ready for ingathering, realization, who desire to repent, turn to the Lord, return to be One.

Ignorance and darkness rule this world. Unenlightened society is dominated by the influences of archonic, even demonic forces. Much of humankind is bound up in that ignorance, that darkness, and embodies those impure and dark forces. Most of humankind loves the darkness and does not want to come into the light, let alone be filled with the Holy Light and Spirit.

To see people suffering so, when the kingdom of heaven has come near, and their salvation and realization are at hand is indeed a vision of sorrow to the messengers, to spiritual people having faith and love, who are in anointed community. Indeed, they do not look with eyes of judgment and condemnation, but love and compassion, having empathy, feeling with souls who are bound up in the ignorance, lost in aimless wandering, unaware of what they are doing, unable to recognize the cause of their sorrow and suffering, and so are unable to bring it into cessation. Adonai Yeshua prayed on the cross, "Father forgive them, for they do not know what they are doing" (Luke 23:34). Such is the vision of sorrow. The messengers, and faithful and spiritual people—those having received the Holy Light and Spirit—are aware that eventually all will repent and be saved, that all will return to God and reintegrate with the Infinite Light. All will return to be One. Messengers are in the love, the Messiah, of Christ; they have compassion and hold this hope in their heart for all people, all creatures. Through skillful means, guided by the Holy Spirit, they labor to ingather as many souls as possible. Though it may be that relatively few people will be realized amidst the masses in their generation, they labor to relieve whatever suffering of people and creatures they can, for whatever spiritual development and progress of souls is possible, knowing that in grace, with the Holy One, Holy Shekinah, anything is possible. Great leaps of spiritual progress, radical healings, and wonders are happening all of the time.

However dark and perverse the times might be appear to be, they keep awake, abide in faith, hope, and love, and do not lose hope, for their hope is in the Eternal One, that the Eternal One delivers, which is the very meaning of the Blessed Name of Yoshua, Yeshua: Yahweh delivers. They know that in truth, Christ, Messiah is in all people, all creatures, all things. So however impossible, improbable, or hopeless things might seem outwardly, inwardly they know that the darkness is not ultimately true but illusory and unreal. For those who have faith, love, and inward cleaving, in truth with Christ and God—the Messiah and Holy One—anything can happen, anything is possible. So, in the midst of dark and difficult times, the messengers and those ingathered into anointed community, hold sacred space for all people and hope for all people. They are in the love, the compassion of Christ, Messiah being a refuge, a sanctuary, for people. They labor to ingather and uplift people to relieve whatever suffering they can, to give whatever help and comfort they can to people around them.

There is always hope, though our hope is not of this world. Our hope is in the kingdom of heaven—the Messiah and Eternal One. Amen.

Verse 29

Yeshua said, "If the flesh came into being because of the spirit, it is a marvel, but if the spirit came into being because of the body, it is a marvel of marvels. Yet I marvel at how this great wealth has come to dwell in this poverty."

There is no doubt that the soul has an existence beyond the body. In the Eternal One, the soul is without beginning or end. But to propose that the soul or spirit—the intelligence of the soul—generates or creates the body is mistaken and is ignorance. Likewise, those without faith, the materialists, atheists who propose that the body and its material evolution generate or create the intelligence in the brain and that all of this ends with the body are equally mistaken and ignorant. Neither of these views expresses knowledge and understanding of the mystery of how all things come into being from the Infinite and Eternal One, let alone the soul and body of a human being. You see, the soul and body of human beings come into being through the powers of heaven and the Holy One, Holy Shekinah, and the inmost aspects of the soul of human beings emanate from the Holy One and Holy One alone.

Masters of the tradition have seen and known in the Holy Spirit that there are three who are present during the conception of a human child: a woman and man and the Holy One, Holy Shekinah. The conception of a child and so the flesh, the body, happens through the Holy Shekinah— Divine Presence—with and through a woman and man. The soul comes from the Holy One and is woven of the powers of heaven—angels—and therefore it is the Holy One, Holy Shekinah that joins and interweaves the soul and body in incarnations. So the body does not come into being because of the soul nor the soul because of the body, but the Holy One, Holy Shekinah is the cause of the soul and body coming into being, joined as one for the duration of an incarnation.

It is true, however, that holy and enlightened ones—souls having reached supernal realization—with a conscious intention can generate a threefold body, even a body of pure emanation to appear in the world. But understand that they abide in conscious union with the Holy One, Holy Shekinah, having passed away in the Absolute Oneness of the Infinite and Eternal. As such, theirs is the intention of the Holy One: It is from the Holy One, Holy Shekinah that they come into being and appear, no other. Likewise, save for a pure, spontaneous emanation, such as with Melchizedek appearing to Abraham and Sarah or the appearance of the Risen Messiah, until holy and enlightened ones come into being in their incarnation and reach supernal realization again, as in previous lives, their light vestures are left behind when they incarnate. So truly, it is from the Holy One, through the divine powers, actions, of the Holy Shekinah—Divine Presence—that souls and bodies come into being, not through souls in and of themselves, certainly not!

Furthermore, in the Holy Shekinah, there are powers of heaven and various other spiritual forces in the weaving of outer aspects of souls and bodies. As with all things, there is a vast play of co-arising within which the arising of soul and body in an incarnation is interdependent and interconnected with everything else arising in the matrix of creation and this world. In this you may realize that the very thought of the body coming into being because of the soul, or the soul because of the body, does not even hint at how souls and bodies come into being, not in the least! That is all speculation in the ignorance, the illusion of separation, devoid of any understanding of the true mystery.

True knowledge and understanding of this great mystery can only come through the Holy Spirit; it can only be revealed by the Holy One, and the Holy One alone. Even the greatest of archangels cannot reveal this most holy mystery. In truth, no words of anyone here can explain this mystery, but can only point or hint at it in such a way that those who seek knowledge of it can inquire of the Holy One for the revelation of this truth from the Holy Shekinah, Holy Spirit.

Now, there is something more to be said. The kingdom of heaven is inside and is outside. In the Holy One, when souls are unified with the Holy One, the inside and outside are unified: There is no inside or outside, but it is all known to be in the Holy One, all the manifestation of the Holy Shekinah. There is no difference between inside-outside, above-below, before-behind, right-left, and so on. All is in the Holy One, all is the manifestation of the Holy Shekinah—the Divine Presence. This is seen, heard, felt, and known in the experience of pure radiant awareness, nondual gnostic awareness—the dawn of Messianic Consciousness.

In the Holy One, Holy Shekinah is no difference between the body and soul. This is the revelation of the risen and ascended Christ, Messiah—the Living Yeshua, Hayyah Yeshua.

The state of poverty is separation and lack. The state of wealth is unity and fullness. All the while, this wealth is within and behind the apparent poverty, dwelling in it. Isn't that a true marvel, the most amazing and astonishing mystery? What truly good news when this is revealed and realized! Hallelu Yah! Amen.

Verse 30

Yeshua said, "Where there are three [divinities], they are divine. Where there are two or one, I am with that one."

First we may recall a saying of Adonai Yeshua in canonical gospels: "Where two or more are gathered in my name, I am with them."

On one level, we may understand this saying in much the same way, though what is said here is more subtle and sublime, goes far deeper, and speaks a heart-essence teaching of anointed community in the gnostic path, or straight path.

Listen to the saying closely, from inwardness, not outwardness, from oneness, not twoness. Hear this word of God spoken with power: "Where there are three divinities, they are divine"—One Divine—"Where there are two or one, I am that One." Those who receive the Holy Light and Spirit, within whom Christ, Messiah is revealed, who are gathered into anointed community—the Body of Christ, Messiah—they are all one in the Inner Light and Spirit. When they join together in faith and love with inward cleaving in that love, they are of one heart and mind—the Sacred Heart of Christ, the Mind of Christ—no other. This is what is means to be gathered in the Blessed Name of Yeshua.

Understand that when we receive the Holy Light and Spirit, and Christ, Messiah is in us and we are in Christ, Messiah, we are united and filled. Wherever we are, there is the kingdom of heaven—Pleroma of Light— and the Eternal Messiah, the Eternal One. God is always with us, wherever we are, in all that we do. So in the straight path, we are taught to remember that God is always with us, that God is nearer to us that we are to ourselves, and that we are never separate or apart from God, the True Light. Though, in effect, in our relative experience, we can fall into the illusion of separation, the delusion of lack, sin, error, and generate negativity which removes ourselves from the presence of God, God never removes Godself from us and never will. So any time we do stray and err, the moment we repent and turn to God, God is with us. This is the truth of the Name of Christ, Messiah as *Emmanuel*: "God with us."

This is the grace of the Eternal One, the Supreme, manifest in Messiah Yeshua, Christ Jesus: through the Christ Spirit, Holy Spirit, God comes to dwell in us, God gives Godself to us and takes us into Godself. As the image and likeness of God, being transformed by the presence and power of God in us, we are divine, we are divinities, certainly so! But then we must live as such, being the light, the love, and those qualities and attributes that are in Christ and God—the Messiah and Holy One. We will live according to teachings of the Lord within us, the guidance of the Holy Spirit, and sin no more. If we sin, err, we repent and return to be One. When we do, there is complete forgiveness. We are blameless as are the apostles and prophets of God, without sin, as is Christ, Messiah. The Inner Light and Spirit make it so, for in returning to God, we have returned to our innate purity and perfection as we are in God. We return to be One—inseparable from the Holy One, the Shekinah of Messiah.

Yeshua is the Messiah, which is to say the first to enter into supernal realization—Christ Consciousness, God Consciousness. More so, in this, he is the Firstborn Son of a new humanity, supernal and divine—the Elder Brother of the family of sons and daughter of God, the True Light. As he is the Sun of God, so we, like him, are Stars of Heaven. In that he is the Firstborn, having made a complete self-offering of himself and being raised from the dead and glorified, unified with the Infinite Light, filled with the Eternal Spirit, Eternal Life, he is the Christ, Messiah, not you or me. And yet through him, Christ, Messiah has come to be revealed and is realized in us and appears through us. As he is supernal and divine, through the grace of the Supreme made manifest in him, so are we. Where we are, he is, where he is, we are, all in the Holy One, Holy Shekinah. Yeshua lives in us.

Christ, Messiah dwells in us. The Holy Spirit moves with, in, and through us, manifesting as us, according to our progress in the gospel, our progress in our Self-realization in Christ, Messiah.

We are God, Not-God. We are Christ, Not-Christ. God is God, Christ is Christ. Contemplate this well, contemplate deep, and understand! What more can I say? Amen.

Verse 31

Yeshua said, "A prophet is not accepted in his own hometown.
A doctor does not heal those [whom the doctor knows]."

This is simply true as stated. You see, when an apostle or prophet, or anyone is anointed in the Way of the apostles and prophets of God, as are all
who are ingathered into anointed community, the change is inward, not
outward. And outwardly, except for those who have the Holy Spirit and
can see the inwardness of people, who can see the Holy Light and Fire
within and around them, they look the same, like any other ordinary man
or woman. It may be that their thought, speech, and actions change, but
they appear just the same as before as they are in themselves, have the
same voice and mannerisms, and are the person they always were. But
receiving their anointing, the Holy Shekinah, Holy Spirit has taken up their
person and life. The presence and power of God dwells in them such that
those who have known them before are unlikely to believe, just as most
ordinary, unenlightened people are unlikely to believe.

As with all general and common spiritual truths, there are exceptions.
Curiously enough, many of Yeshua's closest disciples were his boyhood
friends. His mother, brothers, and sisters became followers and came to
believe in the Christ, Messiah. And here and there, there have been other
apostles and prophets for whom this was true, some friends or family
members who came to faith through them, believed in them, and believed
in the presence and power of enlightenment or God in them. When this
happens, it is through the Spirit. Through the grace and mercy of the
Supreme, as with anyone able to recognize and receive them as they are in
God, they see, hear, and feel with the Spirit, inwardness to inwardness, and
so know and believe God is with them.

The truth is, unless we are given to a gnostic apostle, prophet, or holy
tzaddik by the Holy Spirit and they are revealed to us by the Spirit to display

the presence and power of God in themselves and engage with us in the light transmission of the Spirit, they would be hidden from us. We would not sense, intuit, believe, or know who and what they are in Christ and God—the Messiah and Holy One. Apart from the Spirit, we would not be able to draw near and have a true bond of sacred friendship with them or be a disciple or companion in the Way within their community. They would not be able to teach, guide, or initiate us.

At the outset, there is no asking to be a disciple, let alone a close spiritual companion any more than one can walk up to a stranger and ask them to be a best friend, let alone our husband or wife! The truth is, we either are or are not. We are either given to them in the Holy One, Holy Shekinah or not. Neither we nor they can make ourselves a disciple, a companion in the Way. This only happens through the grace and mercy of God, through the Holy Spirit, the anointing from God, all in the Holy One, Holy Shekinah. We are given to one another by God, from God, to God, and for God—all in the Holy One, Holy Shekinah. There is no conjuring a movement of the Holy Spirit between us. The Holy Spirit either moves or does not move with and between us.

If there is true faith and love and a heart or soul bond, if it is good and true, the Spirit will move between us and it will be revealed that we are given to one another, destined to be together in Christ, Messiah—anointed community. It happens in no other way. So meeting, becoming acquainted, we wait upon the Holy Spirit, seeking to see the witness of the Holy Spirit, the movement of the Holy Spirit between us. It could happen sooner, later, or not at all. And as the Parable of the Sower of seeds teaches, a movement of the Spirit can happen and there can be light transmission, but it might not take root. Having been given a bond, if we were to willfully turn away, the bond could be broken. If broken, it may be mended if we return. If fully severed, it may be that the mending can only happen when we meet again in a future life. In this is the mercy and compassion of the Eternal One: Once there is a bond in truth, it cannot be broken but will be brought to fruition, if not in this life then in a future life. Just as God never removes

Godself from us even when we go astray, so it is with these heart and soul bonds in God.

As you might intuit, souls may be bonded with a messenger or several messengers, through many lives. Some bonds may spark very deeply, such that at the very outset, meeting our tzaddik and companions around them might feel like coming home. On psychic and spiritual levels, such an immediate bond of close friendship can run far deeper and more intimately than a bond with a partner or spouse. Generally speaking, when messengers are sent from God and holy and enlightened ones appear in the world, other holy and righteous ones appear with them to generate anointed community—a matrix of souls that have been ingathered and realized to various levels in previous lives. This was true with Adonai Yeshua and the souls of the Holy Mother and Holy Bride, the soul of Elijah appearing as Yohanan the Baptist, and Yeshua's close disciples, who themselves were destined to be holy apostles. The same is true of the generation of light transmission lineages and anointed communities to this very day, not only in the Christian stream of revelation and realization but all authentic and living wisdom traditions of the world. All have their origin and foundation in the very same Truth and Light—the Infinite and Eternal One—all having as their heart-essence teaching to be in the love, be the light, be the love: Be One from One.

In this regard, it may be said in truth there is One God, One Enlightenment, One Faith, and One Divine Humanity: One Way! Amen.

Verse 32

Yeshua said, "A city built upon a hill and fortified cannot fall, nor can it be hidden."

You and your life are the kingdom of God, the city of God, the palace of God, the temple of God—the dwelling place of God. Your life display is the kingdom, your body the city, your heart and soul the palace where God dwells and lives. Going within, living within, being inward, you are high above, and you have peace, rest, in the Lord, the Spirit, within you. You are unmoved by what transpires outward, having true refuge, sanctuary, in the Lord—Adonai. You have peace and happiness regardless of what is happening in the world.

The city and palace are indeed fortified. The palace is fortified with all the divine attributes, powers, actions—the presence and power of God—all powers of the Holy Spirit. The city is fortified with the powers of heaven—the angels. Having the presence and power of God in you, and the companionship of angels, neither archons or demons, nor the great enemy, the satan, have power over you, nor can they cause you to fall, or bind or harm your soul, your being as you are in God Most High—the Absolute Light.

You cannot be hidden except for those who are blind. If indeed Christ, Messiah is in you and you are in Christ, Messiah, it will be evident in your way in life itself and all you do. Your very life will be a speaking of the word of God with power. Louder than words, your actions will bear witness to the truth, the reality, of the Inner Light and Spirit you reflect in others, drawing out and so making known to them the same Inner Light and Spirit.

Those who are in Christ, in whom Christ dwells and is revealed, walk in the beauty and holiness of Christ, the glory and power of Christ being inside them and outside them. The inner like the outer, and the outer like the inner, the two made one in the Christ Presence, Christ Spirit.

This is our noble ideal. This is our intention, what we strive for in the Christ Life—the Life Divine. What more can I say? Amen.

Verse 33

Yeshua said, "What you hear in your ear, in the other ear, proclaim from your rooftops. No one lights a lamp and puts it under a basket, nor in a hidden place. You put it on a stand so that all who come and go will see its light."

In the Sermon on the Mount in Matthew, this teaching is joined with the saying, "You are the light of the world, and Let your light shine" (5:16).

Here, this verse is a natural and lovely extension from the previous one. "What you hear in your ear, in the other ear"—your ear, this is the word of God spoken by Adonai Yeshua or holy apostles after him; the word, the gospel, that the Holy Spirit speaks in your heart is your other ear, or inner ear. The revelation of Christ, Messiah within yourself and all people is not for yourself alone but the sake of others as well. Likewise, the word of the Lord—the gospel—spoken by the Spirit in your heart is not to be kept to yourself but to be spoken to others that they might hear, believe, go within, and seek and find God within themselves—the inner Christ, Messiah, the Inner Light and Spirit.

If the Holy Light is in you, then you are a light bearer and it is given that the radiance of the Sun of God shines from within you. If the Holy Spirit is in you, it is given that you share with others and pass the Living Spirit to others around you, to all who may wish to hear the Living Word and desire to receive the Living Spirit. It is not meant to be a secret; it is not meant to be hidden. It is meant to be disclosed and in the open, so that anyone who is seeking or desires it may draw near, hear the word spoken with power, and receive the Holy Light and Spirit—the truth of the inner Christ, Messiah—revealed through you to them, all as the Spirit moves, all as God wills.

To proclaim it from your rooftop means speaking with boldness, confidence, and self-abandon in faith and love, with inward cleaving, letting the

Lord, the Spirit in you speak to the Lord, the Spirit in others, awakening them to the inner Christ, Messiah so that they might be ingathered into anointed community.

Of course, among Christian Gnostics this does not mean going door to door or randomly imposing oneself and one's views upon others as though only we know the Way to enlightenment or God for all people— not in the least! The intention among gnostics is to follow the inspirations and leadings of the Spirit, to be open and sensitive to opportunities that present themselves in life with those around us and those we encounter as we sojourn in this world. When the Spirit moves, we move with the Spirit; we speak with the Spirit. There is guidance in the Spirit, a sense of feeling in the Spirit, a knowing in the Spirit—an intuitive intelligence of the heart. Being in the Spirit and the light and love of Christ, Messiah, we share the word of the Lord spoken in our hearts of the inner Christ, Messiah and inward communion with God—the gospel of the second coming of Christ, Messiah in glory, the Christ, Messiah appearing again through many.

What we wish to share is the love, the Way of inward communion, an experiential knowledge of Christ and God—the Messiah and Holy One— not a religious doctrine to be agreed with and believed, but the Truth and Light that are seen, heard, felt, and known with the Spirit and in the Spirit.

Know and understand that it is not only messengers who are to ingather souls, through whom light transmission and the passing of the Spirit happens. But in Christ, Messiah, we are all ordained in a holy and sacred priesthood. If indeed we have received the Holy Light and Spirit ourselves, having been ingathered into anointed community when the Spirit moves, light transmission and the passing of the Spirit can take place through us as well.

As has been said, we first and foremost seek to communicate the Truth and Light through our actions: how we live our lives, how we interact with others, and how we love. Actions speak louder than words, yet also with words: speaking the word of God, the Truth and Light of the inner Christ, Messiah revealed to us, the Way of the gnostic path, the straight path— inward communion with God in intimate nearness and oneness, unity.

There is a great influx of the Supernal Light and Spirit happening today among all peoples in all lands, but as we know, a great darkness is overcoming many people; a time of great trials and tribulations has come into the world. There is a need for many voices and witnesses proclaiming the great outpouring of the Holy Light and Spirit that is underway, the truth of the Inner Light and Spirit within people, and how those who have faith and desire it may abide in direct, inward communion with the Eternal One. There is a need for voices of hope, those who embody the fullness of the Holy Light and Spirit and can share it with others and all who desire to receive it. Amen.

Verse 34

Yeshua said, "If a blind person leads a blind person, both will fall in
a hole."

This verse also appears in canonical gospels. On the surface, its meaning
is straightforward and simple. Many people are religious but not spiritual,
and likewise there are many religious leaders and religious scholars who
are not spiritual. They have not received the Holy Light and Spirit and cannot see, hear, or feel with the Spirit and as yet do not have true knowledge
of God. The blind lead the blind throughout much of religion, and relatively few have experienced the revelation of the presence and power of
God in their hearts and souls or the Inner Light and Spirit, let alone seeing
with the eyes of God, hearing with the ears of God, and feeling with the
heart of God, feeling the love and being love. As yet, they grope in darkness
as though blind; they are ignorant and do not know God. They remain in
separation and lack, cleaving to man-made dogmas and doctrines, rites and
rituals born of human invention and speculation, not from the revelation
and realization of God—true knowledge of God, da'at, Gnosis.

Yeshua was not a teacher of religion but a mystical spirituality of the
direct experience of God and communion with God that opened the way
of apostles and prophets to experience revelations of God, to see visions of
heaven and God, to hear the word of God, to feel the presence and power
of God within and around themselves. Yeshua baptized with the Holy
Light and Spirit of God who anoints apostles and prophets. While all those
with him were not called to the outward works and mission of an apostle or prophet, all shared in the same anointing with the Holy Light and
Spirit and were able to see, hear, and feel with the Spirit in their own way
and according to the works and mission the Eternal One gave them. Mass
religion is devoid of living messengers and true initiation—the imparting
of the Holy Light and Spirit. It is like a shadow or partial reflection of the

knowledge of God held by the anointed apostles and prophets of whom they preach. Generally speaking, these leaders do not see, hear, or feel with the Spirit, nor do they carry the presence and power of God in worship. Though perhaps seeking God, mass religion is not worship in spirit or truth because it lacks the finding of God—the Eternal Spirit and Truth.

In this regard, the god of religion is dead, just as religion is dead, devoid of living revelation and realization of God.

Yeshua brought grace, light transmission, the passing of the Spirit, and freedom from the law of religion. Through faith, inward cleaving, and most especially love come knowledge of Christ and God—the Messiah and Holy One. Know and understand that the very nature of the Holy Light and Spirit is the love of God; in knowing God, we will be light and love—such is the nature of true knowledge of God.

In that love we are in the light, the kingdom of heaven. But if we are not in that love, we are in darkness and the fire of hell. If we are not in that love, we are in the fire, right here, right now, in this life, in this world. There are spiritual people who live in the love and therefore in the light, but there are many who instead live in the opposite and thus in the fire. Heaven and hell are here in this world, not just in the afterlife. Where we live is where we are going.

Yeshua said, "Do not judge, for as you judge you will be judged." Yeshua also said, "Love one another as I have loved you." If you are in judgment, you are in the fire. If you are love, you are in the light. So do not be in the fire—be in the light. Do not judge; instead be in the love and forgive. Have mercy and compassion and you will be in the light—heaven—here and now, today. Don't wait—be the light, be the love today! Be in heaven, be in God—the Divine Life!

We can see where religious fundamentalism leads: venomous teachings of a god of judgment, condemnation, damnation, and laws that lead to judging and hating others, and great violence—the fire, hell on earth. There is only sin, error, death, and destruction in it; immeasurable sorrow and suffering in that way. That path leads to a very big hole, a great abyss into which many souls fall. It is the complete opposite of the way Messiah Yeshua taught and lived.

There is a better way. There is good news. As John taught: God is love. God loves the world. God loves people, so God sent Christ, Messiah—the Holy Light and Spirit—not to judge but to love, heal, and enlighten people and all creatures, bringing revelation and knowledge of God, the True Light. In truth, there is no judgment in the Infinite and Eternal One as we would conceive of it. There is supernal grace, supernal love—complete mercy, compassion, and forgiveness. If we judge and condemn ourselves and others, we are in the fire, in hell. But if we love, we are in the light, heaven. This is the judgment, in this life and the afterlife. It is ours to choose. We create the reality of our experience, light or fire, heaven or hell from moment to moment, day to day. All the while, the Eternal One loves us regardless of what we choose to be and do. Any time we return to the love, so we are in the light, in heaven and God. It really is that simple!

Know and understand that all knowledge of heaven and God is in the love. The knowledge of all secrets is in the love. In the love, all the knowledge, understanding, and wisdom of God is yours; indeed all attributes, powers, actions of God are yours. In the love is seeing with the eyes of God, hearing with the ears of God, feeling with the heart of God—God being the seeing, hearing, and feeling through your mind, heart, and life.

In the love is unity and fullness—right here, right now!

Those who are blind are those of limited love, who are unloving. Those who see are those who are loving as the Messiah and Holy One loves! It is that simple. Amen.

Verse 35

"You cannot enter the home of the strong and take it by force without binding the owners' hands. Then you can loot the house."

This saying is intended to shock those who hear it. After all, who would ever think a righteous and holy one would give an essential instruction on how to commit robbery? There is no doubt that people hearing this saying from the mouth of Adonai Yeshua would have been very surprised, such that for a moment their minds might have been silenced as they paused and waited for him to explain what he was actually saying.

The "house" of course is you and your life. The strong man or woman is your ego and self-cherishing, and more so, your inclination to violence and evil. It is the desire to receive for oneself alone, to get one's own way or what is desired, regardless if others are harmed or deprived of happiness and satisfaction. For the most part, this bestial tendency rules the world, rules unenlightened society, and is the complete opposite of the way of holy and enlightened ones, or the family of God.

There are essentially two inclinations in us: the evil inclination—*sitra ahara*—and the good inclination—*sitra tov*. Basically speaking, they are the desire to receive and give, respectively. When the desire to receive is divorced from the desire to give and dominates our person and life, it leads to sin, error, evil, and violence in thoughts, words, and actions. However, when joined with the desire to share and give, brought into submission to that good inclination, the desire to receive is good and integral to doing what is good and true. After all, unless we receive, we have nothing to give.

The submission of the desire to receive to the desire to give—love—is the binding of the strong man or woman. Once in submission, integrated with the desire to give, sharing, giving becomes the primary motivation in life, taking all that is received and sharing it, giving it—being love—looting the house.

We may take note that this saying speaks of binding, not killing the strong man or woman. You see, there is no cutting off the ego or the evil inclination, because it is part of us, an inseparable part of our soul, our being, and consciousness. There is no getting rid of it as such; rather, we can let go of ego-cherishing and its play of desire and fear. We can bring our ego into submission to our inner being, the Inner Light and Spirit. We can unite our desire to receive with the desire to give. We can bring our vital soul, *nefesh*, into submission to our intelligence, *ruach*, and our intelligence into submission to our divine nature, *neshamah*, and so be in an active and dynamic surrender to the indwelling Messiah and Holy Spirit. This is righteousness, the state of a holy and righteous one—a holy tzaddik.

When we let go of ego-grasping and the ego surrenders to the Lord, the Spirit within us and serves the kingdom of heaven and the Lord, the ego is redeemed and is righteous. There is its nobility and light. When the desire to receive is unified with the desire to share and give, the desire to receive is redeemed. When joined with giving, there is nothing wrong with receiving. As an example, after acquiring money, food, and such, we are able to share and give to those who are in need. Being grounded empowers our active compassion to be love in a most practical way, to relieve suffering. Likewise, we must desire to receive the Holy Light and Spirit so that we can impart the Holy Light and Spirit to others. Our desire for greater gifts, powers of the Spirit, and realization amplify our greater service to others and brings greater glory to God. Receiving is good.

In the depth of our soul, in the Holy One, in the love, there is no receiving and no giving, no receiver and no giver. All is from the One, to the One, for the One, no other. In the fullness of love there is unity, no giver and no receiver. There is just love, the delight of loving—the radiance of the Holy One, the complete and perfect union of receiving and giving as one holy desire, the desire of the Holy One. Amen.

Verse 36

Yeshua said, "From morning to evening and from evening to morning, do not worry about what you will wear."

This teaching is drawn out in greater detail in the Sermon on the Mount in the Gospel of Matthew. It begins with Yeshua saying: "Therefore I tell you, do not worry about your own life, what you will eat or what you will drink, or about your body, and what you will wear" (6:25). At the conclusion of the teaching Yeshua continues, "but strive first or the kingdom of God and his righteousness, and all of these things will be given to you as well" (6:33). Among gnostics, this singular focus upon not worrying about material clothing alludes to secret mysteries of the resurrection and ascension, as well as entering into the kingdom of heaven in the World to Come.

Within and behind the physical, material body is a subtle body and a glow from it that surrounds people—an aura. In ordinary people in the unenlightened condition, that subtle body and aura is moonlike, which is to say a relatively dim self-radiance. That subtle body is often impaired with turbulent and dimmer spaces, voids, holes, and various anomalies; sometimes other things can be attached to or appear within it, usually various kinds of impure and dark spirits. When a person receives the Holy Light and Spirit as their inward communion deepens and they progress in their realization, however, that subtle body is healed and transformed into a body of light that is first a body of brighter astral light, then even more glorious spiritual light, and thereafter it is brilliant supernal light, becoming sunlike. The generation of a body of astral light, spiritual light, and supernal light in gnostic scriptures are often called light vestures or heavenly garments. In saying not to worry about what you will wear implies a focus upon the generation of a spiritual and supernal body of light, which is the body of the resurrection and ascension, the appearance of the soul in the kingdom of heaven—the Pleroma of Light.

Who from morning to evening and evening to morning actually worries about what they will wear? That would be very unusual. But those very words connote an abiding in inward communion, invoking often and praying without ceasing, through which greater and greater influxes of the Holy Light and Spirit transpire. With these influxes come the power of the divine attributes, generating the fuller body of light. In the dawn of Messianic Consciousness, the threefold body of Melchizedek emanates, corresponding with a gnostic understanding of striving first for the kingdom of God and his righteousness.

Understand that it is not we who generate the body of light; it happens through Divine Grace, the Holy Spirit. For the generation of the body of light to occur, we must engage in an active and dynamic surrender to Divine Grace and strive and co-labor with the Spirit for its generation and a greater realization in Christ, Messiah.

When speaking of resurrection and ascension, gnostics are not just speaking of an experience following death in the afterlife. Rather with the generation of a body of light, astral, spiritual, and supernal, there can be corresponding mystical ascensions of the soul—*aliyat neshamah*—into the heavens, the light realms of the Pleroma, and various other realms and worlds of the inner, metaphysical dimensions of creation. There are those among mystics and gnostics who are gifted with the power to engage in a transference of consciousness, the ability to shift their soul or center of consciousness from the material body into a body of light and so ascend and travel beyond the body in inner dimensions. When the Spirit leads them to do so, some who master this gift may even send the soul of another sister or brother beyond the body into astral and spiritual heavens or into light realms of the Pleroma. This is a common gift of true apostles and prophets. In this regard, you may recall Paul in his second letter to the Corinthians writing of being carried up into the third heaven by the Holy Spirit (12:2), he, by his own account, being the least of apostles.

There is something to be said about this ability, because for such things to happen with us, for the presence and power of the Holy One to move with us in this way of healing, prophecy, wonderworking, and such, we cannot live in outwardness or be obsessed with material and worldly concerns. We need to be inward and live from deep inwardness, no longer cleaving to and being self-identified with things of the world: We cleave to the inner Christ, Messiah, oriented more and more to the kingdom of heaven—the Pleroma of Light.

Besides, worrying is a waste of time and changes nothing. Worse than that, falling into fear, doubt, and anxiety is a negation of faith and a generation of negativity that opposes the movement of the presence and power of the Holy One with us, the divine action of the Holy Spirit with, in, and through us. There is a great manifesting power in us, the power of a co-creator and co-redeemer. But if in negation, doubt, or fear rather than affirmation, faith, and love that power may become a harmful, self-fulfilling prophecy that undermines or even destroys the good of ourselves and others. There is a great power within our soul, consciousness, and mind, so we need to learn how to focus it and bring it into harmony and resonance with the Messiah and Holy One in us, the will of God—this is the very purpose of prayer. Prayer is not for God, but for us; it is not to change God, but to change ourselves, to bring us into harmony and resonance with the presence and power of God so that the Spirit of God can move with, in, and through us, along with the powers of heaven to fulfill the will of God and our very own Divine Self.

Rather than worrying, faithful and spiritual people invoke, pray, and meditate, uplifting all concerns to God, intending that God's will be done, and knowing that God will provide. Amen.

Verse 37

His disciples said, "When will you appear to us and when shall we see you?" Yeshua said, "When you strip naked without being ashamed and take your clothes and put them under your feet like small children and trample them, then you will see the Son of the Living One and you will not be afraid."

This verse flows from the previous saying and it affirms the gnostic teaching about material clothes, bodies, light vestures, light bodies, and the spiritual practice of the transference of consciousness or mystical ascensions of the soul: *aliyat neshamah*. It is a delightful exchange between the disciples and the Master, for it reflects an understanding that while embodied in Yeshua, the Christ, Messiah is beyond Yeshua. Yeshua's "I am" statements in the Gospel of John are not him speaking of himself as he is but of Christ, Messiah within and beyond him: who and what he was, and is, and forever shall be in the Eternal One.

Regarding these "I am" statements, much of Christendom—outer and unspiritual churches—have made an idol out of Jesus the man and missed the greater revelation of Christ and the true word of God of the Christ in all people. In the outer and unspiritual churches, it is very rare if it happens at all for anyone to preach or teach of a direct revelation of the indwelling Christ, Messiah with an actual light transmission and an actual—not symbolic—imparting of the Holy Spirit. Rarer still is it for anyone to demonstrate how to go deeper inward to pray and meditate, experience direct revelation of the risen and ascended Messiah, the Christ in full supernal glory in all of the countless emanations of that presence and power, the reality of the Cosmic or Universal and Primordial Christ, Messiah.

This is beyond Yeshua, Jesus, though the Spirit and Soul of the Messiah, the fullness of that Holy Light and Spirit, was embodied, incarnate in him. This is the gnostic understanding and experience of the risen and ascended

Christ, Messiah and the word of God—the gospel—that Adonai Yeshua preached. Yeshua was an apostle and prophet through whom Christ, Messiah appeared, lived, and moved among us. He was the firstborn of a new humanity, supernal and divine: the divine-human. So now it is given that Christ, Messiah appears through us, more or less, all according to our realization of Christ, Messiah within us, our living the Christ Life, the Life Divine.

In devotions of mystical ascent or the practice of transference of consciousness is an envisioning or spontaneous arising of an appearance; a body of light and glory before and above the gnostic initiate, often in the form of one of the great holy and enlightened ones, or a divine personification—*partzuf*—such as Yeshua Messiah in glory, the Holy Bride, or Holy Mother in glory, or others. The sister or brother will pray and meditate upon this glorious image and presence while envisioning light and glory streaming from that presence upon them, transforming their own body and appearance into the image and likeness of that Divine Presence. When transformed and with conscious intention, they will rise up, dissolving into fluid flowing light and merge with that Divine Presence, shifting their soul into that appearance, that body of light and glory becoming that aspect of the Divine Presence, of Christ, Messiah. They may ascend through conscious intention into heavens and light realms of the Pleroma to commune with saints and angels or pass beyond into a direct communion with the presence of the Eternal One. Rather than ascend, however, they may also pass away completely in the Absolute Oneness of the Infinite and Eternal One, dissolving into and merging with the Clear Light, Perfect Light, Infinite Light, like a rainbow dissolving into the sky within which it appeared. This is what it means to strip naked and be unashamed.

As was mentioned in an earlier saying of Thomas, this process gives rise to the Great Vision of Melchizedek: a vision or awareness of the Supernal and Primordial Christ, Messiah—the Cosmic Christ. As was shared, parallel with this Great Vision is the arising of three pure light bodies—the threefold body of Melchizedek—and the experience of conscious union with the Messiah in the Eternal One: the dawn of Christ Consciousness,

Messianic Consciousness. This is the inmost manifestation of the gnostic experience and is the realization of gnostic masters, gnostic apostles.

At the outset, such grand mystical experiences might sound very remote or removed and unattainable to you. But in Christ, Messiah with the Holy Spirit, nothing could be further from the truth. What we are speaking about is the divine or enlightened nature—*neshamah*—of all souls, the reality of souls of meta-dimensional being, meta-dimensional consciousness, that are completely capable of rising into higher, more expanded states of mental and supramental consciousness into the experience of Reality as It Is and God as God Is. They are able not only to entertain a communion with Christ and God in nearness, but in oneness—conscious union.

Receiving the Holy Light and Spirit, cultivating and abiding in an inward communion—worshipping God in spirit and truth—all manner of direct spiritual and mystical experiences can and do happen. In living gnostic community, sisters and brothers are bearing witness to this all of the time. They often share experiences of the Holy Spirit and powers of heaven uplifting their souls in ascent into the realities of the inner dimensions, visions of the heavenly realms and realms of the Pleroma of Light.

Quite naturally, we must let go of grasping at the ego and name, form, personal history, and the lower, more limited ordinary states of vital and mental consciousness. Instead, we must cleave to and identify with the inner Christ, Messiah—Inner Light and Spirit—our fully evolved, realized, divine, and enlightened being—the Divine Self, the Divine I Am—taking off our clothes, stripping naked.

As has been said previously, the Inner Light is the very same Infinite Light and Love souls encounter in the afterlife in the judgment or life review, seeing, hearing, and feeling with great intensity everything done in their lives. If in separation and lack and life has not been lived well, it becomes a judgment; there is shame, the light becomes like fire. But if in nearness, oneness, and fullness, then there is mercy and compassion, a heavenly and delightful experience, even an experience of full reintegration with the Infinite Light or the realization of unity with Christ in God—

the Messiah in the Eternal One. The latter is stripping naked and being unashamed. This not only happens when our souls pass beyond when we die, but when we go deep within to the very depths of our soul, here in this life and this world.

There is supernal grace, complete mercy, compassion, and forgiveness in Christ, Messiah—this Inner Light, Infinite Light—the love. If only we have true faith and open to it, understanding in the love there is nothing to be ashamed of, being in the love, there is only immeasurable love, endless light. Hallelu Yah! Praise the Lord! Amen.

Verse 38

"Often you wanted to hear these sayings I am telling you, and you have no one else from whom to hear them. There will be days when you seek me and will not find me."

What is taught in these sayings the depths of souls yearn to hear, to remember, and realize in incarnation. This knowledge is in the heart of souls. But when souls incarnate and merge with the flesh in the dullness and density of matter, they forget. In outwardness, they are overcome with the illusion of separation, the delusion of lack. There is a need for messengers to remind them and reveal the Inner Light and Spirit that is their true, divine, and enlightened nature. There were many prophets before Yeshua, including the lawgiver Moses and the great prophet Elijah, but none of them revealed and spoke of the innate unity of souls with the Eternal One or imparted the fullness of the Supernal Light and Eternal Spirit, let alone taught the Way for the realization of conscious communion and union with the Holy One, Holy Shekinah. They were not the Christ, Messiah: Yeshua was. There was indeed no other apostle or prophet of God from whom this revelation and realization of Christ, Messiah in us could be heard.

To this very day, most outer and unspiritual churches do not accept the sayings of Thomas. For those few progressive and liberal churches that do, it is rare for anyone in them to preach or teach these sayings with experiential knowledge and understanding of their true meaning. Only from those who have realized and manifest the inner Christ, Messiah can we hear something of the true meaning of these sayings, true knowledge of them. It is through the Christ Spirit, Holy Spirit speaking through them that the inner and secret meanings of these sayings can be heard, not only outwardly but also inwardly, in our very own hearts, as the Lord in them speaks to the Lord in us. As the true hearing comes from within, from the

Lord, the Spirit, so within us the Spirit speaks through apostles, prophets, tzaddikim, awakening us, certainly so!

Only from Christ, Messiah within Yeshua, messengers, and us is there speaking and hearing of these sayings—revelation of the Truth and Light in them: only from the Christ, Messiah, no other. Know and understand that if we ever encounter a gnostic apostle or gnostic preacher, it will not be a human who speaks, preaches, or engages in light transmission and the imparting of the Holy Spirit; rather it will be the Christ Presence, Christ Spirit—the Messiah and Holy Spirit moving with, in, and through them.

Our aim and intention in our own lives is that in union with the Lord, the Spirit, within us, abiding in an inward communion, we are no longer the doer. Instead, the Lord, the Spirit is the doer, the Lord, the Spirit, taking up our person and life, living with, in, and through us.

"There will be days when you seek me and do not find me." On the surface, this may of course be read as the days that pass before Yeshua's resurrection and his reappearance to the disciples after his death. However, there is much deeper wisdom in these words regarding spiritual life and practice, our inward communion. Quite naturally, there will be an ebb and flow in our experience of the presence and power of God with us and mystical experiences and revelations of God in our hearts and souls. There will be times when we will be profoundly aware of the Christ Presence, Christ Spirit with us, seeing, hearing, feeling with the Spirit, and experiencing powerful revelations and movements of the Holy Spirit. Our devotion will be in awareness, in knowledge, knowing Christ and God with us—this Light-presence and Light-power. At other times in our devotions and worship, we may not be aware of the Divine Presence with us or feel much in the way of any movement of the Holy Spirit and powers of heaven with us: Christ, Messiah being hidden from us.

When there is not direct awareness or knowledge, we invoke, pray, meditate, and worship in faith, remembering the truth of Christ, Messiah within us, God, the Holy One, with us, and our innate unity and fullness in Christ, Messiah. At times our devotions and communion are in faith because there are days we cannot find or feel the Inner Light and Spirit.

But there are times our devotions and communion are in our knowledge because we are aware of the Inner Light and Spirit. Whether in faith or knowledge, it is no different; whether we are aware of it or not, having received the Holy Light and Spirit and the inner Christ, Messiah having been revealed to us, we know that the Messiah and Holy One and the powers of heaven are always with us, wherever we are. Amen.

Verse 39

Yeshua said, "The Pharisees and scholars have taken the keys of knowledge and have hidden them. They have not entered, nor have they allowed those who want to enter to go inside. You should be shrewd as snakes and innocent as doves."

This could not be any more straightforward. Generally speaking, religious authorities and theologians are outside the spiritual mysteries of creation, revelation, and God whom they speak and teach about. They have not entered into the spiritual and mystical experience of the messengers, the apostles, and prophets of God, have not experienced direct revelation of Christ and God in their heart and soul, nor have experienced the disclosure the secrets of God from God, or from the Holy Spirit. Therefore, being outside the ongoing revelation and realization of Christ and God, unaware of the Inner Light and Spirit within themselves, they theorize about the experience of the messengers, mystics, and gnostics; they speculate about the meaning of the word of God that the messengers spoke and lived; they seek to know God only through their mortal, finite intellect and reason, not the intuitive intelligence of their heart and soul. They are outside, not inside. Their so-called knowledge is conceptual, not experiential, revealed, or realized.

Without having received the Holy Light and Spirit or experienced the full revelation of the inner Christ, Messiah or powerful movements of the Holy Spirit in the play of light transmission, prophecy, revelation, healings, and wonders, many authorities today deny such things are possible. They dismiss and even ridicule the witness of those who have and do, those who are inside, those who have an intimate, inward communion with Christ in God and the powers of heaven. Worse, religious leaders discourage the faithful from going inside and seeking true faith in the presence and power of God, dissuading others from having faith in the living messenger of the

Pleroma of Light, proposing instead that various events and wonders that have been recounted of messengers in the past are metaphorical and symbolic, mythical sorts of primitive imaginings. If miracles happened once upon a time long ago, they cannot happen now. Many religious leaders are mistaken. Many scholars are ignorant—the blind leading the blind.

Of course the same is true of fundamentalist theology and so-called literal interpretations of the Bible as the absolute word of God for all time. This way of thinking is simply the opposite pole of the very same ignorance, made of speculations devoid of experiential knowledge, direct revelation, and realization.

This ignorance was the problem infesting large institutions of religion, their authorities, and scholars in the time of Yeshua, and the same is true today. It is not that religious authorities and scholars hide the truth, but that they've either lost it or never had it to start with. If one has never been inside, ingathered, and come to know the Inner Light and Spirit within themselves and within all people, how can they preach or teach of it, initiate or guide others in the Way of direct revelation and realization? One cannot share or give what they do not know or have.

That the problem has increased these days is obvious; more and more churches go further away from the light and love of Christ, Messiah into the darkness and hate of what can only be called the antichrist spirit. Many churches and their priests or pastors and congregations are in great trouble and great spiritual peril. Believing as they do in false, man-made doctrines but thinking they have the true teaching of Christ and are privy to the only way to God, it is very unlikely that they would be able to hear the Living Presence, Living Spirit speaking the Word and Wisdom of the Eternal One. False leaders will be unable to receive the Holy Light and Spirit and experience the actual revelation of Christ, Messiah within them, to be in the light, to be in the love.

Those who wish to go inside, however, are to be "wise as serpents and gentle as doves," as is translated in canonical scriptures. Generally speaking, serpents will abide, coiled in waiting for their prey or stalking them with great stealth, vigilance, and acute sensitivity and awareness. In the same way, seeking to be an insider, we must be inward, deep within, and learn to wait upon the Holy Spirit, the revelation of Christ, Messiah within us; upon receiving it, we must then keep awake, staying open and sensitive to follow the leadings of the Spirit wherever she leads us. Let us remember that serpents never close their eyes and are driven by warmth, heat, light! As for being gentle as doves, it means being nonviolent, the inward resolution of any conflict, but more so it is being in the love, having compassion and forgiveness, and seeking to be very, very kind. If you are in the love you will not err; you will not stray from the straight path. But if you do, very swiftly you will return to be in the love again and so be in Christ, Messiah. This is the Way of insiders, knowers of Christ and God—gnostics.

Similar challenges are occurring in all faiths and wisdom traditions today, as many religious faithful remain outside; but then, so too there are insiders in them all, knowers of enlightenment or God—gnostics. We may speak a Gnostic Christian language, but this isn't just a Christian thing—it's an everybody thing, among all faithful and spiritual peoples. Amen.

Verse 40

Yeshua said, "A grapevine has been planted far from the Father, since it is not strong it will be pulled up by the root and perish."

This verse continues the rebuke of religious institutions, and specifically alludes to a gnostic view of the god worshipped by many religious faithful. While one and the same God—the Eternal One—was within and behind the revelations within the Torah and Gospel, unless there is an experience of direct revelation of God and a spirituality of direct experience, there is no knowledge of God, no true communion with God. What is worshipped are concepts of God born of ignorance, separation, and lack: all manner of projections of the mortal, human ego upon God, as though the Infinite and Eternal One is anything like us as we are in the flesh and this world. What is often worshipped in religion is the demiurge—half maker—distorted, partial, concepts and vital sentiments of the Divine arising from an ignorant, unenlightened state. It is god in the image of man, rather than God as God is and the awareness of human beings created in the image and likeness of God—the Eternal One.

It may be said that until the Christ, Messiah appeared and engaged in teachings and revelations of the Eternal One in conscious union with the One, embodying the fullness of the Divine Presence, the Holy Light and Spirit, all revelations and realizations of the Holy One were partial and incomplete, in separation and lack. Though indeed the greatest among the prophets may have received revelation in intimate nearness, there remained a subtle and sublime separation from the Holy One. It was in dualism. Therefore, along with the truth and wisdom of the Divine that was revealed, so also were created impurities of falsehood and folly. Among the children of Israel with Moses, instead of the revelation of grace and covenant of love, a revelation of law of the knowledge of sin was given, a covenant of fearing God.

Although the Christian faith was established in a revelation of grace and covenant of love, with the dawn of orthodoxy and the corresponding man-made religious institution, very swiftly was the giving of the law, rules, regulations: teachings of a judgmental god to fear. As we know, when another great prophet appeared and another religion of the Abrahamic faiths was formed—Islam—once again it was for the masses, the mixed multitude; yet again was another giving of law, teachings of a judgmental god to fear. This is the plight of mass religion: it tends to fall under the law, the knowledge of sin, evil, and judgment, not grace and mercy or true salvation—true and full knowledge of God, enlightenment and liberation.

Blind belief is taught in place of a seeing faith, a knowing faith: a spirituality of direct spiritual and mystical experience of the Divine, of actual revelation and realization of Enlightened Being. This blind belief is a grapevine planted far from the Living Father—the Eternal One—that is not strong and thus will be pulled up by the root. It leads to little, if any, actual spiritual or supernal realization, not being conceived from it. This is far from the Eternal One, for it is not born from an intimate nearness, let alone oneness—conscious union.

As we know, Yeshua speaks of Christ, Messiah in himself in the Gospel of John, saying "I am the True Vine"; he is in harmony and unity with the Eternal One, rooted in the Living Father, inseparable from the Living One—alive, enduring, everlasting.

Now what is in Christ, Messiah is a revelation of grace and a covenant of love—being in grace, being in love. As the gnostic Gospel of Truth teaches, the Living Father—the Eternal One—does not see people and creatures in their sins, errors, imperfection, but in their innate and natural perfection as they are in the Father—the Supreme—in the eternal realm—Pleroma of Light. Neither the Father nor the Son judge: There is no judgment in the Eternal One, the Infinite Light. Rather, the Supreme is supernal grace, supernal love, complete mercy, compassion, and forgiveness. Given how much we have heard of the judgmental god—demiurge—and have been taught to fear that god, we cannot hear the truth enough, the reality again and again that God is love, that we are to be in the love, not fear.

At points in our experience of the overwhelming presence and power of God early on, we will experience fear and be troubled, and that is fine. It is a natural and integral part of our experience of drawing near, coming into being, and the sense that arises of our need to pass away to enter into the most intimate nearness and oneness with Christ and God—the Messiah and Holy One. At the outset, there are natural resistances to passing away, the complete self-offering to God. However, we are not to stay in that fear of God, but go deeper still: being in the Inner Light and Spirit, we will experience the unconditional love of Christ, Messiah as were called to be in that love of God, to be the light and the love.

As the Supreme, the Eternal One is supernal love, complete mercy, compassion, and forgiveness, so we are called to be love, to be merciful, compassionate, and forgiving. In a manner of speaking, this and this alone is True Religion. In the grace, in the love, there is no need for law; keeping to outward doctrine is not at issue. Rather, abiding in inward communion is the essential focus—being united and filled, being light, being love. In this is True Doctrine. What else do we need? What more is there? What else brings salvation, enlightenment, and liberation, simple lasting peace and happiness?

Such is a grapevine planted near the Living Father, rooted in the Eternal One.

Be strong and passionate in love! Amen.

Verse 41

Yeshua said, "Whoever has something in hand will be given more and whoever has nothing will be deprived of the paltry things possessed."

This teaching appears in the Parable of Talents in Matthew 25. As the story goes, a master intended to depart for a time and gave three servants different sums of money to tend to his affairs while he was away. When he returned, he went to his servants so they could return the money they kept for him. Two of them had invested it well and doubled what they had been given; they were praised as good and faithful servants. The one given the least feared losing what he had been given. In fear of his master, the servant buried his one talent and simply handed it back, having done nothing with it. That servant was rebuked as unfaithful and the talent he had was taken from him and was given to the servant with the most. All that he had was taken from him, leaving him with nothing.

In their simple and plain meaning, both this saying in Thomas and the Parable of Talents teach us to make full and skillful use of all that our life offers and all that God provides, whether on a spiritual or material level. Our intention in the Divine Life is love, compassion, and self-offering, using all of our abilities, skills, and our resources—all that we have and are—to be of benefit to people around us. We must be a blessing to all of our relations and the environment around us, serving the kingdom of heaven, seeking to ingather and uplift living spirits and souls in Christ, Messiah. When we do so, having received the Holy Light and Spirit and the Holy Spirit having taken up our person and life, there will be a greater flow of blessings.

Blessings will increase as we engage in the various works and missions given to us so that we will have more to offer and give, and we will be of greater benefit, able to accomplish greater divine actions and works. Basically speaking, the more we make good use of who we are and what we have in our lives, the more we will have to work with and the greater the flow of blessings with, in, and through us: the greater the divine action of the Holy Spirit with, in, and through us.

This is an expression of living in unity and fullness, aware that God will provide, rather than separation and lack. We are aware that when we exhaust our efforts, abilities, energy, and resources, the Holy Spirit will take up our divine actions and works to complete and perfect them, fulfilling our heart's desire and the will of the Holy One.

There is, of course, something more that gnostics hear in this saying of Thomas and the Parable of Talents from canonical gospels, for the gnostic path is initiatory. In gnostic community, initiation is founded upon discipleship, sacred friendship with living messengers—apostles and prophets—and involvement in the gatherings of gnostic community for sacred discourse, invocation, prayer, meditation, and sacred ceremony or charismatic, Spirit-filled worship. Through the messengers and mature, experienced sisters and brothers in community, there is the play of light transmission and powerful movements of the Living Presence, Living Spirit. Likewise, being ingathered into anointed community in that matrix of light, there can be direct influxes of the Spirit and light transmission, blessings from the spirits of tzaddikim and powers of heaven, or saints and angels.

Understand that there are many gradations of light transmission, different possible movements, actions of the Holy Spirit through messengers and anointed community for those who are ingathered. Our initiation is when we first receive the Holy Light and Spirit, but then after experiencing different manifestations of light transmission and passings of the Spirit, we receive various spiritual empowerments corresponding with openings of new cycles of our coming into being, new progressions in our realization, and the reaching of higher, inner stations and states of the soul.

In a manner of speaking, when we receive initiation, we must put to use what we have received: We need to surrender to the Lord, the Spirit to follow the teachings of the inner Christ, Messiah and leadings of the Spirit in our lives. We need to actively strive with the Spirit to bring our initiation to fruition and to progress in our spiritual and ultimately supernal realization in Christ, Messiah. We must seek to be in the light and in the love to grow a faithful and sincere spiritual life and practice: to remember and keep Shabbat, engage in daily devotions, spiritual practices, and gather with our community for devotion and Spirit-filled worship to truly take up the Christ Life, the Divine Life.

We need to abide in inward communion, invoke often, pray often, meditate often, and study and contemplate in the Spirit often, seeking to be in the love, being kind, and engaging in good works, living in the Way of the Anointed—Christ, Messiah. If we do, there will be an experience of ongoing influxes of the Holy Light and Spirit, ongoing experiences of light transmission and passings of the Holy Spirit, and ongoing empowerments. As with our initiation, it is the same with the empowerments we receive; we co-labor with the Spirit to actualize and realize them and bring them to fruition. As various blessings, empowerments, and gifts of the Spirit are given to us, we take them up and make use of them in various divine actions and spiritual works for ourselves and for the sake of others. If we do not use the empowerments, knowledge, and power given to us, we cannot receive greater empowerments or greater gifts.

In fact, as we saw in the Parable of the Sower of Seeds, if initiation and empowerments are not made to take root, they will bear no fruit. The light power and spiritual power given to us will be removed from us; having neither integrated nor made it our own, we will have given it away.

Our initiation, the initial reception of the Holy Light and Spirit and revelation of the Christ, Messiah in us is a beginning. From it, we must sojourn in the Way and strive always with the Spirit for a greater revelation and realization of Christ, Messiah in us. Likewise, the spiritual empowerments we receive are openings. We must go forward, go to God, and strive with the Spirit for that evolution and expansion of the Divine Life.

It may be said that as in material life, so also in the spiritual life: growth, expansion, is living; cessation of growth, expansion, is dying and death. So we always strive for progress—growth, expansion—in the Life Divine. Amen.

Verse 42

Yeshua said, "Be passersby."

This is a very delightful and beautiful saying; though only two words, its wisdom runs deep. There are layers of meaning in it. We may be reminded of the shortest verse, also of two words, in canonical gospels, in the Gospel of John at the raising of St. Lazarus. When Yeshua saw the people grieving for Lazarus, it says, "Yeshua wept" (11:33). On one hand, perhaps Yeshua wept in compassion, having empathy and feeling with the people mourning so deeply, many of them followers of his. On the other hand, for three days he was aware of the resurrection of Lazarus that was intended in the Holy One; Yeshua postponed coming until he had been dead for some time. Perhaps he wept because as yet, they did not realize who he was and who they were in the Eternal One; they did not come from that place and were just passersby, briefly stopping in this world on a far longer journey. In this sense, this world is not their home or a place of rest.

Our home is the kingdom of heaven and our place is God; we are just passersby here, travelers away from home, as it were, until eventually we remember where our home is when we return. But then, as the saying goes, home is where the heart is. What we most desire and love, we become. If that is the body, life in this world, not the kingdom of heaven and God, rather than a full and true return to God—reintegration with the Infinite Light—we will return to incarnation again, bound up in the ignorance, separation, and lack. It is with this in mind that a very old sacred text of the Kabbalah—the *Sefer Yetzirah, Book of Formation*—says: "If your heart runs, return it to the Place." The Place is God. So when Yeshua says to be passersby, it is essentially the same teaching. Turn away from creatures and creation and go straight to God—seeking and desiring God and nothing else.

Of course, when we are deeply inward and rest in Christ and God in us, unified with Christ in God, the True Light, and aware of God in us, we are aware of God in all things in their inwardness. Looking outward, we no longer see people and creatures but all in their inwardness, in God, God in them. Then we see their outwardness as they are in themselves. We are aware of creatures and creation in God, and God in creatures and creation, inward, outward, in every direction. There is nothing other than the Holy One, Holy Shekinah. So we are passersby, living and moving and having our being in the Holy One, not of this world and the things of this world but of the kingdom of heaven and God—the Eternal One.

There is another open secret here, one well known to apostles and prophets. As it is recounted of Moses when he was on the sacred mountain in revelation of the Holy One, the Holy Shekinah, the presence, glory, power, of the Holy One passed by. And as the Holy Shekinah was passing by, the word of the Holy One was spoken. After the Shekinah had passed by, the prophet was able to see the back side of the Holy One, in retrospect. In the movements of the Holy Spirit, Holy Shekinah passing by, the Holy One is revealed and realized.

Now among even the greatest of prophets, this vision was always in twoness, separation, dualism, and they did not see the Eternal One face to face, in oneness, union. In Christ, Messiah however, there is seeing face to face, in oneness and unity, the faces of God being in our face. The fullness of the Holy Shekinah—the Holy Light and Spirit—is in us. In revelations and transmissions of the Holy Shekinah, Holy Spirit initiation, the imparting of blessings, empowerments, healing, and the divine play of wonders, miracles, magic—in all of this, the Shekinah moves with, in, and through us, and passes by as us. So we are passersby, the Holy Shekinah of Messiah passing by. As Christ, Messiah is appearing and being revealed through us, so the Holy Light and Spirit is being imparted, blessings and empowerments are given, healing and wonders transpire. Be passersby, be vehicles of the Shekinah, the Divine Presence passing by, facilitating the revelation and realization of God with those who are around you, uplifting them in the resurrection and ascension, ingathering them into Christ, Messiah— the Inner Light and Spirit. Amen.

Verse 43

His disciples said to him, "Who are you to say these things to us?"
Yeshua said, "From what I tell you, you do not know who I am, but
you have become like Jews. They love the tree but hate the fruit, or
love the fruit but hate the tree."

Yeshua and his disciples were of course Jews, but in gnostic scriptures
the term "Jews" is often used to refer to the outward religious faithful. In
Christian Gnosticism, there are three races of humankind, or three states
of souls within humans: the bestial and material human, the faithful and
psychic human, and the spiritual human being or spiritual elect who, having received the Spirit, have knowledge of God and is gnostic. "Jew" indicates those faithful and psychic humans, the state of most religious people.
So to say to his disciples that they have become like Jews means that they
have become like those who as yet do not have the Holy Spirit and so are
unable to see, hear, and feel with the Spirit to know and unite with God.

"They love the tree but hate the fruit" may be understood as loving
God and religion but hating or lacking love and compassion for people.
And to "love the fruit but hate the tree" may be understood to love people
but lack love for God, a true seeking or desire for God, and the revelation
and realization of God. Such love of God is not a true love of God, and
such love of people is not a true love of people; both are partial and incomplete, in outwardness, from self-cherishing. In the fullness of love, there
are no differences between loving God and loving people—friends, strangers, or enemies. There is just love: being love. The very nature of unity
and fullness is love; if we are not in the love, we are in separation and lack.
If we consider this question from the disciples, it is not in the love, unity,
or fullness, but separation and lack; while they have affection for Yeshua,

apparently they were disturbed by his teachings, the word of God being spoken to them.

In this regard, people speak of their love for Messiah Yeshua but do not follow the teachings of Christ, Messiah. They quote scripture but strive neither to live according to them nor for an actual spiritual, let alone a supernal realization. This is not loving Yeshua. And so with living messengers of God, some might like them but not the word of God in them or their teachings; others might like their teachings but not the messenger. These are all vital tangles and mentalities that prevent listening and hearing the word of God as it is spoken that create barriers to spiritual progress, spiritual realization. They correspond with conditions of a compromised faith and love and inward cleaving, a lack of faith and lack of love.

"From what I tell you, you do not know who I am." Yeshua was and is the word being spoken, the wisdom, enlightenment, being revealed. He is the living teachings of truth, living word, living wisdom, the Way revealing the Way, leading in the Way. So it is with the true apostles and messengers of God, the holy and enlightened ones through whom God is being revealed, all in the Holy One. In Christ, Messiah, we also are called to be the living teachings, embodying the Living Presence, Living Spirit: being the light, being the love.

Now there is also something that may be said regarding a spirituality of direct experience, inward communion, and Spirit-filled, Spirit-led devotions and worship. We do not want to become religious with our devotions or our worship, stuck in repeating a routine or closed off to change, progress, or evolution in our daily devotions, gatherings for worship, or celebrations of the mysteries. We do not want to become like the outward religious faithful in that way, but we want to follow the inspirations and leadings of the Spirit, to be open to new movements of the Spirit, and to new ways of devotion and worship.

From the perspective of our gnostic lineage and tradition in our gnostic experience, devotions and gatherings for worship and sacred ceremony are a creative affair; all are open to improvisation as the Living Presence,

Living Spirit inspires in the movement and in the moment. It is all about being in the Spirit and moving with the Spirit, whether inward or outward. Among gnostics, the intention is for the Spirit to speak in sacred discourse, for the Spirit to move in sacred ceremony: for God to invoke God through us, for God to pray to God through us, and for God to meditate upon God in us as we pass away in union with the Divine Presence. Amen.

Verse 44

Yeshua said, "Whoever blasphemes against the Father will be for-given, and whoever blasphemes against the Son will be forgiven, but whoever blasphemes against the Holy Spirit will not be forgiven, either on earth or in heaven."

This verse also appears in canonical gospels. It is perplexing to many who hear it, because never having received the Holy Spirit or witnessed power-ful movements of the Spirit, the reality of the Spirit and what it means to blaspheme or go against the Spirit is not understood. In many outer and unspiritual churches, the unforgivable blasphemy is taught to be suicide, self-murder, and to some extent there is truth in this, especially if a person who kills themselves had received the Holy Spirit or witnessed the reality and power of the Spirit but then turned away. However, there is something more to the blasphemy of the Holy Spirit and why it is an unforgivable sin, or error, such that the negative karma generated will have to play out in the afterlife states and be worked out in future lives.

First, understand that Christ and God—the Messiah and Eternal One—are revealed through the Holy Spirit. Apart from the Spirit, the Messiah and Eternal One are hidden and unknown to people in this world. So, in effect, if one has never received the Holy Spirit or witnessed the reality and power of the Spirit, which is the presence and power of the Messiah and Holy One, whatever blasphemy or opposition there may be toward the Messiah or Holy One is done in ignorance, unknowingly, not will-fully. Likewise, in the Eternal Messiah and Eternal One, there is supernal grace, supernal love, complete mercy, compassion, and forgiveness. In the Messiah and Holy One, all is forgiven. However, if a person received the Holy Spirit or witnessed the reality and power of the Spirit and then went against a messenger of the Messiah and Holy One or the Holy Spirit, it would be knowingly and willfully done; they would know what they had done. In effect, it would haunt them. If they were unrepentant and refused to return to be One, they would be unforgiven. If they died in that state, they would be unforgiven in the afterlife; that negative karma would play out in the afterlife states, and it would need to be worked out in future lives.

There is a mystery to understand about the Spirit, however. It is like a Great Force within all things, flowing through all things. It can manifest in mercy and severity, creation or destruction, light or darkness, good or evil. The Holy Spirit in herself is primordial and supernal, completely Divine and beyond the dualism of light and darkness, good and evil. But as the Spirit is manifest in people, creatures, things of creation, in the illusion of separation and lack, this power of the Eternal One can manifest in mercy or judgment, all as living spirits and souls create for themselves. Understand that just as there is no judgment in the Messiah and Holy One, the same is true of the Holy Spirit. If there is judgment or evil, it is we who manifest it.

You see, the Holy Spirit is the light and life in all people, but the question remains what people do, how they live their lives, and what they do with the light and life within them.

When a person receives the Holy Light and Spirit, a great power is awakened in them, the light and life in them are increased and amplified; they move with greater force and there is a greater play of cause and effect with them. If a person were to turn away and go far astray to blaspheme the Holy Spirit or use this force in a destructive way or for evil, going to the other side as it were, they would become bound up in the other side—the archonic and demonic—and experience the reality they created for themselves and others in their lives. It is not that there is no forgiveness in Christ and God for them—there is complete forgiveness for all. But those who turn away are unable and unwilling to receive it, having gone so far from the light, from the love.

In various ways, having received the Holy Spirit or witnessed the reality of the Spirit, it is possible for faithful and spiritual people to go astray, blaspheme, or go against the Spirit. Generally speaking, actual blasphemy of the Holy Spirit corresponds with extreme circumstances and a willful generation of great negativity and harm toward others. But of course to do so is to go against ourselves! If we are going against ourselves, who can stop us? From whom can we receive forgiveness? This exactly is the plight of blasphemy of the Holy Spirit: Going against ourselves and gravely harming ourselves is tantamount to spiritual suicide.

It really is going against our own light and life—the Inner Light and Spirit.

Abiding in faith and love and an inward communion, this is not a great concern to us. Falling into extreme negativity and opposition to the Spirit to such an extent is very unlikely. Likewise, being in the company of messengers and anointed community with spiritual sisters and brothers who strive to live in faith and love and have received the Holy Light and Spirit, following the guidance of the Spirit in their lives, and through whom the Spirit moves—is a great guardianship against going astray from the gnostic path, the straight path. There is indeed sanctuary in anointed community from many negative influences and deceptions. Amen.

Verse 45

Yeshua said, "Grapes are not harvested from thorn trees, nor are figs gathered from thistles. They yield no fruit. A good person brings forth good from the storehouse. A bad person brings forth evil things from the corrupt storehouse of the heart and says evil things. From the abundance of the heart such a person brings forth evil."

When a wicked and evil ruler ascends to power in the world and suddenly great crowds of people are breaking out with evil words and evil actions, the cause is not the wicked and evil ruler but instead the wickedness and evil that was already held in the hearts of many people. That is how evil people come to power.

When there is a great influx of the Supernal Force happening in the collective consciousness of humankind in the end times, what is held in peoples' hearts is intensified, amplified, and brought forth and revealed. For those with righteousness in their hearts, what is good and true in their hearts takes them up in the influxes of the Supernal Light and Spirit. For those with wickedness in their hearts, falsehood and evil carries them away in the increasing darkness. The Supernal Force becomes light for those who have light within them, who are in the light and the love. The same Supernal Force becomes darkness and fire for those who have darkness in them, who are in the fire, fear, anger, and hate. This is the judgment in the end of days: not in the Messiah and Eternal One but in people to whatever they cleave and cherish in their hearts, their spirits, and their vital souls. If there is heaven on earth, it is people who make it so. If there is hell on earth, it is people who make it so. Know that in the Messiah, in the Holy One, all are loved and held in the heart of the Eternal One. This is the most essential truth of Christ and God: God is love. As you are loved, God is in you; being in the love, you are in God, the True Light.

Quite naturally, if we are faithful and spiritual, awake and aware of Christ, Messiah within us—the Inner Light and Spirit—we need to pay attention to what we hold in our hearts and the thoughts, mentalities, we entertain in our minds. We want to be inward, deep within, and let our hearts and minds be uplifted to those things that are above, where the Messiah is, where we are in the Eternal One—the Infinite Light. Look at what is good and true in yourself and bring that forward. What is neither good nor true, let go as you go forward to God, the True Light. Do not pay attention to or worry about the darkness, wickedness, or evil that may arise in heart and mind: Do not give it your soul power, your light power. Rather, see the good in you. Pay attention to the good, be concerned with the good, and bring forth that good from within you, all of it. Let your light shine brightly: be the light and the love, nothing else. In the same way, do not focus upon or concern yourself with the wickedness and evil in others. Rather, seek to see the good in them, seek to see them in their inwardness as they are in the Eternal One. As you are able, do what you can to reflect that good to them. Help and encourage them to draw out their good—something of the Inner Light and Spirit.

This is not to say that you will fail to see and know righteousness and goodness as righteousness and goodness or wickedness and evil as wickedness and evil. Being aware of the inwardness of people and things does not mean you are not aware of the outwardness of people and things or who and what they are in themselves—not in the least. In the love of Christ and God, you will simply love without differentiating between people, neither in judgment nor condemnation but in compassion and forgiveness.

If you hate the hateful and judge them, then you are being hateful and in judgment; you have been infected by that very wickedness and evil. You are in the fire, not the light or the love. Know and understand that this is the greatest and most lethal pandemic in these times: not only does it harm the body and ends with the body, but it also harms the soul. This suffering goes beyond the body, into future lives. It is truly a dreadful psychic and spiritual sickness, a dis-ease. Guard yourself against this: be on watch, be mindful, and do not give way to it. But if you do, as soon as awareness is restored and you see what is happening, leave it. Return to the love, the mercy, compassion, and forgiveness. See the good and draw out the good from within you and others around you.

Remember that in the Inner Light and Spirit, we are aware that many people are unaware of what they are doing and the realities they are creating for themselves; they are bound up in ignorance, separation, and lack. This fact is a cause for compassion and forgiveness; they really do not know what they are doing!

There is a simple gnostic devotion connected with this truth called giving and receiving. In it, we energetically take up the cross with Yeshua and engage in the action of co-redeemers, being light, being love, and having compassion and forgiveness for those bound up in darkness and caught up in great sorrow and suffering. Taking up this mystical way of prayer and meditation, we envision a Spiritual Sun in our heart—the Sun of the Eternal One—and behold our body as brilliant light, glory. Merged with the Spiritual Sun and being inward, our breath becomes as the radiant holy breath of that Divine Sun, a fluid, flowing light. Next, we envision those in need before or around us, those bound in darkness and suffering in body, heart, mind, and soul. We see them as shadowy or dimly glowing figures filled with something like sooty smoke or flaming fire and such. When we inhale, we take all that negativity into the Sun of the Divine in our heart, envisioning ourselves breathing in the sooty smoke or flames and envision it transformed into the radiance of that Holy Star in us, completely unharmed. When we exhale, we breathe light and love, all of our good and the good of that star of heaven upon them and into them. In so doing, we take from them the negativity, suffering, and evil and give them what is good and true: the light and love of Christ, Messiah, mercy, compassion, forgiveness, peace, and joy. We continue in this way until they appear like us, like the Sun of God, Human One of Light, delivered, healed, and enlightened in the Spirit.

Many sisters and brothers have experienced greater healing and realization themselves while giving and receiving. Likewise, powerful movements of the Holy Spirit actually touch people at a distance. Know that within this gnostic devotion is a secret key to the play of light transmission and passing of the Spirit among us. This practice is similar to how we move in the Living Presence, Living Spirit: with the conscious intention of light transmission and passing the Spirit, forgiving and releasing sin, and anointing with the Holy Light and Spirit in Christ, Messiah. Amen.

Verse 46

Yeshua said, "From Adam to Yohanan the Baptist, among those born of woman, no one of you is so much greater that your eyes should not be averted. But I have said that whoever among you becomes a child will know the kingdom and become greater than Yohanan."

In this saying, Yeshua praises Yohanan the Baptist as the greatest soul born of women. As Yeshua was also born of a woman, the Holy Mother, that would include himself. As we know, the soul of Elijah—the *neshamah* of Elijah—was incarnate as Yohanan, a truly great and holy soul indeed, one taken up into heaven through divine rapture, not tasting death. But Yeshua's praise of Yohanan is not about that, for as we know there was another holy prophet taken up into heaven through divine rapture: Enoch the Initiate. Rather, this is traditional praise of a disciple for the spiritual master who taught, initiated, and served as the spiritual guide in their process of coming into being and realization. According to oral tradition in the Christian Kabbalah, Yohanan was the holy tzaddik of Yeshua, Yeshua having been his disciple before coming into being as the Messiah.

The above verse in Thomas and similar ones in canonical gospels supports this gnostic view. Yeshua was fully human and fully divine; like all human beings, he had to seek and find gnosis, enlightenment, or God. Virtually all who become fully realized and enlightened have relied upon a spiritual master, someone holy and realized to serve as teacher and guide with whom they were a disciple. The same remains true to this very day. The Holy One continues to send anointed messengers—apostles, prophets, tzaddikim—to teach, initiate, and generate lineages of light transmission and true anointed community. This was the way of the original church, the first anointed community. There were apostles and prophets among the various gatherings of the community. Following the Way was founded upon actual discipleship—companionship in the Way.

While Yohanan was only six months older than Yeshua, he was sent along another path. According to our Christian Kabbalah, as soon as he was weaned and old enough and after receiving word from God through an archangel, Zachariah and Elizabeth sent him to live with and be raised by a community of desert prophets. Among them, the head of the prophets of their generation, the *Baal Shem*—"Master of the Name"—received Yohanan as his protégé. After the death of his master, Yohanan came into being as Baal Shem, just as in the incarnation of Elijah. He had come into being and became realized before Yeshua to serve as Yeshua's tzaddik, opening the Way for him, the coming of Christ, Messiah, the first divine human to embody supernal realization, conscious union with the Holy One, Holy Shekinah.

Their deep and intimate soul connection, however, did not begin in that life. As Yohanan was the reincarnation of Elijah, Yeshua was the reincarnation of Elisha, to whom, before his ascension, Elijah promised twice his knowledge and power (2 Kings 2:9). That sacred promise and word in the Divine Presence was only partially fulfilled in the lifetime of Elisha, for Elisha did display twice the wonders as Elijah. Its complete fulfillment, however, happened in the Sacred Jordan between Yohanan and Yeshua, when the Spirit and Soul of the Messiah came into Adonai Yeshua, who reached supernal realization. It is on account of this that in canonical gospels, Yohanan praised Yeshua, the holy one coming after him, as greater than himself. Truly so, for Yeshua was the Presence and Power of the Name and was the Christ, the Messiah.

Quite naturally, when Yeshua was taken up in supernal realization, so was Yohanan, though he was not the Messiah. Such is the Way of inmost grade of light transmission within which tzaddik and disciple disappear: They merge and pass away in the Holy One, Holy Shekinah—two being one, and then two again, each One from One. In this regard, those who become little children in the Way we have previously discussed, who enter into a supernal realization in this life or at the time of their crossing over, they will know the Pleroma of Light most intimately, in unity, and will be greater than Yohanan was before the Sacred Jordan, greater than a Master of the Name or those of the prophetic succession before the coming of Messiah.

As has been said, there is a greater revelation and realization of the Eternal One—Yahweh—in Messiah Yeshua than in the prophets who came before him. Though gnostic apostles and masters teach that there are holy and enlightened souls who will be the Christ, Messiah to other worlds in the matrix of creation, it was through Yeshua in this universe that a great divine action was accomplished, and no one after him shall accomplish the same in this world. Amen.

Verse 47

Yeshua said, "A person cannot ride two horses or bend two bows, and a servant cannot serve two masters, or the servant will honor one and offend the other. No one who drinks aged wine suddenly wants to drink new wine. New wine is not poured into aged wineskins, or they may break, and aged wine is not poured into new wineskins, or it may spoil. A new patch is not sown onto an old garment or it may tear."

This verse seems like two joined together, making two teachings. But given the subject of the previous saying, their union can be interpreted as the spiritual guidance and discipleship in addition to the reception of teachings.

First: "a person cannot ride two horses or bend two bows" can be interpreted to be a very important teaching for our times. Today there is a wealth of information available of spiritual and esoteric teachings from many diverse wisdom traditions, perhaps more than ever before. There are indeed many true paths to enlightenment or God and actual realization of souls. Often, many seekers are attracted to numerous paths and draw teachings and practices that they like from them, but they never actually journey very far or immerse themselves completely in any path or wisdom tradition, let alone seek out a true guide—holy tzaddik—and spiritual community. This behavior tends to keep many seekers outside, on the surface of teachings. This forms a barrier that limits their spiritual life and obstructs the deeper inwardness that grows from more fruitful devotions and spiritual practices.

Flirting with spirituality does not bring about much progress in actual spiritual and supernal realization. In a manner of speaking, how many boats does it take to get to the other shore? If you keep going from boat to boat but do not set sail, how will you get out of the harbor into the open sea, let alone reach the other shore where the boat may be left behind? If seeking actual spiritual and supernal realization, whether the gnostic path and Christian Kabbalah or another that has true initiation—light transmission—it is best to find a path that deeply resonates with you. Commit yourself to it, become fully immersed and involved in it, and if possible, seek a living spiritual master—holy tzaddik—and spiritual community to receive teachings, initiation, and guidance.

"A servant cannot serve two masters, or the servant will honor one and offend the other." In canonical gospels, this saying is linked to seeking and serving God or money; we either love God and the Way of the family of God, or we love the world and the way of unenlightened society. Obviously, if a person is going to seek and find enlightenment or God, they need to have faith, a passionate desire for enlightenment or God, and to seek to live in the Way of the holy and enlightened ones, not like the unenlightened society, certainly so! Likewise, having a single path or vehicle for realization, it is wise to have a single spiritual teacher and guide—holy tzaddik—and community and become a true disciple, a spiritual companion to them, following their teachings and guidance closely and with zeal.

If you were to meet more than one realized individual who served as spiritual guide to people, each would have a different style of teaching and initiating. Even in teaching the same path or vehicle, they would have a different timing in giving reflections and instruction. To have two or more guides can create conflict in a seeker, which might prevent them from being a true disciple and drawing close to either of them. Indeed, as the saying states, they may honor one and dishonor the other. There is only a need for one and one alone. In this way, a more rapid spiritual progress and deeper realization becomes more likely, if indeed we follow the direction of our guide and come to know the true guide within us.

It is true that we may have what is called a heart master or tzaddik, a deep inward heart or soul connection to an apostle, prophet, tzaddik, of the past. That is not uncommon among mystics and gnostics; there is a communion with the spirits of tzaddikim or saints as with angels. However, our principle guide will be a living one, a root master or tzaddik, and it is with that living one whom we have discipleship and companionship in this life; it is their word, their teaching, and guidance that we follow first and foremost.

If we encounter a realized individual of any authentic wisdom tradition, they will have an ancient teaching and a new teaching. The revelation and realization of enlightenment or God will be unique and individual to them, for there is never repetition in divine revelation. Each is a unique and individual embodiment of enlightened or divine being, as are each of us as we come into being and are realized. In the Christian stream, each will have their own gospel, their own realization and knowledge of Christ and God—the Messiah and Holy One. If teaching Christian Kabbalah, they will teach their own Kabbalah as it has been revealed to them by heaven and God, the True Light. It will be an ancient teaching and a new teaching. If indeed they and others around them are realized, there will be ongoing new and innovative teachings and revelations, progressions and evolutions of their gospel and Kabbalah, naturally so. New teachings, new revelations, generate new ways. As new ways come into being, some old ways will necessarily pass away and be shed by their community. They and their community teach a living tradition in an experience of living revelation and realization, inwardness and not outwardness from the indwelling Messiah and Holy Spirit. The word of God is spoken with power through them, the play of light transmission and passing of the Spirit. Amen.

Verse 48

Yeshua said, "If two make peace with each other in one house, they will tell the mountain, 'Move,' and the mountain will move."

In canonical gospels, moving mountains is connected with faith the size of a mustard seed. When speaking of invoking and praying in faith, the apostle James wrote that we are to have complete faith, free from doubt. He then went on to speak of being double-minded, how those who are divided can neither expect to receive answer to their prayers, nor anything from God or the powers of heaven. Two making peace with each other in one house is single-mindedness, having complete faith that is free from any shadow of doubt. When we invoke and pray in complete faith with inward cleaving, in the love, and with a clear conscious intention, unifying and focusing the force of our will in harmony with the Inner Light and Spirit, nothing is impossible for us. The Holy Spirit can move with, in, and through us and accomplish wonders, miracles. Likewise, in the Spirit, the powers of heaven and angels will move and take action with us, all as God wills and ordains.

In the Way of the straight path, the Way of mystics and gnostics, something more is happening in this singularity of mind and heart and the force of will-desire in us. When there is a deep inward communion, when invoking and praying in Spirit-filled worship, in celebration of the mysteries of Christ and God, often there is the experience of passing away, merging with the inner Christ, Messiah and Holy Shekinah, Holy Spirit, the seeming two becoming one. When unified with the Holy Shekinah, Holy Spirit, so also with the array of divine attributes, powers, actions: the Sefirot. In oneness, in unity, it is the Spirit that invokes and prays, wills and desires, moving the powers of heaven to fulfill the will of the Holy One; the force of will of the Holy One being merged with the will-desire of that holy and righteous person. Quite naturally, any of the attributes, powers, and actions of the Holy One, the Holy Shekinah, the Holy Spirit, can be manifested through that faithful and spiritual person as needed to fulfill this true will, the true desire of their soul in the Messiah and Holy One.

Such prayer, of course, cannot be conjured, but comes from God. It is the manifestation of the grace and love of God with those who have complete faith. Those in the love and devotion of God in spirit and truth experience the mystical and magical reality of Spirit-filled worship. When the Spirit takes up those who are worshipping, such that the One who is worshipped is worshipping, in effect God delights in God, God knows God; God invokes, prays, and moves the powers of heaven. The Christ, Messiah and Holy Spirit in us communes with and in God ever beyond—the Eternal One—and the full presence and power of God is made manifest with us. Indeed, there may be the moving of mountains: prophecy, revelation, healing, all manner of wonders, various grades of light transmission, passings of the Spirit—blessings and empowerments.

The Spirit naturally and spontaneously takes up those in their devotions and worship who have the fullness of faith with inward cleaving, who are in the light, in the love. As faith and love matures, as the inward communion deepens, and there is progress in spiritual and supernal realization, it becomes more and more common in devotion and worship that a holy woman or man is able to pass away, to merge with this Living Presence, the Living Spirit with a simple conscious intention to do so. These have come into being as tzaddikim, holy and righteous ones, holy and enlightened ones.

There is something to be said about the holy tzaddikim who are called by the Lord, the Spirit, to be revealed tzaddikim, to make themselves known as they are in God, to reveal the presence and power of God that is with them, and to serve as teachers and guides to others in anointed community. There are also concealed tzaddikim in anointed community who are not called by the Lord, the Spirit to reveal the presence and power of God that is in them, but to instead remain concealed as they engage in their spiritual works and mission in secret, known only to God and the angels. They are able to see, hear, and feel with the Spirit and know others in their inwardness.

In gnostic community, in the gnostic path—the straight path—all of us are called to strive to be and become a holy tzaddik. All are called to take up the works of their tzaddik, their teacher and guide. Know and understand that anytime the Holy Spirit takes us up and the powers of the Holy Spirit are manifest with, in, and through us, the Holy Spirit has uplifted our soul into the station and state of the holy tzaddikim. In such a moment, we are glimpsing, tasting, who and what we are in the Eternal One—a holy and anointed tzaddik, a righteous one, a perfect one in Messiah. Amen.

Verse 49

Yeshua said, "Blessing on you when you are alone and chosen, for you will find the kingdom of heaven. You have come from it and you will return there again."

In other translations of Thomas, this verse is a blessing on those who are solitary or single, of course speaking of the two becoming one, or two making peace with each other as in the previous saying—therefore being alone, solitary, single: one.

When we receive the Holy Light and Spirit, we are reborn from above, from heaven and God, the True Light. We are sons and daughters of light, sons and daughters of God, members of the family of God. When we receive the Holy Light and Spirit, we are united and filled, newborns of the enlightened family. Although perhaps glimpsing, tasting, our innate unity with Christ in God and the fullness of the Holy Light and Spirit in us, it has not been realized. We must learn how to be deep inward, to be the light and love, and to learn how to pass away and merge with the Christ Presence, Christ Spirit.

When we pass away, merge with the inner Christ, Messiah and Holy Spirit, we are alone, solitary, single—one with the Living Presence, Living Spirit. There is the Divine Presence alone, no other, nothing else. Understand, conscious union with the Divine Presence is the experience of the true kingdom of heaven: Being merged with and inseparable from the Divine Presence and Power is being reborn from above, coming from above, coming from the Pleroma of Light, the Divine Presence—the Shekinah of Messiah.

Though it may be said that in the Eternal One, Eternal Now, it is all one rebirth and is singular in the Holy Light and Spirit, perhaps you will understand that being born again is not an isolated or singular event; in truth we are born again and again and again. As this happens and we abide in an inward communion with the Holy Spirit, progressing in our realization, the Holy Shekinah more and more will take up her full divine action with, in, and through us: We will return to this mystical experience of being merged, unified with the Messiah and Holy Spirit. And so we will return there again. If it becomes common in our devotions and worship and various situations and circumstances of our lives, naturally this experience will arise for us in the afterlife states. When we pass beyond, we will indeed return to the kingdom of heaven—the Pleroma of Light, certainly so!

As we learned in a previous saying, whether we experience a spiritual or supernal realization in this life, through the grace and love of the Eternal One, in Christ, Messiah passing beyond, all will be a single one. Such is the truth and reality of who and what we are in Christ and God—the Messiah and Holy One. Through Divine Grace, the Holy Spirit, that Divine Self will be realized. Even if on their deathbed, a person open to the Holy Light and Spirit, through the Holy Spirit, through the grace and love of the Eternal One in Yeshua Messiah—the Anointed—may be ingathered to the kingdom of heaven, the Pleroma of Light.

The truth is that all souls in their essence and nature come from the Pleroma of Light. This Inner Light and Spirit is in all people, whether or not it is realized and embodied in their lives. In one incarnation or another, in this world or another, all will eventually become realized and return to the kingdom of heaven, the Pleroma of Light. Christ is universal, salvation is universal. Hallelu Yah! Praise the Lord! Amen.

Verse 50

Yeshua said, "If they say to you, 'Where have you come from?' say to them, 'We have come from the light, from the place where the light came into being by itself, established itself, and appeared in their image.' If they say, 'Is it you?' say, 'We are its children and the chosen of the Living Father.' If they ask you, 'What is the evidence of the Living Father in you?' say to them, 'It is motion and rest.'"

This is a lovely, deep and esoteric saying from which many teachings may be drawn and many interpretations given.

In the Holy Kabbalah, the Infinite One—*Ain Sof*—is often spoken of as Radiant Nothingness, and that holy radiance is Infinite Light—*Ain Sof Or*. From that Infinite Light emanates ten Holy Sefirot—divine attributes—which are themselves infinities of light. Within those ten are ten and within those are ten, ad infinitum. The Infinite Light appears and is revealed as the Sefirot in their image, and they are the Pleroma of Light, the outermost of them being called *Malkut*—Kingdom. Malkut in the Reality of the Holy Sefirot called *Atzilut*—Emanation, Everflow—corresponds with the true kingdom of heaven, or, according to the Christian Kabbalah, the heaven of heavens.

We come from the light, from the place where the light came into being by itself and appeared in their image, the inmost of the Sefirot, called Keter-Crown—corresponding with the Will-Desire of the Infinite One, through which the entire array of the Sefirot emanates and flows. According to the Holy Kabbalah, the Spirit and Soul of the Messiah emanates from the interiors of Keter. This is the place from which our divine spark or unique essence emanates, our soul being woven of the Sefirot—divine attributes, powers, actions. We are indeed from this Infinity of Light, and these emanations of the Infinite Light are within us, our souls. When we receive the Holy Light and Spirit and we are reborn from the true kingdom of heaven, this reality of the Inner Light and Spirit is awakened in us. We come into being as sons and daughters of light, sons and daughters of the Eternal One.

The chosen are those who receive the Holy Light and Spirit: children of the Living Father—Hayyah Abba—and true brothers and sisters of the Living Yeshua—Hayyah Yeshua.

As for movement and rest being the sign of the Living Father in us, recall that going deep inward and abiding in an inward communion, passing away, merging with the Inner Light and Spirit, Divine Presence, is rest in the Holy One, Holy Shekinah. The Holy Light shines from within us; the Holy Spirit moves with, in, and through us, accomplishing all manner of divine actions, spiritual works. Merged with, resting in, the Messiah and Holy One within us, we are no longer the doer, but the Holy Shekinah, the Holy Spirit is the doer. This is motion and rest.

The presence and power of God manifest within and around us is the evidence or sign of God being in us, and we being in God, the True Light.

In the Gospel of John, Adonai Yeshua gives another teaching of the sign of God in us, saying to his disciples, "Love one another as I have loved you" (John 13:34). Be in the love, be love: In you and through you, God will be revealed, God will be glorified. Being in the light is being in the love, so it could be said: We have come from the love, from the place where the love came into being by itself, and appeared in their image. You see, coming from light, we come from love: As we are guided by the light, we are guided by the love. One who is guided by the light, guided by the love, will not sin, will not err. As the Gospel of Philip teaches, they will have put on the perfect light and will be among the perfect ones.

In this regard, we may recall the teaching of Yeshua Messiah in canonical gospels: "Be perfect as your Father in heaven is perfect." Amen.

Verse 51

His disciples asked him, "When will the dead rest? When will the new world come?" He said to them, "What you look for has come, but you do not know it."

This verse, along with its other variants, is a question that might arise in the hearts of many religious faithful to this very day, and the answer given would be the same.

When you go within, deep within, and die to yourself to be reborn in Christ, Messiah, you will have rest. But then being alive, resurrected in Christ, Messiah, you glimpse and taste the delight and sweetness of the World-to-Come in this world: You know the kingdom of heaven inside and outside—within and all around you.

Many among the religious faithful are awaiting the second coming of Christ, Messiah in glory some day in the future, but what they look forward to has come and is transpiring among us this very day. They could very well ask, "When will the Lord appear? When will New Jerusalem come?" But in truth, Christ, Messiah is appearing again through various messengers in supernal glory. The Inner Light and Spirit is awakening in many people, and true anointed communities are being generated among all peoples and in all lands. Supernal grace and love abound; the light transmission and supernal radiance pass between people even at great distances with no need for physical presence or anything outward. Consider New Jerusalem, an image given in revelation of the kingdom of heaven to indicate secret mysteries of the eternal realm and its reality, within which all is self-radiant in glory. There is neither a single source of light nor an outward temple; the Eternal One and Eternal Messiah is the place of worship and communion within souls and souls within them, the Holy One, Holy Shekinah.

This very day, Yeshua lives within and all around us as long as we have the eyes of the Holy One to see, the ears of the Holy One to hear the Living Word spoken, and the heart of the Holy One to feel and know the endless light and immeasurable love of the Eternal God—Yahweh Elohim—the Almighty—Shaddai, all in the Lamb of God. The Messiah has come and is coming. There are many who are seeing, hearing, and feeling it with the Spirit, but there are also many who do not yet know this; they do not see, hear, or feel with the Spirit.

If you die before you die and are resurrected in Christ, Messiah, reborn from heaven, in the depths of your soul, deep inward, you will find rest, the most subtle and sublime peace and joy, here and now, regardless of what is transpiring outward—happiness or sadness, wellness or illness, auspicious or inauspicious circumstances, light or darkness, good or evil, living or dying, or whatever might be happening on the surface. There is indeed resting in the Eternal One, reintegration with the Infinite Light, knowledge of the Holy One, Holy Shekinah, most intimately in oneness, complete unity. This is the very nature of the true kingdom of heaven. What more is there? What more could you want?

If this is in you and you are in this, if the end of days were to come while you are traveling here, there would be no end for you. Rather, a Continuum of Life and Light without End—the experience of bornless being in union with the Eternal One—Yahweh, Yeshua.

As we know in what has come to be known as the Lord's Prayer, many faithful pray every day that the kingdom be manifest on earth as it is in heaven. Many praying for this are waiting for it to happen someday. Yet if Christ, Messiah is in you and you are in Christ, Messiah—if this Inner Light and Spirit is awakened in you—the kingdom *is* on earth as it is in heaven; the kingdom of heaven is within and all around you. Wherever you are is the true Dwelling Place of God and the true Holy Land. Wherever and whenever there is a manifestation of true anointed community—Body of Christ, Messiah—there is the kingdom of heaven on earth.

If you have received the Holy Light and Spirit and Christ, Messiah has been revealed in you, the Inner Light and Spirit has been awakened in you, your life is the kingdom of God: God ruling in it and bringing prosperity, happiness, and peace. Your body is as the city of God, through which the living presence and power of God moves and is revealed and realized. Your very heart is as the palace of God—the Dwelling—and in it is the bridal chamber, the holy of holies, filled with love, within which your soul is united with Christ, Messiah in the Infinite and Eternal One—the Living Father, the Living Mother, the Holy One of Being.

What you've been looking for has come: See, hear, feel, and know it. Knowing it, be the light, be the love, be the living presence of the Holy One. Return to be One! Amen.

Verse 52

His disciples said to him, "Twenty-four prophets have spoken in Israel and they have all spoken of you." He said to them, "You have disregarded the living one among you and have spoken of the dead."

On the surface, this saying may seem to be a curious response to the rec- ognition being spoken by the disciples; to say that all the prophets have spoken of Yeshua reflects that they are realizing that he is the Messiah, the most holy Anointed One of God. Yet he says to them, "You have disre- garded the living one and have spoken of the dead."

It must first be understood that a living apostle, prophet, tzaddik—let alone the Messiah—is not justified or validated by those who have gone before them. Their anointing and divine authority and power do not come from men or women, however holy they may be. Instead, it comes from the Holy One and Holy Shekinah, the Holy Spirit. What they are is from God and God alone, no other. Even if a holy man, woman, or angel was sent to initiate them and speak the word of the Holy One to them, it is God's doing, an action of the presence and power of God, the Holy Spirit.

In the midst of the manifestation of the Living Presence of the Eternal One or in the presence of a living revelation and realization of the Eternal One, why look elsewhere, to the past or to the future? Why remove your- self from the present and the Divine Presence with you in this moment, this very day? The place or event of revelation and realization of the Eter- nal One, Eternal Now, is in the present—in the moment, here and now. For those present in what is happening with faith, love, and inward cleav- ing, revelation and realization—enlightenment—is always transpiring from moment to moment.

Curiously enough, much of religion is always oriented to the past and the dead. Even if a living messenger is encountered—an apostle, prophet or tzaddik, assuming the living messenger is recognized as such—most religious seekers will have greater veneration for and devotion to those of the past than the living one. You see, one can make realized beings of the past say or be whatever one wants. One can also interpret their teachings and word of God spoken however one wishes because that one does not encounter the direct intensity of their presence and the knowledge and power of God that was in them. In the presence of a living messenger, however, one must deal with their divinity and humanity—the reality of a divine-human—and take direction or correction from them. There is no making them be, say, or do anything that the Holy One, Holy Shekinah does not call them to be, say, or do, not in the least. Generally speaking, the dead tend to be comforting to us early on the path, and the living tend to be troubling. The dead are easier for us to love in the way they love as we are in ourselves, in the flesh. Adonai Yeshua calls this out and gives an essential correction regarding disciples comforting themselves and shielding themselves from the Living Presence with them by invoking the names of the dead and cleaving to them.

As has been said, there can be heart tzaddikim as well as secret tzaddikim who may visit us in dream and vision and are part of our communion as with angels, but our devotion and our cleaving belongs to the living one, the root tzaddik, the Living Presence. Understand it is through a living messenger, a living lineage, a living community, that the light transmission and passing of the Spirit happens on earth. Living tzaddikim are like mirrors within which we behold the face of God, in whose reflection we behold ourselves, the image of God in us, the Inner Light and Spirit in us. However glorious an appearance of a great holy and enlightened one in vision and dream, the light transmission that comes from living ones who walk among us affect, penetrate, and pervade our body and soul more powerfully. Their empowerments radically accelerate our spiritual development, evolution, and realization. After all, it is one thing to encounter a divine-human in dream, vision, or in the imagination, but another thing entirely to encounter them in the flesh as we are in the flesh and receive a clear reflection and witness of the divinity within our humanity. You see, if this realization can happen in any one of us, this realization, embodiment, can happen in any of us. It is possible for all of us!

Understand that as much as speaking of the living one with regard to himself, Yeshua may also be understood to be speaking of the living one within his disciples. The very intention and purpose of the outer tzaddik, root tzaddik, is the realization of the inner tzaddik within us, the inner Christ, Messiah—Inner Light and Sprit—and our own Divine Self, Divine I Am. Know and understand that the outer tzaddik and inner tzaddik are one Holy Tzaddik in the Messiah and Holy One. Amen.

Verse 53

His disciples said to him, "Is circumcision useful or not?" He said to them, "If it were useful, fathers would produce their children already circumcised from their mothers. But the true circumcision in the spirit is altogether valuable."

The true circumcision is in the spirit, intelligence—*ruach*—which resides in the heart. A circumcision or purification and opening of the heart is necessary so that Holy One can be revealed in the heart, so that Messiah and Holy Spirit can dwell in the heart. Unlike the outward circumcision only of men under the law, this is a circumcision for men and women alike, allowing all to be one and the same in Christ, Messiah as spiritual human beings of light, all in the love of the Supreme—*El Elyon*.

At the outset of our spiritual journey, what we often call our heart is not our heart but something like a vital husk or shell encasing it: the *klippah* of the heart. It is composed of a lot of falsehoods and misunderstandings of ourselves and others, along with various impure desires, fears of surface consciousness, and all manner of things we hold on to from the past: various psychic wounds, injuries, and grievances about how others have let us down, harmed us, or did not give us what we wanted, or betrayal, judgment, or persecution, and so on. Accompanying this shell around the heart are many insecurities, self-judgments, negativities, doubts, and feelings of not being good, smart, or worthy enough. These tend to encrust and harden the heart, closing it. Hiding our true heart from ourselves and shielding it from others is a principle barrier blocking out light and love, whether from people in our life or God. This barrier often includes all manner of false beliefs and misconceptions about God that man-made religion in fundamentalism plays upon through its teachings of a very severe and judgmental god. In this falsehood, humans are nothing more than miserable sinners.

To receive the Holy Light and Spirit and experience the revelation of the inner Christ, Messiah and the light and love of Christ, Messiah within out heart, it must be circumcised, purified, shed. This is why the baptism of water of Christian initiation precedes the chrism or anointing with the Holy Light and Spirit. Going down into the living waters of baptism and being immersed in them, the old self—the name, form, and personal history of which it is concocted—is dead and buried with Christ, Messiah, shedding this *klippah* of the heart. Rising from the waters, we are resurrected and ascended with Christ, Messiah. A new self emerges in Christ, Messiah, a divine-human. As we receive the Holy Light and Spirit, Christ, Messiah is revealed in us. Our circumcised heart is purified and opened.

It is said in scripture that to come to the Lord and draw near to God, we need to have a broken heart and contrite spirit; we need to be surrendered. This is true, but understand that the heart that breaks is not our true heart—it is the husk or shell of the heart. Our true heart is spacious, radiant, and aware; it is compassionate. Our true heart has room in it for everyone and everything, including the Holy One, the fullness of the Holy Shekinah, the presence and power of the Living God. It cannot be broken! Therefore, when your heart breaks, do not try to mend it. Leave it broken. Your heart is opening. Let it open and turn to the Lord within you, to the Holy Light and Spirit. Let that Holy Light and Spirit fill, heal, and enlighten you. When your heart is circumcised, God will unveil and disclose Godself in your heart. God will give Godself to you and replace your human attributes with the attributes of Christ and God, the Messiah and Holy One. It is through the opening of the heart and coming to faith and love, that you are truly reborn from heaven, the Inner Light shining from within you and the Spirit moving with, in, and through you. It is all about the generation of the sacred heart—spacious, radiant awareness, love, and compassion. It is in this that we not only become truly human but we also become truly divine. Amen.

Verse 54

Yeshua said, "Blessings on you the poor, for yours is the kingdom of heaven."

This is the first beatitude of the Sermon on the Mount in the gospel of Matthew. As the first of them, understand that all blessings that follow—which correspond with the full array of the divine attributes, essential stations, and states of the soul—are in and accessed by the very first beatitude: being poor, or knowing that you are poor.

As is known, faith is the very first station and state in the ascent and realization of the soul. Without faith, souls cannot ascend; they will not seek and find God or return to be One. Yeshua spoke of faith as an essential and great spiritual power, such that with faith the size of a mustard seed, with a mere wish or thought, mountains can be moved. In itself, faith is the outermost divine attribute, power, and action, but it is through faith that we are able to access every other attribute, power, and action, able to ascend and reach all stations and states of the soul. Truly, while seeming outermost, faith is a great power. All the powers of the Holy Shekinah, Holy Spirit are in true faith.

Parallel with faith and one of its more sublime elements is the station and state of poverty, being poor. Having faith, turning to the Lord—being inward—seeking and finding God, you will discover that in reality, you are nothing, empty—completely impoverished—and that God is everything. In reality, you have nothing of your own—no existence, light, life, intelligence, or anything apart from God. You may recall the second saying of Thomas and Yeshua, on becoming troubled when you find. Understand that underlying virtually all our fears, the deepest fear is that in reality, we are nothing, nobody. This feeling of being nothing is what drives self-will, extreme self-cherishing, and all the desires and fears that avoid looking into this place of nothingness—the underlying emptiness of oneself and all that arises and appears. Against this is the constant striving to prove that one is something or somebody, special and great.

Deep down, people fear being alone and that they are nothing. But understand that if you are willing to look into being nothing and embrace and go into it—accepting this reality of yourself—in that deep, deep fear is the truth that will set you free. You are nothing, you are empty of any substantial and independent self-existence: you are poverty, you are poor!

But wait! From that nothingness, that emptiness, that poverty, the nothingness that you are, everything you are and everything in your experience of being arises from it, self-generating and radiant! And as you go deeper still, embracing and going into this, you will find an empty radiant awareness—spacious radiant awareness—a primordial and supernal Radiant Nothingness within you and ever beyond you. You will see the Living Father, the Infinite and Eternal, the Holy One of Being. You will become aware that the only Reality or True Existence is the Holy One, and the Holy One alone. There is no other; there is nothing else—there never has been!

The open secret to this lies in being willing to pass away. Being nothing, you will find that you are everything.

You and all things are emanations of this Radiant Nothingness—the Eternal One—manifest as countless many in infinite diversity in an endless, exhaustless self-generation: an endless arising of self-awareness, intelligence. While appearing as countless many, all are the Holy One, and the Holy One is indeed alone. There is no other.

Being poor, as such, yours is the kingdom of heaven, certainly so! Amen.

Verse 55

Yeshua said, "Those who do not hate their father and mother cannot be my disciples, and those who do not hate brothers or sisters and bear the cross as I do will not be worthy of me."

Something similar to this saying is taught in canonical gospels. In them, Yeshua speaks of leaving family and friends to follow him and be of the family of God. But here his words are recounted as stronger and more severe, speaking of hating family. Given that Adonai Yeshua was adamant about having mercy, compassion, and forgiveness, being generous in self-offering to friends, strangers, and enemies alike—being in the love—it is impossible to imagine him hating anyone, let alone teaching his followers and disciples to hate. Naturally, we must look deeper to understand what he is saying.

When we first come to faith and begin the gnostic path, we receive teachings and initiation. It is a wonderful time. Receiving the Holy Light and Spirit is delightful—we taste something of the peace and joy in Christ, Messiah and experience something of the light and love of Christ, Messiah. But as we know in canonical gospels, when Yeshua came into being at the Sacred Jordan, the Spirit and Soul of the Messiah came into him and the Spirit immediately drove him into the wilderness of the desert to be tempted by the satan—the enemy, adversary. The same is true when we receive the Holy Light and Spirit and are set upon the gnostic path of Christ: an ordeal of initiation follows with challenges and temptations that arise from inside and outside. From inside, old habitual patterns of thought and patterns in our vital being, impure desires, fears, and our various selves test us. From outside—the satan—others are disturbed because we are changing and they do not want us to change; they want us to live like they do, outside, in the darkness, in the way of the unenlightened culture and society.

Some people who become the voice of the archons and the satan may be strangers, but the more common and powerful ones are friends and family who may discourage our faith, spiritual life, and practice. They may tell us we are not going the right way, that the gnostic path is wrong for us, and so on. At the same time, we will encounter vital resistances and rebellions from within ourselves: thoughts that echo the satan, speaking with the same voice as the satan, telling us we have better things to do than keep the Holy Shabbat, that prayer, invocation, and meditation are a waste of time, and spiritual study, contemplation, and sacred discourse is not for us. This voice may say that such things as love, compassion, and forgiveness are foolishness. Reaching the station of faith, moving into its interiors and growing, maturing in faith, is a very real challenge early in our journey to ourselves and God. As the Parable of the Sower makes clear, many do not make it through this ordeal or temptation: instead succumbing to it and falling asleep again, into the darkness, the outside, and thus not becoming true insiders let alone gnostics—knowers of Christ and God.

When we are tested in this way, we must pay attention and strive with the Spirit to make changes in our lives. We need to stand strong in the Lord—Adonai—because the first holy war has broken out inside of us. The evil and good inclinations battle with one another; our bestial nature strives with our divine nature. There is no way around this great conflict, none whatsoever. If Jesus, Yeshua went out into the wilderness and waged battle against the forces of the archons and the satan, then so must we.

The first holy war is the most challenging because at the outset, our faith is weak and immature; we have not reached many stations and states of the soul. We are very vulnerable on a psychic and spiritual level. All the same, we must listen not to the voice of the satan but the voice of our Lord within us. We must not follow the spirit of the Other Side, but the Spirit of the Lord—the Holy Spirit. We need to invoke the Name of the Lord, the Name of God often, remember the Name, pray and pray and pray, and have an inward communion. We need to follow the instruction of our guide, our holy tzaddik, and let them help us and walk us through this time of temptation.

The voice of God is in our heart. We must listen and submit to the guidance of the Lord from within; the voice of God is in the voice of our tzaddik and our brothers and sisters in the enlightened family—anointed community. We must listen, hear, and follow the guidance we receive. Our earthly mother, father, sisters, brothers are no longer our guides: the Lord is, the family of God is. Indeed we turn away from the advice and guidance of our earthly family, as well as former friends who are naysayers with regards to our faith and spirituality. While we do not hate people by any means, we despise and consider foolish any voice of the satan, outside or inside, and we do not listen to the voices of the satan, let alone submit ourselves to them again. We cannot turn aside or turn back; we must go straight to God and ourselves: who and what we are in God.

This is not an easy time. There is much work to do that requires much effort. We need to make many changes. We need to be strong, disciplined, vigilant, and push forward to higher inner stations, going to our true self and God. But we are not alone. God is with us. If we invoke and pray, and ask for help, God will help us draw nearer and nearer and will give us strength. The Holy Spirit will be our comforter, helper, protector, and guide if only we abide in faith with inward cleaving, cleaving to the Inner Light and Spirit. Quite naturally, gathering with our tzaddik and family of God for sacred discourse, ingathered communion, sacred ceremony, and Spirit-filled worship will be of great help and give us refuge, sanctuary. It is no longer our earthly family we turn to for refuge, sanctuary, and support in our lives but our enlightened family, our family of God. Amen.

𝔙erse 56

Yeshua said, "Whoever has come to know the world has discovered a carcass, and whoever has discovered a carcass, of that person the world is not worthy."

This world is impermanent; it and all things in it will pass away. Whatever passing pleasures this world may offer, life in this world and throughout the great matrix of creation, in the unenlightened condition, in separation and lack, is pervaded with great sorrow and suffering. As it is in itself, this world and life in it, is no more desirable than a carcass, a corpse. Apart from the Spirit, it is neither able to see, hear, and feel with the Spirit, nor smell, taste, and touch with the Spirit. Many people and creatures in this world have no True Light and life in them but are like corpses, dead. And whether caused by human beings in their ignorance or by some cosmic event, the end of days is near. If not that collective event in our lifetime, the day of our death is coming and is growing near. So one way or the other in this world, there will be an end of days for us who live in the end times. That is life here!

Perhaps these words are unpleasant and hard to hear. Perhaps they are depressing to you and you want to move on to one of the more upbeat and affirmative teachings in this gospel about how you are light, divinity, and so on. But understand that only those who are willing and able to look and see, listen and hear, the truth of what is being spoken here will have the drive and passion to realize and embody the light and divinity in them. They will be resurrected and ascended, enlightened and liberated. Apart from finding God and acquiring wisdom, enlightenment, this awareness of the world and its unenlightened society as utter vanity and futility of everything under the sun is a key driving force for those who seek enlightenment or God. It is why those zealous for God will not turn aside or turn back until true spiritual and supernal realization dawn.

Unless a person gets this truth, sees and recognizes it for themselves, they will have little or no zeal for the gnostic path or the spiritual life and practice. If they are involved in spirituality, it will be half-hearted and luke-warm, just another activity in their mundane life. But they will neither really change nor have a passionate desire for God and God alone. They will not go very far in the gnostic path or the ascension into higher, inner stations and states of the soul. Without the motivation to put forth the great effort it takes to do so much work on themselves or to strive for an actual spiritual or supernal realization and the corresponding knowledge of God—True Gnosis—they will not have a reason to.

Yeshua was born into a very poor family and lived in a poor village in the hills of Galilee. He saw the dominion of the rulers—the archons—and the very wealthy over the common people. He witnessed all the injustice and oppression of unenlightened society and the cruelty of fundamentalist religious authorities so prevalent in his day. Being who he was, he was very moved. It set into his heart and belly a fiery passion to seek and bring true salvation—enlightenment and liberation—to all people. He would bring God down to them, so that everyone might be free to worship God in spirit and truth in an inward, personal communion relationship and communion with the Eternal One—Yahweh. This world was truly worthy neither of him nor anyone in whom this passion for enlightenment or God ignites!

Integral to coming to faith is beginning to question the true purpose and meaning of life, human existence, and a growing dissatisfaction with life in the unenlightened condition, unenlightened culture, and society while having a deep desire for something better, something more, some-thing good and true, something real, and being in the real. Truly faithful and spiritual people have realized that the world and its unenlightened society are fundamentally unreal, so they seek to find the real, enlighten-ment, God. They are holy people: The world as it is in itself is not worthy of them, not in the least! Amen.

Verse 57

Yeshua said, "The Father's kingdom is like someone with good seed. His enemy came at night and sowed weeds among the good seed. He did not pull up the weeds but said to his servants, 'No, or you might go to pull up weeds and pull up the wheat along with them. On the day of the harvest the weeds will be conspicuous and will be pulled up and burned.'"

This parable of wheat and weeds appears in canonical gospels, though it is told with more elegant wording for the sake of clarity. The meaning, however, is clear: There are seeds of light and seeds of darkness; each comes to its corresponding fruition, whether love and thus in the light or judgment, thus in the fire. Those who do what is good and true bear sweet fruit for themselves; those who do what is false and evil bear toxic fruit for themselves. Each comes to their own end, experiencing the reality they have woven and created for themselves. In the Eternal One, Eternal Messiah, there is no judgment—just love, mercy, compassion, complete forgiveness. If there is judgment, it is we who judge ourselves and others, experiencing the reality we have created—judgment, fire.

The teaching of this parable goes much deeper, because who is to say who is faithful and who is an infidel, or who is righteous and who is wicked? According to this parable, the radical fundamentalist who believes and preaches a violent eradication of all infidels and who believes they are righteous and serving God in so doing is sorely mistaken. Rather than following the voice and word of God, they listen and follow the voice of the satan—the opponent of God. Assuming there was anything righteous and godly in such violence—there is not—while killing infidels, they also kill those who are faithful and righteous in the process in addition to those who, given time, would repent, and turn to seek and find God. Pulling up the weeds also pulls up the wheat.

Let us remember that we all begin in ignorance, darkness here. We all begin as infidels. Who are we to judge? As there is in reality no judgment in the Eternal One, the Infinite Light, why are we judging? It is the complete opposite of the Holy One. And if it is opposite the Holy One, who are we? To be in the light is to love, to have mercy, compassion, and forgiveness. This is the Way of the Messiah and Holy One.

Look and see! According to this teaching of Yeshua, the Eternal One has everlasting patience and is lovingly waiting upon all living spirits and souls to awaken, to seek and find the Holy One, Holy Shekinah, to be ingathered, and return to being One. So much so that souls do not live only to either go to heaven or to hell for all eternity. Rather, they sojourn through many lives, having many opportunities to awaken and return. So it is until they are realized, reintegrated with the Infinite Light. The Holy One is very, very patient, kind, and loving, completely so!

People can change at any time. If a person ever repents, turns to the Lord, opens to the Holy Light and Spirit, the good seed of light will be implanted in them. If they tend it with the Spirit, striving with the Spirit for a spiritual realization, it will take root in them, grow, and mature into a Tree of Life. Divine attributes, powers, actions will be made manifest in them as they bear good fruit. If we are inside, in the light and the love, we will neither judge people who are outside in darkness, bound up in wickedness and evildoing, nor assume that is all they are and is the end of their story. Rather, we will invoke and pray for them, seeking their good and to draw it out, actively hoping for their awakening and ingathering, their salvation—their enlightenment and liberation. As this is the intention and desire of the Eternal One for all who sees everyone and everything in their innate perfection as it is in the Holy One, this is to be our intention and desire as well, that all might experience enlightenment or come to God. If we are in the light and love of Christ, Messiah, what else would be our heart-wish for all people, all creatures, all living spirits and souls? Remember, this is why messengers appear in every generation. We are called to be as they are: lovers of God and people, light-bearers, healers, and peacemakers. Amen.

Verse 58

Yeshua said, "Blessing upon the person who has labored and found life."

There is indeed salvation through Supernal Grace if we believe, having faith and inward cleaving. But in order for Supernal Grace to come into effect, in order for the Holy Spirit to take up her full divine action in us, we must engage in an active and dynamic surrender to Supernal Grace, the Holy Spirit and co-labor with the Spirit to work out our salvation, to bring our realization to fruition in Christ, Messiah.

This labor is a life of devotion: invocation, prayer, meditation, and inward communion. Equally, we must work on ourselves and be willing to change and change and change in active cultivation of the qualities of Christ and God—the Messiah and Holy One. With it, we are all given messianic works and a mission to accomplish in our lives: working on ourselves and working to relieve the suffering of others to ingather them into Christ, Messiah. As the Secret Book of James teaches, "You are not saved for yourself alone but for the sake of the salvation of others"—their realization in Messiah.

While we have the help of the Lord, the Spirit and can receive help, encouragement, and support from others, we must each work out our salvation for ourselves—there is no way around that. As understood by gnostics, salvation is not a vicarious affair but active and participatory. As Yeshua teaches, "Take up your cross and follow me." We therefore need to co-labor with the Spirit to redeem ourselves and others. We are to engage in the labor and works of a co-redeemer with Yeshua, as the Magdala and Holy Apostles did. In this way we find True Light and Life, living the Truth and Light revealed to us, thus realizing and embodying it.

This labor in the Spirit is well known by those who are called to teach and initiate. Save that a person has faith and love, they cannot teach and initiate them. Unless a brother or sister will help themselves and others, their guide cannot help them. You can only help those who help themselves and cooperate; there is no other way. There is no vicarious salvation or spiritual realization through mere sentimental belief or a conceptual agreement and recitation of a creed and doctrine. Creeds and doctrines bring neither salvation nor realization. Only direct experience of the Truth and Light, the integration of your person and life with the Truth and Light, the Messiah and Holy Spirit, brings salvation: the realization of bornless being, eternal life.

Those who labor are blessed. For in Christ, Messiah, we engage in our works and take up various divine actions with ourselves and others, giving our all. When our means and energy are exhausted, the Holy Spirit will take up, perfect, and complete those works, actions, so that they will bear an abundance of good fruit—much merit, much light and life power.

In Christ, Messiah, we do not labor alone. We labor with the Holy Spirit and the powers of heaven. In laboring, we are blessed. Amen.

Verse 59

Yeshua said, "Look to the living one as long as you live or you may die and try to see the living one and you will not be able to see."

This saying may be understood on many levels but first and foremost is the Lord within you, the inner Christ, Messiah. From the moment you first receive the Holy Light and Spirit and Christ, Messiah is revealed in you, you must look to that true Living One to be deep inward and abide in inward communion. Unless you do, you might depart from that true, holy communion and sanctuary of grace to be led astray, not uplifted in the resurrection and ascension when you pass beyond.

And so we are taught in the Christian Kabbalah: Let the Blessed Name of Yoshua, Yeshua, and the Great Name of Yahweh, be always before you. Abide in remembrance of the Name and invoke the Name often. This is an essential devotion among Christian gnostics.

Living One—*Achad Hayyim*—is a variant of Living Yeshua—*Hayyah Yeshua*. While this holy name denotes Yeshua living in you as inner Christ, Messiah, it also denotes the risen and ascended Christ, Messiah. Along with seeking an actual revelation, realization, of the inner Christ, Messiah, gnostic Christians also seek a direct revelation of the reality of the risen and ascended Christ, Messiah so that with faith in the resurrection of Yeshua Messiah from the dead and in his ascension, we may also have knowledge of that supernal reality. We believe and receive teachings in faith, and we also invoke, pray, and meditate to seek revelation from the Holy One, the Holy Spirit and powers of heaven. Ours is not a blind faith; it is a seeing, hearing, feeling faith—a knowing faith.

Of course, experiences of light transmission and revelations of the Inner Light and Spirit in us are glimpses, tastes of the reality of the risen and ascended Christ, Messiah. But we seek a revelation of the Great Resurrection and Ascension as known in the World-That-Is-Coming.

Then there is another truth of looking to the living one: seeing and knowing the presence and power of God within a living messenger, our holy tzaddik. Knowing through them who is speaking to us, teaching and initiating us, guiding us, we are faithful to them as true disciples, true spiritual companions in the Way. Likewise, joined with this is seeing the face of God, the image of God in all our brothers and sisters in anointed community and being aware of the revelation and appearance of Christ, Messiah through them and as them. A holy tzaddik and their community are inseparable from one another. The gnostic apostle, gnostic master, is the Heart, their community the Body, and Christ, Messiah the Head. We look to the Living One in ourselves and all who are in anointed community—the Body of Christ, Messiah. We do not separate ourselves from the Holy Body, but instead hold our place and perform the work we are given to do in it, whatever part of the Holy Body we may be—an eye, hand, foot, liver, sinew, and so on. We seek to be who and what we are—the Messiah and Holy One—and thus who and what we are in this Divine Order, this Living Body of God. Amen.

Verse 60

He saw a Samaritan carrying a lamb as he was going to the land of Judea. He said to his disciples, "…that person…around the lamb." They said to him, "So that he may kill it and eat it." He said to them, "He will not eat it while it is alive, but only after he has killed it and it has become a carcass." They said to him, "Otherwise he cannot [eat] it." He said to them, "So with you. Seek a place of rest or you will become a carcass and be eaten."

In this saying, Yeshua puts an emphasis on finding the place of rest. Rest or repose is essential. Living in separation and lack, self-will and self-grasping, there is sin, error, and the generation of karma: cause and effect. There is a play of mercy and judgment, the experience of the consequences of our thoughts, words, and actions along with the realities we create for ourselves and others. As has been said before, in the Eternal One there is no judgment, only complete mercy and compassion. But in the matrix of creation and in the transmigration of souls—*gilgulim*—or the realm of separation, there is the play of the law and cause and effect in a karmic continuum. In the relative reality of our experience is mercy and judgment, the experience of being in the light or the fire, all manner of realities in the afterlife states—heavens, hells, and various realities in between—and any circumstances of reincarnation, from very auspicious and fortunate to very inauspicious and unfortunate. In this mix, we form various kinds of energetic connections, exchanges of soul sparks both positive and negative with other living spirits and souls, as well as with other types of spiritual forces—divine, archonic, and demonic. Souls therefore become bound up, entangled in this karmic web, unable to escape, thus creating the need for the Savior and Gnostic Revealer who brings salvation and reveals the Way to enlightenment or God.

As long as you or I are the doer in self-will and self-grasping, remaining bound up in the unconscious play of desire and fear, law and karma exist. We will remain tangled in this great karmic web. If, however, self-will and self-grasping are brought into cessation, along with their play of desire and fear, and the Lord, the Spirit, within us is the doer, we are blameless, without sin. There is no karma or judgment, only the supernal grace and mercy of the Eternal One, Eternal Messiah. This is rest, repose—not being the doer.

In canonical gospels, Yeshua Messiah speaks of this rest when he says, "I do nothing of myself, but I do what I see my Father doing" (John 5:19). He was neither the seeing, hearing, and feeling, the smelling, tasting, and touching, nor the speaking, acting, or moving: The Holy One, Holy Shekinah, was the doer. Thus do the scriptures speak of Adonai Yeshua as being without sin. This itself made the resurrection and ascension possible, the offering of a Lamb of God without blemish—without sin or karma.

Yeshua says, "If you do not find the place of rest, you will become a carcass and be eaten." When he tells us as his followers and disciples to deny ourselves and take up our cross to follow him, this is bringing self-will, self-cherishing to cessation. It is passing away, merging with Christ, Messiah within us and therefore with the Eternal One: this self-offering, passing away, being rest, repose, in the Holy One, Holy Shekinah.

The image of someone carrying a lamb wrapped around their neck on their shoulders connotes a state of resting in God, a complete self-offering to God of one's person and life, such that one is eaten by God, absorbed in God. Conversely, this image may connote serving archonic and demonic powers—spiritual forces of the Other Side. In this world, many people feed and are consumed by impure and dark forces that absorb the spirit and vital soul and keep beings bound to the gilgulim—potentially endless rounds of birth, life, aging, illness, and death.

Nature, our supernal and heavenly soul—*neshamah*—generates a new emanation of spirit and vital soul—*ruach* and *nefesh*. In the afterlife states the spirit and vital soul dissolve from one incarnation to another, and only the karmic continuum of the soul is preserved in the outer aspects of the supernal soul. Until something of the supernal soul, divine nature is realized and embodied through the spirit, intelligence, and vital soul in an incarnation, the connection between incarnations is this karmic continuum, whether positive or negative or some admixture. However, as the supernal soul, divine nature begins to be realized and embodied in the incarnations of the soul—the intelligence and vital soul being manifestations of our supernal soul, who and what we are in the Eternal One—such realized souls endure, passing beyond to have eternal life. They are living, immortal in the supernal soul and the Eternal One, not carcasses to be eaten.

Remember, going to God is going to yourself—your divine nature, the Divine Self. Resting in God is resting in the Divine Self, the Divine Self being realized and embodied and thus living your life—being the doer. This freedom from sin, karma is enlightenment and liberation! Amen.

Verse 61

Yeshua said, "Two will rest on a couch, one will die and one will live." Salome said, "Who are you, mister? You have climbed on my couch and eaten from my table as if you are from someone." Yeshua said to her, "I am the one who has come from what is whole. I was given of the things from my Father." Salome said, "I am your disciple." Yeshua said, "I say, if you are whole, you will be filled with light but if divided, you will be filled with darkness."

This is perhaps Thomas's most curious and esoteric saying. On one hand, it can be interpreted as an encounter with Salome the Maiden, who according to our gnostic oral tradition was the inmost disciple of Mirya the Magdala and thus a close disciple of Adonai Yeshua. As such, what he says to her in this private and intimate exchange would be his essential heart-essence teachings for her, a common occurrence between apostles and prophets and their close spiritual companions. According to the same oral tradition, Yeshua gave a very specific heart-essence teaching that was very straightforward but most sublime and deep to Mirya the Magdala just after she and Yeshua met one another in this world.

On the other hand, it is not uncommon in gnostic scriptures for disciples to tell of interactions of Christ and various cosmic figures or personification of the Divine or divine attributes. For example, one very esoteric gnostic scripture speaks of Christ coming to redeem an aspect of Wisdom called *Pistis Sophia*—Faith-Wisdom—and so with her redemption is the redemption of all souls, all creation. Gnostics teach not only of an earthly ministry of Christ, Messiah but also a heavenly ministry and a ministry in worlds of inner dimensions among various spiritual forces—angelic, archonic, and demonic—that brings the True Light and Holy Spirit to all who desire to receive it, bringing salvation to them.

In gnostic teachings and the Christian Kabbalah, to bring about a shift in the world or engage in a powerful divine action and movement in the material dimension, there must be a parallel corresponding shift or divine action in the matrix of spiritual forces within the inner dimensions, specifically the astral and spiritual. Understanding this, Salome may be interpreted as a divine personification, an aspect of Wisdom—Sophia, Hokmah—to connote parallel divine actions in the inner dimensions within and behind his appearance and actions in the world, the material dimension. In fact, this is always going on with messengers of the Pleroma of Light.

Regardless of how we interpret Salome and this interaction, the heart-essence teaching remains the same: As it appears in Thomas, it is for all disciples of the Master.

Yeshua first proclaims he is from the Pleroma of Light—from what is whole, and goes on to say that he was given things from his Father—the full array of light emanations, or divine attributes, powers, actions—Sefirot, or Aeons.

Such a statement or proclamation from a messenger of the Pleroma, a light-bearer or Christ-bearer to a disciple would be understood to correspond with a revelation of the Light-presence and Light-power in them—the presence and power of God with them—and so a movement of light transmission or spiritual empowerment. When this happens, followed by teaching or revelation of secret mysteries—or as here an essential heart-essence teaching—the disciple is taken up in that very experience. It is not conceptual but experiential, becoming truly known to them and their own. It is a mind-to-mind, heart-to-heart, or soul-to-soul communication beyond spoken words: the very knowledge spoken dawns in the mind, heart, or soul of the disciples. In this, perhaps, you may understand that this passage alludes to experiences of light transmission and how movements of light transmission are engaged with conscious intention.

The messenger, holy tzaddik is completely unified with the Divine Presence and Power, such that the Divine Presence manifests as them. As the Divine Presence, they uplift and ingather their spiritual friend, merging with the soul of their friend and so with the Divine Presence in that moment. Thus is there a most intimate transmission, revelation on psychic and spiritual levels, a powerful communion of two becoming one in the Holy One, Holy Shekinah. In inner gradation of light transmission, to which this saying points, it is far more intimate and blissful than any romantic, physical intimacy. There is no comparison, none at all!

The essential teaching here is this: Being whole, unified, one is being in the love. Being in the love, you are in the light, filled with light. If divided, separated, two, not in the love, you are in the fire, the darkness, filled with the darkness. It is that simple. Be in the love, be in the light! What more do you need to know? What more can I say? Amen.

Verse 62

Yeshua said, "I disclose my mysteries to those who are worthy of my mysteries. Do not let your left hand know what your right hand is doing."

Who is worthy to listen and hear such holy utterances and revelations of secret mysteries of creation, Christ, and God—the Messiah and Holy One? You and I as we are in ourselves are not worthy. No one is worthy as they are in themselves. And yet as we are in Christ and God, and as Christ and God is in us, we have been purified and consecrated, sanctified and ordained to experience the revelation of the secret mysteries of Christ and God. Through grace we become worthy; through faith, love, and inward cleaving we become worthy. As we are in God, the True Light, we are worthy.

Most essentially is being in the love, for it is in the love that intimate nearness and oneness open the secrets that can be spoken in our heart and soul; the full unveiling and self-disclosure of Christ and God are revealed within us.

Who is speaking, who is listening? Who is writing, who is reading? If I am and you are, then while the word of God might be spoken and written, it is not with power. No secrets are revealed. If the Lord, the Spirit is speaking, writing through me, and the Lord, the Spirit is listening, reading through you, then the word of God is being spoken with power. Secrets are revealed. Contemplate this well, and understand!

When there is speaking and listening in the love, it is in the Holy One, Holy Shekinah: inwardness speaks to inwardness, souls speak to souls, God speaks to God. This happens when we have true faith, in the love and light together, unified in the Messiah and Holy One, of one mind, one heart, one soul. This is the only way secrets are revealed and made known. Are you feeling it in the Spirit? I pray that you are in the love with me, as I am with you!

Do not let the left hand know what the right hand is doing. Understand that to know the secrets, you must be able to keep a secret. Receiving inner and secret teachings, revelations of secret mysteries, you need to be mindful of when and with whom they are shared, whether the speaking is from the Lord, the Spirit or from some other place, your ego. Is it in the power of the moment. Is there a clear leading of the Spirit to share? Are you in the space and the love with whomever you are speaking for them to hear and receive what is being spoken? Is it good and beneficial for your sister or brother, or is it a progression of a mystery that they are not ready for? Is it for them, from the Lord, the Spirit?

In gnostic community and Christian Kabbalah, there are outer, inner, and secret teachings. With newcomers and novice initiates we generally begin with the outer, hinting at the inner. And as they progress in knowledge, understanding, and inward communion, so do we progress into the inner teachings, hinting at the secret. As for the secret, in the way that has been shared, ultimately they are revealed by God and God alone. Inner and secret teachings venture into what is very holy, very powerful. To be received with proper understanding rather than with misconceptions or misunderstandings that lead astray and from which strange and false teachings are born, inner and secret teachings require progression and maturation in faith, love, and inward communion and realization. There needs to be a strong foundation, stability in the spiritual life and practice to venture deeper into inner mystical teachings, let alone the secrets. All in due season.

It is also true that sisters and brothers do not need the same things. Some teachings and devotions may have nothing to do with us, our way, or our works and mission. It is all a question of what is good to give to each person we are with and what is needed, following the leading of the Spirit and being in the Lord, the Spirit.

The same is true for sharing mystical experiences, dreams, visions, inner revelations, and the inner knowings that arise from the Spirit. When the Spirit inspires and leads us to speak and share, we speak and share; if not, we do not. We are quiet and private about them.

If you come to know a living messenger and draw close to them, they may likely share some things in private with you that are not intended to be shared with anyone else: They are words of the Lord for you and you alone, no other. Amen.

Verse 63

Yeshua said, "There was a rich person who was very wealthy. He said, 'I will invest my money so that I may sow, reap, plant, and fill my storehouse with produce. Then I shall lack nothing.' This is what he was thinking in his heart, but that night he died. Whoever has ear should hear!"

This is the way it is in ignorance, the illusion of separation and delusion of lack. Even the wealthiest in the world often never feel they have enough. Frequently they are always driven and occupied with acquiring more from the world. They have little to no thought of the afterlife, enlightenment, or God. Remaining in separation and lack and having no experience of enlightenment or God, they will be separate and lacking when they die, which will shape their experience in the afterlife states. It will continue in their next life as the wheel of reincarnations goes round and they remain bound up in it.

We have spoken previously of the need to fast from the world and the wisdom of keeping the Holy Shabbat, but something more is touched upon in this saying that also appears in canonical gospels. In ignorance, people seek happiness and satisfaction from the outside, from all manner of outward things in a failure to understand that there is no lasting happiness and satisfaction to be found in them, that the true source of happiness and satisfaction is in fact within themselves. If you were to ask a group of people what their favorite color or food was, perhaps a couple of people might share the same favorite but not everyone; you would hear different answers. If the happiness were in things themselves, everyone would have the same favorite things, but it is not in things themselves. People do not have the same favorites. While things in life may become vehicles for the expression of happiness, true happiness comes from within you as a choice, a view, and as a power you have. The power of your view, how you interpret things, and how you relate with things in your life, whether positive or negative, is your choice. That power is within your own heart and mind.

In this regard, the Kabbalah has a wisdom teaching about dream interpretation. Given that all the realities of our experience are dreamlike, there is wisdom in how we interpret the situations, circumstances, and events in our life. The Kabbalah says that there is great manifesting or even prophetic power in dreams, subject to how we interpret them. It teaches us to interpret all dreams, even those which seem ill-omened, in a completely positive way in faith, not doubt.

As an example, if a person had a fitful, dark dream of being unable to run while chased by some monster, a wise interpretation could say that they are receiving an empowerment to overcome a powerful fear that is holding them back in life; now is the time to turn and face their fear, to see its emptiness, nothingness. It also teaches us to be careful with whom we share our dreams and their interpretations—never with naysayers or those who will not affirm them—only with those who love and care about us, who will affirm and support a positive interpretation. Choosing to interpret dreams only in a positive way could be said to be a happy-making way, a choice to be happy, positive. As in dream, so in life and waking consciousness: Our view and interpretations of things is a great manifesting power that may even be said to be prophetic when taken up from deep inwardness.

There is something more, however—our deepest heart's desire, our soul's desire—is enlightenment or God, though many people are as yet unaware of this inmost desire. As we know in our own experience, when there is a stirring and sparking of faith and we begin to become conscious of this deep desire in separation and lack, we generally go seeking enlightenment, God outside of ourselves, not thinking or knowing to seek the enlightened nature or God within ourselves. The enlightened nature, God, is the source of all and the source of lasting happiness and satisfaction. Unless we seek and find our Lord within us—the Inner Light and Spirit— we will not find our Lord outside. Unless we find the source of lasting happiness and satisfaction—true fulfillment—within us, whatever passing happiness and satisfaction we have will lead to feelings of loss, lack, sorrow, and suffering. We need to go within, deep within, to discover our divine or enlightened nature, to find and know our Lord within us and so be united and filled, truly happy and satisfied.

Here and now, you have a precious opportunity. Having come to some degree of faith or intuitive sense of the truth of enlightenment, the reality of God, it is possible for you to experience enlightenment, nearness, and oneness with God, true knowledge of God. If something of this has not been glimpsed or tasted, know it is very near and can happen any day, at any moment. If you turn to the Lord, go inward, open to the Holy Light and Spirit, invoke and pray, and just be in the Holy One with faith that the Holy One is indeed within and all around you, while holding that faithful and hopeful view, enlightenment can happen today! But as we know, life is short. There is no telling what day will be our last. There is no time to waste. Go to God, go straight to God today: Be inward, deep inward, and seek until you find, until the Lord within you—the Inner Light and Spirit— is revealed to you and you are established in an inward communion. What are you waiting for? Why wait? Seek to be in the light and the love today, aware of the Divine Presence within you and surrounding you on all sides. Believe and know, whether you are aware or not, that the Lord is with you, God is with you. Live, move, and have your being in the Holy One. You've never been nor ever will be separate and apart from the Eternal One.

This saying points to a very powerful view and practice often taken up by mystics and gnostics: living each day as though it is your last or you have a terminal illness. In denial of the impermanence and brevity of life, we waste a lot of time on unimportant, even vain and futile things and often do not tend to what is truly important. However, if we knew we were living our last day, or that we had a terminal illness and our time was short, we would likely pay more attention to how we spent what time we had left. Unimport- ant things would neither attract nor distract us so much, and we would be inclined to tend to those things that were important, that were real and have true value to our soul that might bring some real happiness and satisfaction.

As with true mystics and gnostics, perhaps we might not wish to waste a moment of our time on the nonessentials in the world. Instead, we may tend only to things that are essential, necessary for life, freeing us to give as much time as possible seeking to love and know God most intimately, so that passing beyond we might go straight to God—the Pleroma of Light. Amen.

Verse 64

Yeshua said, "A person was receiving guests. When they prepared the dinner, they sent their servant to invite the guests. The servant went to the first and said, 'My master invites you.' That person said, 'Some merchants owe me money. They are coming tonight. I must go and give them instructions. Please excuse me from dinner.' The servant went to another and said, 'My master invites you.' He said to the servant, 'I have bought a house and I've been called away for a day. I have no time.' The servant went to another and said, 'My master invites you.' He said to the servant, 'My friend is getting married and I am to arrange a banquet. I can't come. Please excuse me from dinner.' The servant went to another and said, 'My master invites you.' He said to the servant, 'I have bought an estate and am going to collect rent. I shall not be able to come. Please excuse me.' The servant returned and said to his master, 'Those you invited to dinner have asked to be excused.' The master said to the servant, 'Go out into the streets and invite whomever you find for the dinner. Buyers and merchants will not enter the places of my father.'"

From canonical gospels we may recall that Yeshua speaks of the wealthy who are unable to enter the kingdom of heaven, but here it is buyers and merchants or businesspeople. This is in fact a more insightful wording due to the nature of business in the world and how businesspeople are esteemed. The motive in business is making a profit; the greater the profit margin, the more successful and esteemed the businessperson is in the world. What profit means is taking more than is given; to have high profit margins, you seek to give less and take more. It is the play of the evil inclination, the desire to receive for oneself alone or to receive more than others. Profit is the complete opposite of the kingdom of heaven, within which love, freely giving, and complete self-offering are held in high esteem, exalted and glorified.

This saying isn't speaking only of literal businesspeople—it applies to all who receive and do not give so much, those who remain dominated by selfishness in a desire to receive for self alone in separation and lack. As long as people are in such worldly and unenlightened mentalities, they will not be able to conceive or perceive anything of heaven, let alone enter it. They will have no resonance with the Pleroma of Light.

The Eternal One is the source of all. God gives of Godself freely, without reservation, and so is the All-Giver, the very first emanation of the Infinite Light, the inmost divine attribute. Keter-Crown, is the principle of the All-Giver—supernal grace, supernal love—because all the other attributes and the entire play of creation and revelation that follows, come from and will return to it. Yeshua was the Messiah because he enacted a total and complete self-offering for the sake of the salvation of all living spirits and souls, making him the perfect and complete image and likeness of the Eternal One, such that those who had seen the Son had seen the Father. This is the very nature of the true kingdom of heaven, the Pleroma of Light, and it is through love and complete self-offering that souls enter it in this world and in the hereafter. Yeshua's most essential teaching to his disciples is: "Love one another as I have loved you" (John 13:34). "No one has greater love than this, laying down their life for their friends" (John 15:13).

As we know on a spiritual level, similitude, likeness, resemblance all correspond with proximity. The greater the resemblance, the closer the proximity, the nearer souls draw to Christ and God. When there is a complete resemblance, there is union with Christ in God, the True Light. Through love and self-offering comes complete resemblance to the Christ, the Messiah and union with God, the Eternal One.

The open secret is this: When you give yourself to God, God gives Godself to you and gives you divine attributes, powers, and actions. When you give all of yourself and all of your life to God, God gives all of Godself to you. You will have the full and complete image of God in you, God's countenance, and the ability to see with the eyes of God, hear with the ears of God, know with the mind of God, love with the heart of God, and be as a body of God, embodying the fullness of the presence and power of God, the Holy Light and Spirit.

Of course, when you realize there is God and God alone and no other, you will realize that you have given nothing but God has given all. It has all been from God, to God, and for God all the while, the seeker having been the One who was sought. Amen.

Verse 65

"A [person] owned a vineyard and rented it to some farm workers to work it, and from them he would collect its produce. He sent his servant to the farmers to give him the produce of the vineyard. They seized, beat, and almost killed the servant, who returned and told his master. He said, 'Perhaps he did not know them.' And he sent another servant, but they beat him as well. Then the master sent his son and said, 'Perhaps they will respect my son.' Since they knew the son was the heir of the vineyard they seized and killed him. Whoever has ears should hear."

This parable, of course, is speaking about the Eternal One sending first prophets and then the Messiah to the people, and is prophetic of what happened to Adonai Yeshua at the hands of rulers and religious authorities. Generally speaking, religious authorities are hostile toward mystics and gnostics, let alone living apostles and prophets; in fundamentalism, such rulers can be outright violent toward anyone who does not believe in the doctrine of their particular sect. Over the ages, countless truly faithful people have been persecuted, oppressed, tortured, and killed in the name of religion and God. Many so-called holy wars have been fought between peoples of different faiths. So this parable speaks not only of the past but also what is ongoing to this very day: a great ignorance and evil that brings much sorrow and suffering, rather than spiritual realization, healing, and peace.

From a mystical and gnostic perspective, living messengers continue to appear, and Christ, Messiah continues to come through those who open to the Holy Light and Spirit, thus embodying the Christ Presence, Christ Spirit.

It is this parable's latter truth that needs to be our focus: living messengers continue to appear, Christ, Messiah continues to be revealed and realized among us, and the revelation of the Divine is ongoing. Through the grace and mercy of the Eternal One, we can be among the living ones; experience the Inner Light and Spirit in us to see, hear, and feel with the Spirit; and have true knowledge of God beyond doctrines, God beyond God.

If we are inward, abide in an inward communion, and are in the love and the light, what creed or doctrine do we need? The essence of all true religion and truth of all authentic spirituality in its origin is the love. Being in the love, we are in the light of all knowledge, all power. In the love and the light, we are united and filled, lacking nothing. In the love, there is a worship in spirit and truth, in oneness, unity, not twoness or separation as in outer and unspiritual religion. And we do not seek our Lord, our God, outside, but inside. It is in being light, love, and the divine qualities and attributes that we find, realize, and embody that Truth and Light, being and doing in the Holy One, Holy Shekinah what is good and true.

Another teaching in this parable is on the spiritual and messianic works we are given to do. They are ours to do, but the fruit of those works, the praise and glory, belongs to God. Indeed, ours is the work, the fruit is God's. When our works bear good fruit, it is the Spirit of God and powers of heaven that labor with us; the Spirit that has moved with, in, and through us, and taken up, completed and perfected, those works in God, the True Light. If in the light, in the love, we are being and doing, the Living Presence, Living Spirit is the doer who is and does through us. God has brought forth the good fruits! Amen.

Verse 66

Yeshua said, "Show me the stone the builders rejected. That is the cornerstone."

In ancient architecture, the setting of a properly cut cornerstone was essential for a building's alignment and stability. Everything else was measured and set into place based upon it, so selecting the cornerstone and setting it in its place was critical. This saying, which is based upon teachings and revelations from the ancient prophets of Israel, is a metaphor of Yeshua Messiah and his rejection by the elite, wealthy, and educated religious authorities.

The Eternal One raised Yeshua up from poverty, from the lowest level of society. The word for his earthly father's trade in Greek so often translated as "carpenter" actually denotes something more like a laborer or handyman of the time, an unskilled and low-paid worker. Not only that, Yeshua came from Nazareth, in the hill country of Judea from which nothing good can come, to quote the rabbis of the time. From the perspective of the Jews of Jerusalem and religious authorities of the temple cult, people from that region were regarded by the elite as uncouth and uneducated. Someone from Nazareth spoke the language of the Jews poorly and could not practice the religion correctly, let alone be a proper messenger of God or true teacher of the law and religion. Naturally, this was their view of Yeshua and of most of his close disciples, which caused the elite to take all that much more offense and to engage his spiritual movement with outrage and hostility. Remember, the image of the Messiah held in their minds was one of royalty, anointed and uplifted from a well-to-do family with the right pedigree, like the legendary King David. Yeshua definitely did not match that picture in their heads, so they naturally wrote off and rejected him, despite the very uncanny and disturbing charisma he had with people, his more radical manifestation of the knowledge of God, and the presence and power of God that was with him.

That the great apostle and prophet, the one who was the Messiah—the Savior—would appear as the person of Yeshua has deep meaning, and is a message for us all. Apart from God, those who raise themselves up are in the unreal and will not endure. But anyone and everyone can receive the anointing from God, the Holy Light and Spirit, to be uplifted, divinized, and indwelled by Christ, Messiah. The Divine Presence, Shekinah of Messiah can appear through anyone the Supreme ordains—rich or poor, educated or uneducated all the same. It isn't just the apparently righteous that God anoints as messengers but also the apparently wicked who turn to God and are redeemed. Anybody who turns to the Lord in faith and love is inward, opening themselves and their lives to the Holy Light and Spirit, living in submission to the Lord, the Spirit, that indwells them.

Being who he was in himself, Yeshua is a vision of great hope for us all!

We must believe and have faith, not reject the cornerstone. We must be inward and seek until we find. Upon receiving the Holy Light and Spirit, Christ, Messiah revealed in us, we must labor to integrate every aspect of our soul, our being and consciousness, our person and life with the Holy Light and Spirit, and live the Divine Life—the Christ Life.

Regardless of their spiritual and symbolic language or what faith or religion they practice, if souls have sincere faith and see the Truth and the Truth alone, seek to be in the light and in the love and live according to the Truth and Light revealed to them, and are willing to change as that revelation and realization progresses with them, this grace of the Eternal One is present for all people. This grace is present for you, me, everybody who desires this. This grace is for everyone who has faith and seeks until they find, or, more truly, until they are found! Amen.

Verse 67

Yeshua said, "One who knows all but lacks within is utterly lacking."

There is a problem with many religious authorities, scholars, and theologians, including many who are experts on mystical and gnostic spirituality. Even if they are correct in their speculations, apart from true mystical experience—the revelation and realization of the Inner Light and Spirit—there is neither salvation nor actual spiritual or supernal realization. All speculative knowledge on the surface is conceptual. What experts have is empty husks or shells—*klippot*—of *da'at,* knowledge. They have nothing.

The same is true of those who study deep mystical and esoteric teachings but as yet have neither true mystical experience of the secret mysteries nor the revelation of the secrets from God, let alone the realization of those secrets. It is not true knowledge of the mysteries and God, but only information, worldly trivia that is of no use to the soul when they pass beyond.

In receiving inner and secret teachings of the gnostic path and Holy Kabbalah, we venture into very holy things. If we seek the revelation and realization of the secrets from and in God—the Eternal One—we need to be in the light and the love in actual inward communion. If we are neither deep within, being changed by the light and love, nor walking in the beauty and holiness of Christ, Messiah living the Divine Life, what good is knowledge of Christian Gnosticism, Christian Kabbalah? Without inwardness, there is nothing good in it; the holy is profaned and bears no good fruit.

Inwardness is all about being in the light, in the love, and in direct communion with the Holy One, Holy Shekinah.

The truth is that if you have the love, you have the light. The Holy Light and Spirit will unite and fill you. You will have everything—all the knowledge, all the power. You will lack nothing at all. If you know all but are lacking the love and the light, you have nothing of God and are completely lacking. You remain in separation.

If we seek teachings and initiation into the gnostic path, receiving inner and secret teachings of the Holy Kabbalah, then first and foremost we must seek to be in the light and the love and be ingathered in inward communion. Amen.

Verse 68

Yeshua said, "Blessings on you who are hated and persecuted, and no place will be found, wherever you have been persecuted."

This teaching is emphasized in a later period within the Beatitudes as recounted in Matthew where those persecuted for righteousness's sake are blessed twice. As we know, many of the original followers of the Way faced great persecution, imprisonment, beatings, and murder. Later, with the emergence of Christian orthodoxy and its false churches, the mystics and gnostics who held to the true spirituality of direct experience that was the foundation of the original Christian faith faced great persecution and were nearly driven into extinction. Fortunately, in secret, some threads of true Christianity—the light transmission and the passing of the Holy Spirit—survived. As it is with the Eternal One and the Messiah, the Anointing, the Holy Light and Spirit, the kingdom of heaven cannot be removed or extinguished from the world: The Holy One continues to raise up and anoint messengers, gnostic apostles, and prophets. As any lineage of light transmission passes away, others emerge through the grace of the Supreme.

As messengers and their anointed communities arise, they will quite naturally encounter strong currents of psychic resistance in this world, hostile psychic atmospheres, environments, and the assaults of impure and dark forces, archons, and demons. Because many people are influenced by those psychic currents and forces, true faithful and spiritual people may face actual outward persecution in this world. So it has always been with messengers of the Pleroma of light, mystics and gnostics of the various faiths and wisdom traditions. Indeed, in the darkness and ignorance that rule this world and its unenlightened societies, there is a very powerful downward and backward pull against the great ascension, something like powerful psychic gravity. To truly strive for enlightenment, an actual spiritual or supernal realization, is like swimming upstream against powerful currents.

To watch natural phenomena in nature such as a salmon run well reflects how things work in this world and the matrix of creation. Anyone who comes to faith, in whom the mystical inclination dawns, and who receives the Holy Light and Spirit will encounter a very strong resistance from outside and inside, a degree of persecution more or less, because of the bestial nature and the darkness of matter. Unless there is strength of faith—deep faith-wisdom—and a passion for enlightenment or God as a full, active striving with the Spirit for an actual spiritual and supernal realization, little, if any, true progress in the realization of the soul will happen. You have to really want and desire this more than anything, putting the full force of your will into this Great Work. If you do, there is grace, the help of the Holy Spirit, and the divine interventions of the powers of heaven. You will be blessed. The Spirit will fill your heart with the light and love of Christ, Messiah and enlighten your mind. You will be healed, resurrected, and ascended.

The verse continues: "…and no place will be found, wherever you are persecuted." Those who engage in such persecutions, being conduits of the impure and dark forces, the archonic and demonic, are bound up in those forces. When they pass beyond, they will have no place in the heavens, let alone the Pleroma of Light. There must be a conscious striving to receive the supernal grace of the Eternal One, an active and conscious evolution to be and become who and what we are in the Eternal One, the Christ, the Messiah. In the Secret Book of James, Yeshua says to James and Peter, "Acquire grace for yourselves."

One thing to understand regarding persecution is that it isn't persecutors outside you that you need to concern yourself with. You cannot control what others do and choose to be. It is the persecutors inside you with which you need to concern yourself. Strive with the resistances and rebellions against the Inner Light, Spirit, and love, against all the little selves of the fragmented consciousness, all the naysaying, negative mentalities or ways of thinking. These are your inner demons, accusing angels, self-doubts, self-judgments, insecurities, fears, and passive or outright anger. It is these inner persecutors that serve as inroads to temptations, the assaults of impure and dark forces, unclean and evil spirits. Likewise, these are what will cause you to care what other people think about you, so that you conform to wrong thought, speech, and action. Listening to your inner persecutors is how you will give your light-power to outward persecutors and attract more persecution to yourself, making you more vulnerable to assaults. If you strive against the inner persecutors, the Spirit will strive alongside you; spiritual assistance will come from spirits of tzaddikim and angels, saints, and angels. And you will be victorious over the enemy—the inner demiurge and satan, the ego and its shadow.

Love conquers all. Staying in the love and the light, you will become immune to the poisonous influences of the Other Side, no longer vulnerable to the assaults of the impure and dark psychic and spiritual forces. Amen.

Verse 69

Yeshua said, "Blessed are you who have been persecuted in your hearts. Only you truly know the Father. Blessed are you who are hungry, that the stomach of someone else may be filled."

In his letter, the Apostle James taught that when we face trials or tribulations of any kind, we are to consider it nothing but joy because through such sufferings in faith and love, our faith is perfected and we become mature and complete, lacking nothing (1:2–4). Love fully blooms in our heart. His teaching is certainly parallel with this saying, though here Yeshua is speaking of the love that shares in the suffering of others, no longer focused upon our own. More so, he is speaking of the willingness to take the sufferings of others upon us, such as being willing to go hungry so that another might be fed and being willing, as discussed in an earlier saying, to the active compassion that arises from the inward devotion of giving and receiving. This is the most essential meaning of taking up your cross.

Being persecuted in your heart is the empathy within love and compassion that makes your heart troubled and pained by the suffering of others. It is true empathy, not in an impure sense in self-cherishing and talking about how much one cares and how hurt and affected one is by all the suffering in the world—it is having actual love and compassion, breaking out of yourself, your ego, and engaging in active compassion and charity. It is loving others around you and taking care of them, surpassing friends and family and extending to neighbors, strangers in need, and even people who act toward you as enemies.

Being in the love is neither a vital sentiment nor a feel-good thing. Love needs to be our way in life, thought, speech, and action through acts of lovingkindness and charity. Love is more than just giving someone money—it is giving our time, attention, and energy, being present with and loving and tending to others, delighting in the image of God in them and loving God through them, as them: loving others as yourself.

The first lesson to learn in the Holy Kabbalah about the Absolute Oneness of the Eternal—Yahweh—is how deeply and intimately creation is interconnected, everyone and everything, inwardly and outwardly, physically and metaphysically. To not have the love or active compassion means the first lesson of the Eternal has not been learned. There is no realization of love.

Without love, the Absolute Oneness is conceptual, not actual. We must be and do. As such, we either are or we are not. We need to choose right thought, right speech, and right action—loving, compassionate, thought, speech, and action. With regard to speaking the word of God with power, actions speak louder than words. In the Holy Kabbalah, the material reality we are in is called the World-Universe of Action, or Asiyah: Making. The very nature of the embodiment of the Truth and Light is being and doing, works and actions. This is why the Apostle James taught that a sister or brother is neither justified by a profession of faith or doctrine nor saved through such—only through works, actions. In their words and deeds, they are loving and compassionate, expressing and embodying the Truth and Light, actually living the Divine Life, or Christ Life.

You either are, or you are not.

These simple, straightforward words occur in the teachings of Yeshua recorded in the Secret Book of James and other scriptures of that gnostic tradition. It is not a harsh or judgmental statement, but is the simple truth and guidance for spiritual discernment. From moment to moment, from day to day, you either are or you are not in the love, and in the light; if you're not, you are in the fire. This can be felt and known. We are either coming from faith and awareness of unity and fullness in the love and the light, or we are coming from separation and lack, not in the love or the light. In every moment, we need to choose to be the light and the love in thought, word, and deed. Every day we must seek to be very kind and have active compassion: acts of lovingkindness and charity.

"Enlightenment" is not a noun—it is a verb. It is not a fixed or static state but an ongoing action, movement, a way of being and living in the Holy One, Holy Shekinah. For example, from the perspective of the gnostic path, we do not engage in devotions or spiritual practices to become enlightened or realized; rather, we engage as an expression of enlightenment, realization, so that invoking and praying itself is enlightenment happening with, in, and through us, Christ, Messiah appearing and being revealed with, in, and through us. By way of good works both spiritual and material, enlightenment is all about being and doing, embodying the light, the love, and all the various qualities of Christ and God, the Messiah and the Holy One.

The truth is that whether you are aware of it or not, you already are enlightened, realized! You only need to be and do to actualize and manifest who and what you already are in the Holy One, Holy Shekinah. Amen.

Verse 70

Yeshua said, "If you bring forth what is within you, what you have will save you. If you have nothing within you, what is [lacking] within you will kill you."

The very essence and nature of your soul, your being and consciousness, is enlightened; it is supernal and divine. Bringing forth the qualities of that intrinsic nature that is inseparable from the Supreme is enlightenment, realization.

The substance of your soul, as it were, is the Holy Light and Spirit. Receiving the Holy Light and Spirit and awakening the Inner Light and Spirit in you allows the supernal radiance to shine from within you. The Spirit will move with, in, and through you; Christ, Messiah will be revealed through you and will appear as you.

Your soul is woven of the Holy Sefirot—divine attributes, powers, actions—and the powers of heaven. These are supernal and spiritual potentials, but they need to be actualized, made manifest, brought forth.

Though you already are, you must be and do. This is true salvation—enlightenment and liberation. It is through embodiment that you ascend!

You have been reading affirmations, but you must affirm and confirm yourself in unity and fullness: You must be and do and bring forth who and what you are in Christ and God—the Messiah and Holy One.

In a manner of speaking, you must give birth to yourself; your spiritual teacher and guide is your midwife. So go within and ask God the Mother how to give birth to yourself as you are in her. Your holy tzaddik and the family of God will be with you in your labor, but it will be your labor giving birth to yourself. You will give birth with the Mother Spirit. You will be and you will do. And as this saying states, if you do not, then you will not be!

Birthing is a wonderful metaphor for our spiritual process of coming into being and realization. As every good mother can tell you, you are not in control in the process of giving birth; you must surrender to the process and be in what is happening as it is happening, doing what you can and need to do. Greater than yourself in control is the power of the Lord, the Spirit within you. You can neither speed up the process of birthing nor slow it down. Birth happens when it happens, as it happens, all as the Spirit moves, as the Lord wills, as is ordained in the Supreme. Yet you are in a co-labor with the Spirit, bringing forth Christ, Messiah from within you, the radiance of the Sun of God. When it is time, you must push and push and push, in spite of whatever resistance there might be to give birth and bring forth that great good from within your heart-womb. Amen.

Verse 71

Yeshua said, "I shall destroy this house and no one will be able to rebuild it."

This verse appears to be a very early and primitive form of later sayings in canonical gospels where Yeshua comments upon the eventual destruction of the temple in Jerusalem. In those versions, however, he speaks of rebuilding it in three days. While prophetic of the eventual fate of the temple and temple cult, he was of course speaking of his body in the canonical gospels and his pending death and resurrection. If we assume the same to be true in this version, we may ponder what he might have meant by saying no one will be able to rebuild it.

First is the obvious truth that no mortal can raise the dead, save through the power of God. In the writings of the prophets is the prophecy of a temple to come not made by human hands but by the word of the Eternal One—Yahweh. Among spiritual Christians, this is understood to be the risen and ascended Messiah, or Hayyah Yeshua.

There is something more than the temple; as we know, in Christ, Messiah there is a new humanity and a new heaven and earth. As these come into being, the old, bestial humankind and the first heaven and earth pass away into destruction, not to be reestablished. The house the Messiah destroys that no one can rebuild may be understood as this world, the seven heavens associated with it, and the humankind of this world.

There is some wisdom in this interpretation for the times we are living in, wisdom that may be hard to hear for some but needs to be spoken, a word of the Lord, a speaking of the Spirit, if you will. What if we are living in the cycles of the end times and the end of days is near, and there is no avoiding it or stopping it?

As we know, there are clear signs that great modern civilization and its unenlightened societies are in decline. Civil unrest is brewing, more and more people are being taken over by the increasing darkness, an insanity of evil. Along with this are clear signs that we are moving toward another great global conflict now with the threat of nuclear weapons that can swiftly and harshly bring most if not all of human existence to an end. We cannot deny the ongoing, catastrophic, human-caused climate change crises progressing far faster than projected; the more it is studied, even if by some impossible miracle where we all radically changed our way of life overnight, climate crises appear to have passed the point of no return for any human effort to reverse. Then of course are all the possible natural and cosmic causes for an end of days. Great extinctions have happened naturally before in this world. What if the duration of the existence of life on earth, specifically the present humankind, is nearing its end one way or the other?

If you study the great prophets and read the Book of Revelation, the Apocalypse is what the prophets have long seen, heard, and felt in the Holy One, Holy Shekinah. This saying in Thomas could be interpreted to speak something of the same vision of the end times and end of days. But what if the divine intention and purpose of this and other worlds of our galaxy and universe within which intelligent, self-aware life evolves isn't about any sort of material perfection or physical immortality? Rather, what if the divine intention is about the spiritual and supernal realization of souls, the great resurrection and ascension, the Great Exodus, Great Liberation? This is the Gnostic Christian understanding of the divine intention of this realm of separation—*perud*—of this and all worlds within the matrix of creation. In a manner of speaking, worlds are like wombs giving birth to spirits and souls to eternity. Just like with the salmon and other creatures in nature who come full cycle or do not, there will always be souls who ascend and some who do not; that is just the way it is, all in its interdependence and interconnection. Life requires all of this to fulfill the intention of the Supreme, the greater realization of the divine fiery intelligence or supramental, supernal consciousness: Christ or God Consciousness. The world as it is, is sacred as it is. Yes, life in it—reality as it is—is a dance of great beauty and great danger or horror—all in the Holy One, Holy Shekinah.

All things material, astral, and spiritual are impermanent. So is this planet and life on it.

This begs the question: If, indeed, we are living in the cycles of the end times and the end of days is coming and is near in one way or another, what should our focus, our drive, our passion in life be? How shall we spend our time? There really is no time to waste, and ultimately there is no saving this world and staying in it; it is physically impossible. We all will pass beyond the body one day. From a gnostic perspective, we are to strive to be resurrected and ascended before we die so that when we pass beyond, we are able to ascend and so be established in the Pleroma of Light, reintegrated with the Infinite Light, in eternal life and bornless being in the Eternal One.

This is why there are many messengers being sent at this time, many voices sharing an essential spirituality of direct experience, direct revelation and realization, teaching a way accessible to all who seek enlightenment, true knowledge of God. Such is the grace and mercy of God in the end times: Along with the increasing darkness are greater and greater influxes of the Supernal Light and Spirit, an outpouring upon all flesh. It is present for all who are inward and open to it. Hallelu Yah! Praise the Lord! Amen.

Verse 72

Someone said to him, "Tell my brothers to divide my father's possessions with me." Yeshua said to that person, "Mister, who made me a divider?" He turned to his disciples and said to them, "I am not a divider, am I?"

In this saying, Messiah Yeshua is distinguished from common teachers and religious authorities of the day who, being under the law and teaching the law as well as being spiritual teachers, were also lawyers and judges. The Messiah is not a lawgiver like Moses or Mohammed but instead brings the grace of the Supreme—God beyond God—the anointing of the Holy Light and Spirit; by Yeshua's own testimony, his kingdom and way is not of this world. His kingdom is the Pleroma of Light and his way is the great resurrection and ascension—the True Exodus. What does he have to do with the apportioning of worldly possession or deciding matters regarding man-made laws of religion and unenlightened society?

We may recall the wealthy young fellow in canonical gospels who sought spiritual guidance from Yeshua. At the conclusion of their exchange, Yeshua told the man to go sell all of his possessions, give the money to those in need, and follow him as a disciple. The fellow left weeping. Some masters of the tradition have said that was Yeshua's first meeting with Lazarus and that his instruction was to prepare for his death. If indeed that was Lazarus, apparently he did as Yeshua directed him, given he was later raised from among the dead in a most miraculous way.

What Yeshua had to say to that young man, whoever he was, reflects his view of wealth and possessions, the need in the spiritual life to give and be charitable.

Being the manifestation of the grace of the Most High, Messiah Yeshua came to unite, fill, and uplift in the resurrection and ascension, not to perpetuate separation, lack, and bondage under the law in the play of cause and effect, of sin and karma.

Perhaps on the surface it might seem very strange that a man would approach an apostle or prophet of God let alone the Messiah and ask them to settle a family squabble over the worldly possessions of an estate. The truth is, however, when first encountering a living messenger or holy tzaddik, we neither know how to relate with them nor what it means to be a disciple or spiritual companion. Generally speaking, we are unclear about what we are seeking. Naturally so, for we have neither experienced light transmission and the imparting of the Holy Spirit, nor the full revelation of the Inner Light and Spirit—Christ, Messiah in us—and so do not yet have a direct inward communion.

Our relationship with enlightenment or God is unclear and impaired. Because we neither know ourselves nor are inward but in separation and lack, we are not really ourselves. Tzaddikim speak from inwardness to inwardness but we meet them in outwardness, just as we tend to relate with people in outwardness. When we meet in outwardness based on what we think we know, who we think we are, what we desire-fear, and what we think reality or the world is, we tend to project things onto people: our preconceptions, preconditions, and expectations, along with what we think enlightenment or God is, what we think holy people are or should be.

When meeting a spiritual teacher and guide, a living tzaddik, we further tend to project on them our ideas of religious authorities and authority figures in general—the roles of parents, therapists, or even romantic partners, and so on. Joined with our desires and fears, these projections will shape how we interact with them and what we expect from them. They are, however, none of these things, they are like no one else in our lives.

The sacred friendship with a messenger, or tzaddik, is like no other. In all of our other relationships, people want something from us, just as we want things from them; based upon whatever they want from us, we can manipulate them. A messenger, a tzaddik, however, desires God and God alone and does not want anything from us for themselves. Instead, what they want is for us and for God. They want our salvation, our enlightenment. They want us to know ourselves and God, to have direct, intimate communion with God and in God, nothing else. Because of this, they cannot be manipulated.

In this regard, it may be said that they are a dangerous friend who is unsettling, unpredictable, uncontrollable. This is very much the case, for they speak from a deep inward communion, a most intimate nearness and oneness; they speak and act with the Holy Shekinah, Holy Spirit, the Living Presence, Living Spirit manifest with, in, and through them. They see everyone and everything in their inwardness and speak and interact with the inwardness of those around them. When we draw near and become more aware of who and what they are, we may get the sense that they see right through us, because in fact, they do! They patiently wait for us to go through our various projections and at times reflect them to us until we can be inward with them in faith and love with inward cleaving, together in the Holy One, Holy Shekinah as a true spiritual companion, a lover of enlightenment or God. Through them, and through our sisters and brothers in anointed community—the family of God—we essentially learn how to relate and commune with God, how to draw near to and unite with God. That is what sacred friendship, discipleship, is all about. In effect they desire to meet the Holy One in us, as we meet the Holy One in them so that the Holy Shekinah may be revealed through us and them, all in the Holy One.

If you go into congregations of outer and unspiritual churches and listen to their prayers and prayer requests, most often you will hear invocations and requests for things of this world: the healing of bodies, finding a job, selling a house, success in some other business venture, and so on. That is all well and good. God provides and it is fine that we invoke and ask for material support, bounty, or blessings. More important than that, however, are spiritual bounty and blessings, first and foremost greater and greater love of God, being filled with love and compassion, and having true knowledge, understanding, and wisdom of God in deeper and more intimate communion, a greater realization. Likewise, it is more important to pray to reach higher, inner stations and states of the soul, to manifest the full array of divine attributes, greater powers, and gifts of the Spirit, to be of greater benefit to others. With this, we pray for knowledge of the powers of heaven and greater communion with the spirits of tzaddikim and angels—saints and angels—to be counted among them. In this light, what do you suppose we are seeking from a living messenger or tzaddik? It is not only material but spiritual bounty, blessings, and empowerments from God.

Pray and pray and pray that the Holy One fills your heart with love, and more love, and more love, an ever more perfect and complete love that fills you with the spiritual and supernal light. With the light and love, so all the qualities, attributes, of the Messiah and Holy One. Pray to be of true benefit to people and true service to the kingdom of heaven and God. Pray to be strengthened in self-offering and be able to completely pass away with the Messiah in the Holy One, Holy Shekinah. Amen.

Verse 73

Yeshua said, "The harvest is large but the workers are few. Beg the Master to send out workers to the harvest."

This is true in every generation, but it is most especially true in these times. There is a plentiful harvest of souls to be ingathered, but while there are living messengers, tzaddikim, they are relatively few compared to all who might be ingathered. There is a need to invoke and pray that the Holy One anoints, empowers, and sends out many more messengers, for time is of the essence. Time is short in these generations. This very invocation and prayer is at the heart of the holy feast in our gnostic tradition celebrating the Apostle of the Apostles, Mirya the Magdala: prayers for the incarnation of souls of higher grades, realized souls, who may live as messengers— apostles, prophets, tzaddikim—that many more people might receive the Holy Light and Spirit and be ingathered into Christ, Messiah, the Pleroma of Light.

There is something more. In anointed community, we all take up the spiritual labor of our holy tzaddik. While we may not all be called out- wardly to be apostles or prophets, we are all called to strive to become tzaddikim, to be the light, be the love, and to labor in the harvest of souls, ingathering people into the family of God. This is not just the labor of the anointed messengers; it is the spiritual labor of us all, each according to our anointing and the skills, powers, and resources given to us. We are to be among the harvesters because our salvation, realization, is not personal. It is not just about us. Our efforts are for the sake of the salvation, realiza- tion, of others along with us in the Holy One, Holy Shekinah.

Yeshua is calling us to pray, that we might be sent as workers to the har- vest and be ready and willing to go to those for whom we are sent. Remem- ber, as Yeshua was speaking to his followers and disciples, many of whom would themselves come into being as apostles and prophets, speakers of the word of God with power, so it is now with us who have received the Holy Light and Spirit, who are anointed and ingathered. With the greater outpouring of Supernal Light and the Holy Spirit on all flesh today, there is indeed a very large harvest and a need for many workers in the harvest of souls. The need is very great! As with prayers for realized souls of higher grades to be incarnate, there is the invocation of our own divine nature, heavenly and supernal soul—holy *neshamah*. Likewise, there are invocations and prayers for an ever-greater manifestation of the light and love of the Messiah in us and all the divine attributes, powers, actions, the fullness of the Divine Presence, Holy Shekinah, along with greater powers of the Spirit for prophetic guidance, healing, and the working of wonders, miracles. We do not ask for these precious gifts for ourselves alone but that they are of the greatest possible benefit and service to people: to ingather, help them know and realize the Inner Light and Spirit in them, and to know God beyond doctrine, God beyond God, the Supreme, the Absolute Light.

These are our prayers: "May the Holy Shekinah, Holy Spirit, take up her full divine action with, in, and through you; with the Shekinah and in the Spirit, may you accomplish the messianic works and mission given to you; that the works and mission of your holy soul in this life be revealed to you; that you be guided by the Inner Light and Spirit in it; and that the Holy One, Holy Shekinah provides all that you need to accomplish your work, your mission."

Not only are prayers for others sent, you also pray that you are prepared by the Holy One, Holy Shekinah, and sent to those given to you in the Spirit. Amen.

Verse 74

"Master, there are many around the drinking trough but nothing in the well."

This saying may also be translated to read "but there is nothing in the well," however no one makes the saying clear; likely, this was the original intention. As the saying is, it appears to be a line from a prayer of Yeshua. With apostles and prophets, it is not uncommon for them to give teachings and revelations through prayers, actively invoking spiritual influxes for those present with them. In this portion of what was no doubt a larger prayer, the intention would be to remove barriers to going deeper within, allowing the ingathering and uplifting of those who were with him so that they might truly hear with understanding

Many may encounter a living messenger—apostle, prophet, tzaddik— and may listen to teachings from them, or even experience moments of light transmission and movements of the Holy Spirit, but as they are outward not inward, they neither hear the inner and secret meaning nor actually receive and integrate the light transmitted or the power of the Spirit imparted. They remain on the surface of teachings in the outer conceptual meanings and stay in the surface of spiritual and mystical experiences that may arise for them. When messengers share teachings and speak words of God, the Spirit, there is light power and energy within and behind their words, and it is the light power and energy of the Spirit that convey the truth, the inner and secret knowledge. The mind, heart, and soul of those who listen and hear in faith and love with inward cleaving are uplifted, elevated to higher inner stations and states, and there is a sense, an experiential or intuitive knowing of the truth being spoken, the secret mysteries being revealed.

This light power, this energetic transmission, is more important than the words themselves. The most eloquently worded teaching without power or the Holy Light and Spirit will not bring true knowledge and understanding of secret mysteries, let alone the wisdom and illumination. Conversely, an apparently clumsily worded teaching spoken with power may communicate volumes and bring wisdom, a full illumination of the mystery. However, unless a person is inward in openness and sensitivity to the Holy Light and Spirit on an energetic or visionary level, they will not receive the light power, energetic transmission and will stay on the surface in conceptual knowledge, lacking actual, experiential and true knowledge of the mystery. More important than the words of living messengers and those through whom the Spirit speaks is the light power they transmit: the power, energy, carrying the real knowledge.

In this regard, we may recall something said of Yeshua in canonical gospels. People marveled because he spoke as one with authority and not like the common, religious teachers they were used to listening to in their synagogues. Being an apostle and prophet, he spoke with divine authority and power, from the presence and power of God within himself and so from true knowledge, understanding, and wisdom of the Holy One, Holy Shekinah. Essentially, God, the Spirit spoke through him. So it is with all true messengers of God—the Pleroma of Light.

As we know, God and God alone reveals the secret or secrets. It is only through the Holy Spirit that secrets of creation, redemption, and God are revealed and known. If a man or woman is preaching or speaking of the great mysteries of creation and God, salvation and realization, their words will be in vain and convey nothing real to those who listen to them. But if it is not a man or woman that is preaching or speaking but the Living Presence, Living Spirit—Holy Shekinah, Holy Spirit—there will be knowledge and power in what is spoken, divine authority and power, unlike that of ordinary religious and academic authorities or theorists and speculators.

Who is speaking? Who is listening? Do you know? Secret mysteries are revealed when inwardness speaks to inwardness, when God, the Spirit speaks and God, the Spirit listens, all depending on the depth of inwardness and the strength of faith, love, and corresponding presence of awareness.

Just as the intention for the Spirit is to speak and act in gnostic discourse as in gnostic worship, so there is intention for the Spirit to listen, hear, and be acted upon, that all who are present are in the Spirit, see, hear, and feel with the Spirit. Such is devotion in spirit and truth as understood among mystics and gnostics.

There is something more to be said regarding receiving teachings and revelations or the experience of sacred and holy discourse. Among gnostics, this itself is a manifestation of devotion, worship, communion with the Holy One, Holy Shekinah: The speaking of teachings and revelations is itself an invocation of what is being spoken about and is a prayer of knowledge. Gnostic apostles, gnostic masters, and those who share teachings and revelations in gnostic community do not prepare sermons or speeches, or concern themselves in advance of a gathering of what they will say. Rather, when they are going to speak, they invoke, open to the Holy Spirit, and bring forward the Holy Shekinah, often with a simple conscious intention to do so. They speak in the power of the moment; it is not them speaking, but the Living Presence, the Living Spirit, of the Holy One speaking through them. We who are with those who are giving discourse, teachings, or revelations, similarly seek to be ingathered, deep inward, as we also invoke and pray at the outset.

When new to a mystical or gnostic community, many will listen to teachings and revelations and even experience energetic transmissions but afterward just walk away or jump back into the mundane or worldly, not dwelling upon, contemplating, or doing anything with what was heard or the energy transmitted to them. They are around the drinking trough but do not go into the well. In order to listen and actually receive the light power transmitted to us and make it our own, we need to contemplate and meditate upon the teachings and revelations given as well as the energetic, spiritual, or mystical experience we have had. We pray for further revelation from the Lord, the Spirit within us, for further insights and illuminations, deeper knowledge, understanding, and wisdom from God, the Spirit. Only then will we hear, receive, and integrate the word and power shared with us and have the blessing, empowerment, intended in what was spoken and shown to us in sacred and holy discourse. Essentially, in this way we must acquire grace and knowledge for ourselves from the Lord, the Spirit within us. Otherwise there will be no grace or knowledge for us. Amen.

Verse 75

Yeshua said, "There are many standing at the door, but those who are alone will enter the bridal chamber."

The mystery of the bridal chamber is at the very heart of gnostic teachings and true gnosticism. The gnostic gospel that speaks in the most deep and detailed way about this inmost secret mystery is Philip, which speaks of three different levels of knowledge of the bridal chamber: guests at the wedding feast, attendants of the bridal chamber, and the lovers—in unity.

First, understand that your heart—the heart of your soul, your divine nature, *neshamah*—is the bridal chamber. In the Gospel of Philip, the bridal chamber is called the true holy of holies, understanding that Christed human beings are living temples, dwellings, of the presence and power of the Holy One, the Holy Shekinah, the Holy Light and Spirit. You, your soul, are the holy bride; Christ, Messiah, inseparable from the Eternal One, the Infinite Light, is the bridegroom, your beloved.

The guests are newcomers and novice initiates in anointed community. As yet they are outsiders who are mostly outward but at times are inward, though not deep inward; these guests experience the presence and power of the Holy One, the light and love in gradations of nearness, but are still in separation and lack. Such is our initial cycle of awakening to the inner Christ, Messiah—the Inner Light and Spirit. If we keep the faith; keep awake; follow the teachings of Christ, Messiah, the messengers, and the leadings of the Holy Spirit; engage in daily devotions; keep the Holy Shabbat; strive with the Spirit to go deeper to progress in our spiritual realization, being ingathered by the Spirit; and abide in an inward communion—we will begin to experience gradations of intimate nearness with Christ, Messiah in the Eternal One. We may even begin to taste the sweetness and delight of oneness, union, with the Messiah in the Eternal One. If we continue to go deeply inward into the very depths of our soul—within, beyond—there may be a dawn of supernal, supramental consciousness, Christ or God Consciousness, realization of conscious union with the Messiah in the Eternal One.

Intimate nearness—being an attendant of the bridal chamber—is the fruition of our spiritual realization in Christ, Messiah. The experience of oneness and union is the dawn of supernal realization in Christ, Messiah.

To be alone is being deeply inward: abiding in an inward communion with Christ and God, the Messiah and Holy One within you, living from inwardness, living from Christ, Messiah within you, the Inner Light and Spirit. When done through the Spirit fully in the love and filled with the light, your interior and exterior life will be aligned and harmonized, unified: You will be solitary, deep within the Inner Light and Spirit. In this way you will find, know, and be most yourself—who and what you are in the Messiah and Eternal One will be joined with who and what you are in yourself. This is true salvation. It is in this that the full, supernal realization of unity and fullness is possible—the dawn of Messianic consciousness or True Gnosis.

A person does not become a gnostic through believing in and agreeing with some doctrine. For example, it is not like becoming a Catholic or Evangelical or similar—not at all! First, we are faithful. Being inward, we begin to have deeper spiritual experiences, true mystical experiences of enlightenment or God. When we become mystics, experiencing more intimate nearness at times with the Divine Presence, when even tasting or glimpsing oneness, then through grace, the Holy Spirit it may come to pass that we realize unity and fullness, our innate oneness with Christ in God— the Messiah in the Holy One—and become gnostic, knowers of God with understanding and wisdom. Truly, it is knowledge of God beyond doctrine or knowledge of God beyond God.

Being and becoming gnostic is a manifestation of supernal grace and is from God, to God, and for God. God and God alone makes people gnostic, no other. Amen.

Verse 76

Yeshua said, "The Father's kingdom is like a merchant who owned a supply of merchandise and found a pearl. He was prudent. He sold all of his goods and bought the single pearl for himself. So with you, seek the treasure that is unfailing and enduring, where no moth comes and no worm [devours]."

This parable, of course, also appears later in canonical gospels, worded much the same. The "pearl of great price" as it is called is salvation, the realization of the soul in Christ, Messiah. It is the enlightenment of the soul, the full realization of unity and fullness, conscious union with Christ in God. Quite naturally, if we desire an actual spiritual realization, and more so a supernal realization, we will need to be very zealous and deeply immersed in our devotions, spiritual life, and practice; we will draw close to our tzaddik and be active in anointed community. We will give to it our all. We will do whatever it takes to bring our realization to fruition, to accomplish our messianic works and mission, all in the Holy One, Holy Shekinah.

If we intend to progress in an actual spiritual or supernal realization, we will need a complete and total surrender to the Messiah and Holy Spirit in us; we will go wherever the Lord sends us, wherever the Spirit carries us to engage in a complete self-offering, the offering of our person and life to enlightenment or God. It is an active and dynamic surrender, co-laboring with the Spirit to bring our realization to fruition and accomplish those works and the mission given to us: Our true will, the true desire of our holy soul, is God's will for us. There is no other way to work out our salvation, to bring about an actual realization in Christ, Messiah.

A half-hearted or lukewarm spirituality or religious observance will accomplish little or nothing in the way of actual progress in the realization of our soul in Christ, Messiah. As was spoken in the Book of Revelation to the angel of the church in Laodicea, it would be better to be hot or cold, and not lukewarm. This is certainly true for anyone seeking a mystical and gnostic spirituality: If there isn't a passionate desire, a zeal, for an actual self-realization in Christ, Messiah, attending a local church would likely be far better than seeking out a gnostic community. Striving individually and collectively for actual realization, spiritual or supernal, is what true gnostic communities are all about: actually seeking to live in the Way of the apostles and prophets, and so zealous, passionate spirituality.

Having said that, abiding in inward communion, engaging in an activate and dynamic surrender, following the guidance of Christ, Messiah and the leadings of the Holy Spirit, we all will have our own way as shown to us by the Lord, the Spirit. We will have our own call, anointing, and the works and mission given to us. There will be those who are called to labor for a spiritual realization, and those who are called to labor for a supernal realization, for there are works and missions for which spiritual realization is needed and is good, just as there are works for which a supernal realization is needed and is good. We sojourn through many lives; it may be that we are not called from within ourselves for a full force push for supernal realization in this life, but the call will come, all in due season. Likewise, as we saw with a previous saying regarding the choosing of souls one out of a thousand or two out of ten thousand and all being made a single one: Through supernal grace in Christ, Messiah, if we keep the faith, keep awake, stay in the love, in the light, and do those works given to us, the Holy Spirit may bring our soul into supernal realization when we pass beyond. It is all about being in the love, being in the light, and living according to the Truth and Light revealed to us. When we do, we abide in the sanctuary of grace that is the Christ, Messiah. Radical transformations and leaps in the realization of our soul can happen. Great, awesome wonders and miracles can and do happen. Hallelu Yah! Praise the Lord!

Give your all as the Spirit leads you to the Life Divine. Give yourself to God and God will give Godself to you. Give yourself completely to God and God will give Godself completely to you. Know that this is one and the same Great Gesture, all in the Holy One! Amen.

Verse 77

Yeshua said, "I am the light over all things. I am all. From me all has come forth, and to me all has reached. Split a piece of wood. I am there. Lift up the stone and you will find me there."

This verse is like the crown jewel of all these sayings, perhaps the most well-known verse of the gospel. This verse is most elegant and precise: It is the truth, the whole truth, and nothing but the truth of Christ, Messiah, the pure emanation of the Infinite Light.

As we contemplate this saying, consider that if the supernal light is in a piece of wood or a creepy crawly thing under a stone, how much more is in you, a human being, who is in the image and likeness of God, the True Light? If the inmost aspect of your soul is a holy spark, a pure emanation of the Infinite Light and therefore itself an infinity of light, you are in essence Endless Light, Endless Life. Yeshua Messiah appeared in the world to reveal this to us so that it might be realized in us.

This may be understood through the universe of the Sefirot—emanations, divine attributes—within Atzilut, the supernal dimension. As has been said, they all are emanations of the Infinite Light—Ain Sof Or—Keter-Crown being the first, inmost emanation, inseparable from the Infinite Light revealed as the I Am: I Am the light above all, and I am all. Indeed, all has come forth from that Infinite Light, primordial and supernal. As the supernal potential of these great, immeasurable lights is actualized and realized through creation and revelation, so those lights return, reach, and are reintegrated with the Infinite Light. The divine sparks of living spirits and souls become realized, reaching and reintegrating with the Infinite Light. All of creation and revelation transpires with, in, and through the Holy Sefirot—the emanations of the Infinite Lights. All creatures and all things in the great matrix of creation are woven of these lights—attributes, powers, actions of the Eternal One, the Infinite Light—so that truly this light is in all things.

Listen, hear, and understand! The Holy and Supernal Light that is above—all the emanations of that Perfect Light—is everywhere here below. That very Light of the Infinite and Eternal One is the secret center of every particle of matter in the material dimension and universe, such that the Pleroma of Light is within and all around you and everything, right here, right now. This was revealed in the empty tomb, the appearing and disappearing of Adonai Yeshua in the resurrection, and again with his ascension when he dissolved, was translated, into pure spirit, glory, light, vanishing into Infinite Light, Radiant Nothingness. Then, with messengers and elder brothers and sisters, we experience something like the transfiguration of Adonai Yeshua on the mountain: We become radiant with light glory in moments of the inner grades of light transmission. The surrounding environment becomes self-radiant and glorious. The Holy Shekinah, Divine Presence is revealed in all, within and surrounding us on all sides: the kingdom of heaven, the Pleroma of Light inside and outside. There are many who can bear witness to experiences of gnosis with living ones among us today. This revelation is ongoing; this play of light transmission and passing of the Spirit continues in the world and will continue until the end of days.

When you become aware of Christ, Messiah within you, the Holy One, Holy Shekinah within you and are inward, with the Spirit you can see, hear, and feel people and things in their inwardness. Being aware of God in you and you in God, you will thus become aware of God in creation, and creation in God. As is said in Job: "from my flesh I will see God-Elohim" (19:26).

Understand that not all seeing is visionary. In fact, luminous dreams and visions are the least manifestation of seeing, hearing, and feeling. There is seeing with the eye of your mind, seeing with the eye of your heart, and seeing with the eye of your soul. As we know, inmost of all is seeing with the eye of God. In the inmost seeing, there is just knowing, the experience of knowing being, gnostic being: God being the seeing, hearing, feeling, and knowing. This knowing being is far beyond and far superior to the psychic visions that so many psychic and occult folk laud and go on and on about as great. Such visions in fact are outermost and generally speaking are very impure, deceptive, mystical experiences. There are gradations of seeing, hearing, feeling, and knowing—gnosis—that go much deeper and are far more subtle, sublime, and pure, venturing into states of pure radiant awareness or nondual gnostic awareness in oneness and conscious union with the Eternal One, the Infinite Light, Radiant Nothingness.

Split a piece of wood, I am there. Turn over a stone and you will find me there. While there naturally may be the opening of sight into the visionary dimension or visionary experiences of realities of inner dimensions, what Hayyah Yeshua is speaking about is something far more direct and immediate—just being in the Holy One, unified with the Holy One; being in that presence of awareness—pure radiant awareness—being aware of the Holy Shekinah in yourself and all things, yourself and all things in the Holy Shekinah, being aware of the Absolute Oneness of the Supreme. In truth, in reality, there is the Holy One and the Holy One alone, no other or anything else. There never has been, is not now, nor ever will be any other or anything else but the Holy One—this is the secret of secrets. But until the Holy One, Holy Shekinah reveals this, we cannot know it. Only the Holy One, Holy Shekinah can reveal and make the secret known to us. Amen.

Verse 78

Yeshua said, "Why have you come out to the countryside? To see a reed shaken in the wind? Or to see a person dressed in soft clothes like your rulers and religious authorities? They are dressed in soft clothes and cannot understand truth."

As we know from canonical gospels, Yeshua is inquiring of people why they went to Yohanan the Baptist to hear him preach, prophesy, and receive initiation—baptism—from him. He was nothing of this world they went out to see, neither an idle-headed person nor an authority and power of this world. Rather, he was a great prophet of the Eternal One, a holy person having divine authority and power in the Name, the Holy Shekinah, to open the Way for the coming of the Messiah. He initiated and prepared the people for their anointing with the Holy Light and Spirit and the revelation of the kingdom of heaven made manifest on earth. He was the one with the authority and power to be the holy tzaddik of Yeshua, guiding him in his coming into being and facilitating his initiation and ascension into the station and state of Messiah.

On a deeper level, we may ask why so many people went out to him. He was a very wild and fierce messenger of God, an apocalyptic prophet of truth who could be swift to rebuke, correct, and warn of the end of days drawing near. He also preached of the kingdom of heaven coming near. People could sense, feel, and witness the presence and power of the Holy One with him. As such, they were called from within themselves to go out and engage with him. The great power in him of the Spirit of God—Ruach Elohim—stirred something inside them, which is exactly what the Holy One intended with the return of Elijah. But then, this is the way it is with all apostles and prophets of God: They stir something inside people, speaking the truth, the word of God with power, imparting something of their knowledge and power to those who are stirred to draw near. Those who draw near and abide with them and those who are their disciples will be guided in the path of return, the path of reintegration. Followers who are more removed or psychically and spiritually distant are given instruction for spiritual life and devotions that are good for them. To those who are mere students, they may speak some words and send them on their way or at times receive them as acquaintances, letting them come to the outer circle of their community. In the gatherings of messengers, there are inmost disciples, followers, and students passing through.

As we have shared, it is a mistake to believe that messengers no longer appear among us or that the revelation of Christ and God, the Messiah and Holy One has ceased in this world. Nothing could be further from the truth. There are always messengers with us, holy tzaddikim revealed and concealed and matrices of souls of lofty grades that gather around them, anointed communities bearing the light transmission and passing of the Spirit. If there were no harvesters engaged in the ingathering of souls teaching, initiating, and offering guidance to people in their process of spiritual and supernal realization, there would be no harvest of souls from one generation to another.

Gnostic apostles, prophets, and the various holy tzaddikim may assume any outward appearance and have many different styles and ways of teaching and initiating. Some might appear more orthodox and work very close to the outer manifestations of faiths and wisdoms while teaching and initiating in an inner and secret way. Others, might appear like Yohanan—more wild, unorthodox, and fierce in their way, to even challenge and criticize orthodoxy. And there is all manner of manifestations of holy and enlightened ones somewhere in between these extremes. Some come from the upper right—mercy—and some from the upper left—severity, fierceness— and some from the upper middle—compassion, a dynamic mix of mercy and severity. Depending upon the movement of the Shekinah, the Spirit with them in the moment, along with what is happening—who they are with, and what the Holy One wills and ordains to be done—all gnostic apostles and prophets are manifestations of the grace and mercy of the Eternal One. All can engage in peaceful, wrathful, and blissful manifestations of the Divine Presence just the same.

If anyone feels a stirring and wishes to seek a messenger, a holy tzaddik, let them be inward, invoke, pray, and ask the Holy One to bless them to find and encounter a living one; let them pray for guidance and follow the guidance of their heart and the Spirit as they set out seeking, probing, to find a living one. Along the way, let them pray that the Holy One, Holy Shekinah prepares them for their meeting their tzaddik, that the meeting be auspicious in the Lord, the Spirit, that they might recognize the tzaddik as tzaddik and be well-received. In a true holy tzaddik, you will find light, love, and compassion and a witness of the Holy Spirit. There will be light and love in their people, their community bearing testimonies of the experience of light transmission and the passing of the Holy Spirit among them who are progressing in their realization among them. Know that the messengers are not about themselves—they are about the Holy One, Holy Shekinah and their community, those given to them in the Spirit. The term "messenger" is about the one who sends the message and the one for whom it is sent—God and the people—not the messenger. Amen.

Verse 79

A woman in the crowd said to him, "Bless[ed is] the womb that bore you and the breasts that fed you." He said to her, "Blessings on those who have heard the word of the Father and have truly kept it. Days will come when you will say, 'Blessed is the womb that has not conceived and the breast that has not given milk.'"

There are stories in the canonical gospels read by those initiated into the mysteries—those with deeper spiritual and mystical experience of the Messiah—not as literal or historical accounts of events but as allegories or metaphors that convey secret mysteries of our process of coming into being in the Messiah, the Anointing.

The stories of the virgin conception with Mother Miriam and the birth of Yeshua in Matthew and Luke are among them. Such stories are a delight to the common faithful reading them, but to those in the gnostic path they glean from them secret wisdom.

The principle of the virgin indicates the reality of the Clear or Perfect Light, the intrinsic nature of our soul, consciousness, and mind that remains ever pure and pristine; it is never tainted, traced, marked, stained, or in any way corrupted or changed by sin or karma.

Being born from a virgin conception connotes the arising of the Great Vision of Melchizedek and the reality of the threefold body generated by holy and enlightened ones in the dawn of supernal realization, Christ, or Messianic Consciousness. The Gospel of Philip addresses this in one passage, asking, "When has a woman ever conceived from a woman?" understanding that, in truth, the Holy Spirit in Hebrew and Aramaic is not male—it is female.

The passage makes clear that gnostic initiates are not to take those stories literally but as something much more wonderful: insights into deep mysteries of our realization in Messiah and the acquisition of true knowledge of

God: gnosis, *da'at*. This saying may be understood to do something similar; and given that this is among the earliest gospels, it may be that stories of the virgin conception and birth of Christ were not fully developed and in circulation at that time. Here we may note that Mark and John do not tell such stories at all but instead begin with Yohanan the Baptist and the great baptism of Adonai Yeshua; of the those two gospels, John is perhaps the most esoteric and profound of the four canonized in the Christian Bible.

If you consider it, this woman in fact praised herself, her flesh, her own self-identity as a woman and in self-cherishing, praised his earthly mother rather than praising God, the Eternal One, the Supreme. Yeshua rightly rebuked and corrected her, reminding her that no woman or man has sent him, but God and God alone. It is God who is to be praised and glorified, not flesh and blood, however blessed and holy it might be. Moreover, he points to hearing the word of God spoken with power, the reception and integration of the Holy Light and Spirit, and living according to the Truth and Light revealed to us. These are the blessed ones, the chosen ones, the living ones, the holy and righteous ones enlightened by God, the Spirit. Then he reminds of mortality, the great troubles of the eventual end times, and the reality of great sorrow and suffering for those who are not resurrected and ascended, enlightened and liberated before they die. It is a very precise and beautiful response. We are wise to take his words to heart!

When we turn to the Lord, when we go to God, when we seek to know the inner Christ, Messiah, when we encounter living messengers, tzaddikim, our self-grasping and play of desire and fear in self-grasping is a great barrier that needs to be overcome. Our strong clinging to and self-identification with name, form, and personal history of being a man or woman, our race, class, or sexual identity and such along with our mortal, finite reason and intellect in its surface consciousness all pose significant barriers. These identities can obstruct and prevent us from experiencing light transmission, the passing of the Spirit, and truly hearing the word of God with understanding and finding and knowing our Lord within us. If our orientation and self-identity are bound up in the flesh, name, form, and personal history, we remain bound up in our sin, our karma and will neither be able to go deep within nor merge with the Lord within us, the Inner Light and Spirit, our Divine or Christ Self. We will not hear the word of the Eternal One to keep it and realize our innate unity with the Messiah in the Eternal One: eternal life, bornless being, enlightenment, and liberation.

We need to break out of ourselves, letting go of our self-will, self-grasping, attachments, and aversions. Instead of self-identifying with name, form, personal history, and whatnot, we need to self-identify with the fully enlightened, divine, and supernal being, Christ, Messiah within us, our Divine Self, the Divine I Am. This is called divine pride or spiritual self-worth; when joined with spiritual humility and full submission to the Spirit in full self-offering, it is essential for an actual realization, spiritual or supernal. So, we are to deny ourselves, take up our cross—merge with the Lord within us, the Inner Light and Spirit—and follow Messiah Yeshua. In this is true salvation, our enlightenment and liberation. Through supernal grace, the Holy Spirit, this is given to us by the Supreme. Amen.

Verse 80

Yeshua said, "Whoever has come to know the world has discovered the body, and whoever has discovered the body, of that person the world is not worthy."

The body and the world in which it appears are inseparable from one another. They are completely interdependent and interconnected, such that the body is the world and the world is the body. Apart from everything else arising, appearing, and existing in the moment, all things are co-arising phenomena, completely empty of any independent, substantial self-existence. In effect, if you look into it from deep within in deep meditation and contemplation, every single thing is actually made up of what it is not—it is made up of everything else in the world, in the universe. Totally!

Take a tree, for example. If you and I were standing by a lovely tree and I asked you to show me a tree or to point to a tree, what you would point to would be its various parts: a branch, a leaf, the trunk, and bark. None of those things, in fact, are the tree but are parts of it and a tree is composed of them. But then a tree is much more than that. To start with, matter is something like frozen light, elements from extinct stars. A tree is rooted in the earth and its soil, and it is composed of minerals, moisture, and lifeforms that have decomposed. Trees depend on clouds, precipitation, air and wind, sun and moon, and everything that is not a tree. On a material level, aside from the source of all—the Eternal One, Infinite Light, Radiant Nothingness—without everything else in the world, the solar system, our galaxy, and universe, there would be no tree. In the very same way, there is no independent, self-existent you or me; all that is within and behind a form depends metaphysically on everything it is not.

You are the world and the world is you; you are other people and other people are you—I am you and you are me! Everything is interdependent and interconnected. There is an underlying Sacred Unity—the Holy One, Clear Light, Radiant Nothingness. Each and all are the emanation, radiance, of the Infinite and Eternal One—the nothingness that is everythingness.

This is Reality as It Is, God as God Is!

This notion gets wilder when you start looking and begin to see, hear, and feel with God. All of this is in the soul, consciousness, mind, of you, me, everybody—even the Holy One. All of this is the radiant, magical display of soul, consciousness, mind. All of this is inseparable from the intrinsic nature of soul, consciousness, mind, of which we can observe three qualities: emptiness—nothingness—and endless self-generation—thinking, imagining—and awareness—intelligence. Whether incarnate in waking life, in sleep, or even death and the afterlife, all is transpiring in the soul, in consciousness and is its own radiant, dreamlike, magical display. Even though all arises in apparent separation, as though things seem to have any independent and substantial self-existence apart from one another or their source, dualism is illusory.

If there is neither you nor me in reality, who or what is there to deny or pass away? Who or what is there other than the Infinite and Eternal One, the Absolute Light, the Radiant Nothingness that is the Father, the Mother, of all—the All-In-All?

Consider this: When you wake up in the morning, where does the dream you with your dream body and all the dream people, things, and its world go? And when someday you die, where do you, your body, and all the people and things and the world go? When people wake up here and individuals are realized, enlightened, it is much the same. It is like awakening in a dream and become fully lucid, with the dreaming power it entails: flying, walking on water, passing through solid objects, transforming a thing into another, bringing about radical transformations in one's form, appearing and disappearing, changing environments or weather, and so on. Compare these dream abilities with the wonders, miracles, Yeshua Messiah and various apostles and prophets of God performed. Moreover, awakening from sleep and dream altogether in the real, when the unreal passes away and ceases to be, all is reintegrated with the source of its arising—the pure radiant awareness: Infinite Light, Radiant Nothingness—the Eternal One, Bornless One.

If one is awake in this way, arising in dream or not, arising in incarnation or not, there is no difference—awake is enlightened and liberated.

Wonders and miracles are moments revealing Reality as It Is, God as God Is, and ourselves as we are in the Real, in God, the Holy and Eternal One. They are wake-up calls, as are moments of light transmission and the passing of the Holy Spirit. As you might intuit, in this saying is the secret of Yeshua nailing the sins of the world to the cross of wood and the forgiveness of sin, karma, that comes through that Great Gesture.

Are you getting the picture? I pray that you are! Amen.

Verse 81

Yeshua said, "Let a person of wealth rule and a person of power renounce it."

On the surface, this saying is enigmatic and curious, like a riddle. The two halves of it appear to contradict one another, but they are actually speaking one and the same truth. First it may be said: Let everyone go their own way. Let the unenlightened go the way of the unenlightened, and let the enlightened to the Way of the enlightened.

My holy tzaddik would say from time to time that there are two paths, two directions, in this world: the path of unenlightened people and the path of the enlightened ones. You must choose between them. You cannot go both directions, only one way or the other. One is good and true, sober and sane; the other is neither good nor true but is intoxicated and insane. They cannot both be right—you must choose between them. You must find your way and live your life, one way or the other.

Let a wealthy person rule, let a person of the world be in the world, in unenlightened society, and let them live in self-will and have the world. Let a person of power renounce it, let a faithful and spiritual person renounce the world, the unenlightened society, and live in submission to God, not their own will, but the will of God, and have God—be in the enlightened family, the family of God.

This is one teaching; allow me to share another. Let the wealthy person rule who has the wisdom treasury of an enlightened one, a realized individual—a holy tzaddik—and a person of power renounce it, who is a true and faithful disciple giving way to the teachings and guidance of the holy tzaddik, the outer and inner tzaddik in Christ, Messiah.

This may also be understood as completely internal, the person of true wealth being Christ, Messiah in you, or your Divine or Christ Self, and the person of power being your ego, its self-will and the play of desire and fear in it.

Yet another teaching is present: When we receive the Holy Light and Spirit, and Christ, Messiah is revealed in us, we are united and filled—wealthy. And with it is a great power awakened in us that needs to be uplifted to the Messiah and Holy One, brought into repose, rest in the Holy One, and thus redeemed. We may read this saying as Let Christ, Messiah rule your life, and let the Holy Spirit take up the great power in you, and with it fulfill the will of God—the true will, true desire of your holy soul, the Divine Self, Divine I Am.

All these interpretations swirl together and overlap, and others are possible, something that is true of all these sayings and inspired scripture. There are many layers of meaning and wisdom; there may be outer, inner, and secret teachings found in them all ranging from plain and straightforward meanings to very deep, hidden meanings.

If we learn to see, hear, and feel with the Spirit and how to study and contemplate scriptures in the Spirit, with the Spirit—the very same Living Presence, Living Spirit, that inspired them—there are endless depths of knowledge, understanding, and wisdom of the Eternal One in them. The Spirit will continue to bring forth new, innovative teachings and revelations from them, all as intended in the Holy One, Holy Shekinah. Amen.

Verse 82

Yeshua said, "Whoever is near me is near fire and whoever is far from me is far from the kingdom."

Truly, whoever is near the Sun of God is near a blazing, spiritual fire, a fire consuming fire making all like unto itself. Whoever is far from the Sun of God is far from the Pleroma of Light; they are in the outer darkness, something like a bottomless pit of abysmal space without light or life. This is completely true—what more can I say?

This Sun of the Eternal One shines within the messengers of the Eternal Pleroma, those who are gathered with them in anointed community. So as with Adonai Yeshua, one near the messenger and anointed community is near fire; one who is far away from the messenger, far from anointed community, is far from the kingdom of heaven—Pleroma of Light. There is an actual baptism of fire and the Spirit within true anointed community, or the imparting of the Holy Light and Spirit. Those receiving it are lit up and set on fire with the Holy Spirit, and they will be transformed by the Spirit to resemble the Sun of God, the stars of heaven. But apart from the Holy Light and Spirit, souls remain outside, in the darkness, ignorance, separation, and lack.

There is something to be said about light and fire, and mercy and judgment. In new ageism and its espousing of spiritual truisms, there are those who say that we all go into the light. This is true, but there is something they do not understand about the supernal light; as such, they are not speaking in knowledge of truth, but in ignorance. When souls go to God—the Infinite Light—to those who have lived in love and light and have done what is good and true, they encounter light, love, mercy, compassion, and complete forgiveness. It is awesome and wonderful, a pure delight: There is rest, peace, complete reintegration with the Infinite Light. However, if that is not the case, if souls have neither learned to live in the love nor the light but have done evil and false things, if they are neither united nor filled but bound in separation and lack, being in the light will be a blazing, consuming fire to them, awful and dreadful.

As has been said, there is no judgment in the Supreme, the Absolute Light—only supernal grace, supernal love, complete mercy, compassion, and forgiveness. The judgment is within souls themselves. Those who are unloving and unmerciful with neither compassion nor forgiveness will not be able to stand or endure such beauty and holiness, glory and power of goodness, righteousness, and truth. They will want to remove themselves far, far away from the light; the fire pains them so deeply. God have mercy upon such troubled souls!

Something similar is true at times in moments of light transmission and the passing of the Holy Spirit. There are those who cannot stand it, who are terribly agitated, disturbed, or pained by the light, even repulsed or repelled by its transmission such that at times, some may literally run and hide. Just as easily, they become angry, aggressive, and insist a light-bearer disengages the transmission. To some who draw near from outside but not inside, the light becomes fire; rather than comfort and light, the fire will burn and injure the individual. Needless to say, in the love it is a great sorrow to see this happen to people; it pains the heart deeply.

To be very close to messengers or holy tzaddikim is to be in a blazing fire. The truth is that very few can endure being too close to them. Few can be inmost disciples to a gnostic apostle, gnostic master. If a sister or brother themselves were fully on fire with the Holy Spirit, it would be a pure delight and would be very good. To be otherwise is quite the opposite. Of course, being too removed or keeping far away from them is not good or useful either: Why have a holy tzaddik and community and not be a true disciple, companion, or faithful follower, in some reasonable proximity to them and some level of involvement in community?

The truth is that for most individuals, the right proximity is somewhere in the middle, between very close and very far. On one level this is naturally determined as the sacred friendship develops and matures, as it tends to do in all human relationships: some are closer friends, some not as close, and some more casual acquaintanceships, all as it naturally self-selects. On another level, a tzaddik may feel led by the Living Presence, Living Spirit, to draw a companion closer, for some duration; likewise, a call may come from within the companion themselves to draw closer or step a bit away, all as the Spirit leads. In truth, there may be shifts in proximity from time to time over years or decades, some closer and not so close, and some closer and closer over time, all as the Spirit leads, all in the Holy One. Holy Shekinah. Amen.

Verse 83

Yeshua said, "You see images, but the light within them is hidden in the image of the Father's light. He will be disclosed, but his image is hidden by his light."

This is a very esoteric and lovely saying. It is a teaching of the Infinite One—Ain Sof—and the emanations—Sefirot—from the Holy Kabbalah.

The "images" may be understood to be the Sefirot—attributes, powers, actions—and their visible outer light, but not their Inner Light because it is hidden in the Father's light, the Light of the Infinite One—Or Ain Sof. He will be disclosed through the Holy Sefirot, but his image—which is no image, no-thingness—is concealed in his supernal glory, supernal radiance—the Infinite Light. This is the secret mystery of the Pleroma of Light, which corresponds with the supernal universe, or Atzilut—universe of emanation, everflow, the eternal realm.

The Infinite One is completely transcendent of creation and revelation, truly God beyond God. As the Infinite One is within the Infinite One, the One is nameless and knowable, without attributes, an unfathomable singularity, that as such is inconceivable to us: No-Thing, like nothing else, incomparable and beyond, the Concealed of the Concealed, thus known only to Itself within Itself. This is the Father Yeshua teaches about, the Soul of the Messiah in him—the One Soul—being the pure emanation of the radiance of the Infinite One—the Infinite Light—and the light of all the Holy Sefirot.

The Infinite One has no attributes whatsoever, and yet in a great and supreme mystery, from the Infinite Radiance of that unfathomable and Primordial One are the pure emanations, the Holy Sefirot—attributes, powers, actions—through which creation and revelation unfold, the Infinite One is revealed and made known through them. But as the Infinite One is Infinite, Endless, Nothingness, however much is revealed and realized, there is evermore that remains concealed, hidden, unknown. There is no end in sight of the revelation and realization of the Infinite One, the Primordial and Supernal One.

This is also true of the Holy Sefirot themselves: While their outer lights are revealed and known, their inner lights are concealed and unknown. What they are in themselves may be revealed and known to us in this world, but what they are in the Light of the Infinite One cannot be known to us. Likewise, as much of their supernal potential or possibility is revealed and realized in creation and creatures, there is evermore that remains to be revealed and realized.

The Sefirot themselves are exhaustless infinities of potentials and possibilities in the Infinite and Eternal. The outer lights of these attributes, powers, and actions manifest in creation and to human beings as archangels, angels, and various divinities, their light hidden in these images appearing as the entire matrix of spiritual forces within and behind the great matrix of creation in the spiritual and astral dimensions. Yet through all of this, something of the Father—the Infinite and Eternal One—is being revealed and realized, as are the Holy Sefirot.

As they are in themselves and in supernal realization, we can reach into the Holy Sefirot, but as they are in the Infinite One, there is no reaching them; they are beyond.

As we know, spiritual realization reaches into the world of angels and archangels. For example, the archangel of the Holy Shekinah spoke to Moses; the archangel Gabriel spoke to Mohammed. In Yeshua Messiah, however, there was the direct speaking of the Holy One, Holy Shekinah, the I Am. He spoke from the Reality of the Holy Sefirot beyond archangels and angels. So indeed, Yeshua saw the Father and what the Father was doing—the Sefirot—and manifested the full array of those emanations of the Infinite Light, those divine attributes, powers, actions. Like the Holy Sefirot, however, while the outer light of the Eternal Messiah is revealed and known to us, the Inner Light of the Primordial Messiah is concealed and unknown, hidden in the Supernal Radiance of the Infinite One, beyond.

Here we may recall Hayyah Yeshua saying, "I am the light above all—the Light of the Infinite One, and I am all—the array of Holy Sefirot." As the Infinite One is revealed and known through the Holy Sefirot, so it is through the Christ, Messiah incarnate, such that Adonai Yeshua spoke truth when he said, "You who have seen me have seen the Father." So too is it true that no one has seen the Father but the Son.

We have progressed a long way through this holy gospel now, well past the second half. As you can see, it is shifting toward very deep things, inmost secret mysteries. Even though it may feel a bit daunting and overwhelming at first, it is time for us to contemplate some of those deep things in the most essential, straightforward way possible. As we go forward with our contemplations, let us pray and continue praying that the Holy One blesses us, that the Holy Spirit gifts us with insight and understanding, all as is good for each of us, all as is ours from the Holy One! Amen.

Verse 84

"When you see your likeness, you are happy. But when you see your images that came into being before you and that neither die nor become visible, how much will you bear!"

This saying flows out of the previous one and speaks a deep mystery about your holy soul—*neshamah*—and your supernal image, the image of the Eternal One within you.

As we contemplate this, be inward. More than thinking about what is being shared and trying to understand or figure it out, seek to feel the truth and the reality the words are pointing to—a truth, reality of your being in the Pleroma of Light and Infinite One known in the depths of your soul, in the very heart of your inner being. Seek to feel with your heart and soul what is being shared. Have a sense of feeling, and see what insights come!

Your heavenly and supernal soul emanates from the One Soul—the First Adam, Human One—the Soul of the Messiah, and at times is also called the Soul of God. The One Soul is inseparable from the Light of the Infinite One and is inseparable from the Holy Sefirot; the One Soul is in the Sefirot and the Sefirot are in the One Soul. The One Soul is the emanation of the Infinite Light, as are the Holy Sefirot. Your holy soul is an emanation of the One Soul—the Soul of the Messiah—filled with supernal light, as are all the lights of the Holy Sefirot. Such is your divine nature and that of all human beings.

That holy soul is the image of God in you. There is a light image of images—like a jeweled being of countless facets—within and behind which is an image that is concealed within the image of the Infinite One within the Infinite Light. That image in the image of the Infinite One is bornless and neither dies nor becomes visible. It is concealed in the supernal radiance, glory, of the Infinite and Eternal One.

As it is with the Infinite One and the Sefirot, so is it also with the One Soul and the countless holy souls—*neshamot*—emanating from the Infinite One in endless diversity. The One Soul is concealed in the supernal radiance and glory of the Infinite One, but is being revealed and realized through all the souls emanating from it. In a similar way, like the Infinite One and Sefirot, the inmost aspects of your soul reach into the Infinite Light while the Infinite One is being revealed and realized through the light image of images; those images are the incarnations within which your holy soul is being realized and embodied, each its own image within your supernal image, each a manifestation of your supernal image in the image and likeness of God, Elohim.

Your holy soul has outer light and Inner Light, just like the Holy Sefirot. The outer light is all that is revealed and realized. The Inner Light is hidden in the Infinite Light and Infinite One. This Inner Light corresponds with the evermore of the inmost aspects within your holy soul that can be revealed and realized without end.

This is mind-blowing, isn't it? It confounds our consciousness. But in the supramental, supernal consciousness is the awareness of this, knowledge of the reality of our soul in the image and likeness of the Eternal God—Yahweh Elohim—in the Infinite Light, Infinite One.

Here we are in self-grasping, clinging to this name, form, and personal history, often thinking this is all we are when in truth, this name and form are something like 1 percent of who and what we actually are in ourselves. How much more is the 99 percent of who and what we are in the Infinite and Eternal One? When you see your likeness, your name and form, you are happy, but when you see your image of images and that hidden image in the Infinite Light, the Infinite and Eternal One, how delightful it is— what inexplicable, immeasurable bliss—how much will you have to bear!

Know that supernal realization corresponds with conscious union with the One Soul—the Messiah in the Eternal One. Amen.

Verse 85

Yeshua said, "Adam came into being from great power and great wealth, but he was not worthy of you. Had he been worthy, he would not have tasted death."

The First Human, *Adam Rishon*, was created in the image and likeness of the powers of heaven and God, having come into being from great power and wealth, the very breath of the Eternal God—Yahweh Elohim—being in this Adam, the Holy Spirit. The Adam in the garden of Eden corresponds with the One Soul in a state of unconscious union, in ignorance or unrealized spiritual and supernal potential, possibility.

As we know, Adam was made to fall into a deep sleep and became two—male and female, Adam and Eve. Reading Genesis, you will find the holy scriptures never say that Adam awoke from that deep sleep. On one level, understanding that if the One Soul is inseparable from the Infinite Light and Sefirot, all of creation and revelation are in the One Soul but only as potential, a possibility in the beginning. All that follows in the scriptures and the reality of our experience and the entirety of creation may be understood to be the One Soul asleep and dreaming, in the process of awakening and becoming realized.

We are the One Soul asleep and dreaming in the process of awakening and becoming actualized and realized. First there is awakening in the dream. Greater yet is lucid dreaming, the realization and embodiment of our holy soul, our *neshamah*, in our incarnations—the realization of Christ, Messiah in us—the Inner Light and Spirit. Greatest of all is awakening from the dream altogether when we pass beyond, not tasting death or falling unconscious but experiencing a conscious, lucid passing into the Pleroma of Light and full reintegration with the Infinite Light. According to gnostic teachings and the Christian Kabbalah, this is what is happening with us: We are awakening, becoming realized—enlightened.

In the Christian Kabbalah, when the One Soul is awake and realized, it is called the Supernal Human—Adam Elyon, the Soul of Messiah and Soul of God in the Holy Kabbalah. Adonai Yeshua entered into full supernal realization at the sacred Jordan, conscious union with the One Soul and the Eternal One, the Infinite Light, and thus embodied the Spirit and Soul of the Messiah. He was the One Soul awakened among us and therefore was called the Son of Man—Human One—and the Son of God. As such, he was the first of a new humanity, supernal and divine: the Second Adam, or Great Seth.

When we receive the Holy Light and Spirit, are reborn from above, and awaken, Christ, Messiah is being revealed in us, our heavenly and supernal soul coming into us. We are conceived in this new humanity of the supernal human, divine-human, and are sons and daughters of light, sons and daughters of the Eternal One. In Christ, Messiah we become more than human; we become supernal and divine. As such, until the old, bestial humankind also receives the Holy Light and Spirit and awakens to be who and what they are in the One Soul and the Eternal One, unenlightened humankind is unworthy of us.

In gnostic teachings, Yeshua Messiah is understood to be the Savior and gnostic Revealer. More than for the sake of the forgiveness of sin, the Christ, Messiah comes to dispel the ignorance, forgetfulness, and slumber that cause sin, karma, bondage to potentially endless rounds of incarnation—the gilgulim. He comes to awaken us within and from the dream, reminding us of ourselves, revealing to us through the cross, resurrection, and ascension who and what we are in the One Soul and Eternal One so that we may be and become Christ, Messiah—the Anointed One.

According to the teachings of gnostic apostles and gnostic masters, there are holy and enlightened ones, realized souls that continue to incarnate for the sake of the harvest of souls. In the love and compassion of Christ, Messiah, they desire the salvation, enlightenment, and liberation of all living souls and actively labor to facilitate their awakening and realization. Among them are those who become the Christ, Messiah to other worlds of creation, as Adonai Yeshua did in ours. When that Great Gesture, that divine action is accomplished, they progress into an even greater realization of the One Soul, the Primordial Human, or Primordial Messiah—Adam Kadmon—complete and total reintegration with the Infinite Light, Radiant Nothingness, completely merging with and being absorbed in the Infinite One—Ain Sof. This is the realization of the image of souls within the image of the Living Father hidden within the Infinite Light. We cannot speak of this primordial realization; it is beyond beyond, only known to those who enter it. It is the ultimate secret of God beyond God. Amen.

Verse 86

Yeshua said, "Foxes have their [holes] and birds have their nests, but the Human [One] has no place to lay his head and rest."

Truly so, the Messiah, the messengers, and all who receive the Holy Light and Spirit, have no place in this world; although in this world, they are no longer of it. They are of the Pleroma of Light and the Eternal One. As taught in an early saying of Thomas, they are passersby. They have no place in this world, and the world is not worthy of them. Their place—Makom—is the Holy One, Holy Shekinah, in whom they rest and with whom they merge, so that they are no longer the doer. The Holy Shekinah, Holy Spirit is the doer of everything—the Messiah and Holy One is living as them!

To be a passerby is to be free from self-grasping, attachment, and aversion to whatever arises, appears, and transpires. One can know what the world and body are and the emptiness of it all. Indeed, everything under the sun is vanity. For passersby, there is no difference whether life gives or takes. If circumstances are auspicious or inauspicious, beautiful or horrible; whether one is living or dying, there is no difference—it is known to be all in the Holy One, Holy Shekinah. In this is true freedom, peace, and joy. To simply abide in the Radiant Nothingness, the Holy One, to be awake in the dance of the Holy Shekinah, Her endless continuum of creation and destruction, is Reality as It Is.

There is neither rest, peace, nor any lasting joy, save in the knowledge and realization of the Messiah and Holy One within you. Just rest in the intrinsic nature of your holy soul, your consciousness and mind free from self-will and self-grasping, desire, and fear. Just be in the Holy One, inseparable from the Holy One. Return to be One.

Being in the love and the light is rest, peace, endless delight, pure and lasting joy. Not being in the love or the light is darkness, fire; no rest, peace, or joy, only perpetual and immeasurable sorrow and suffering. God have mercy!

Be in the love and the light and you will have rest, peace, joy, and all good things in this world. When you pass beyond, you will know the kingdom of heaven within and all around you here. You will be in the kingdom of heaven in the afterlife, in eternity. Amen.

Verse 87

Yeshua said, "How miserable is the body that depends on a body, and how miserable is the soul that depends on both."

This saying flows from the previous one very well.

The body is the world and the world is the body. The body depending upon a body is the body dependent upon the world. Life in this world and all worlds of creation is pervaded with sorrow and suffering: In this respect, it is a miserable condition. For whatever pleasure and good might come, there is much pain and misery. Until our divine nature—*neshamah*—is realized and embodied, our soul is bound up in the gilgulim: potentially endless rounds of birth, life, aging, illness, and death. While many souls are unconsciously compelled into repeated incarnations of self-grasping, desire, and fear, reincarnating is necessary until souls eventually fulfill their divine purpose, their divine destiny. It is through incarnation that souls actualize, realize, and come into being in Christ, Messiah, returning to be One.

When the Inner Light and Spirit are revealed and realized in us and we realize and embody our divine nature, with supernal realization dawning and our divine purpose fulfilled, we transcend the necessity of material, physical incarnation for ourselves. We are fully resurrected and ascended, enlightened and liberated. When, who, and what we are in the Messiah and Eternal One—our Divine Self—is realized and embodied; we are neither compelled to nor in need of reincarnation in the material dimension.

Aware of the plight of souls bound up in the ignorance, separation, and lack, in addition to potentially endless rounds of reincarnation, realized beings strive with the Holy Spirit for supernal realization in Christ, Messiah in a realization of complete unity and fullness and the experience of this greater resurrection and ascension—the Great Exodus, the Great Liberation. In the gnostic path we therefore invoke the Name of the Holy One often. We pray and pray and pray and meditate, contemplating deep and abiding in inward communion. We seek to be in the love and the light, to be very, very kind and forgiving. We strive with the Spirit to ascend the stations of the soul, to manifest the full array of divine qualities.

As has been said, there are many holy and enlightened ones free of the need to incarnate for their own realization, but in their love and compassion they continue to incarnate for the sake of the realization of other living spirits and souls. These are the messengers: prophets, apostles, and holy tzaddikim, revealed and concealed. When they incarnate as Messiah Yeshua, they take upon themselves the sin, the karma of the world around them, suffering with all people and all creatures, engaging in the divine action of a co-redeemer with Adonai Yeshua. But they are not overcome by the darkness of the world and matter, for they are the light and love of the Eternal One. The darkness did not and will not overcome the light, for the light brings darkness—ignorance, the cause of all sorrow and suffering—to an end.

Quite naturally, because messengers have been realized, enlightened in previous incarnations like Yohanan and Yeshua, they tend to swiftly come into being and unfold their realization in their incarnations. Most often, as with Yeshua and those who were close to him, they come in groups, manifesting a matrix of uplifted and realized souls, all taking up various roles in a shared divine action of bringing salvation, light transmission, and the passing of the Spirit.

Some holy ones remain disincarnate to engage in spiritual works through the astral and spiritual inner dimensions. Generally, however, messengers incarnate to be of the greatest benefit and to help as many as possible because when incarnate, they are able to do secret works though the inner dimensions in dreamtime, in mystical ascensions of the soul, and through the transference of consciousness, *aliyat neshamah*. Along with these enlightened ones are holy angels that incarnate as human beings in love and compassion, though when incarnate they are fully human and do not right away bear the knowledge and power of an angelic being. Like realized souls, however, these individuals tend to swiftly enter spiritual realization and are of greater help to people in their lives, very much so! Amen.

Verse 88

Yeshua said, "The apostles and prophets will come to you and give you what is yours. You give them what you have and wonder, 'When will they come and take what is theirs?'"

This is a delightful saying that affirms the ongoing appearance of apostles and prophets who bring light transmission and the passing of the Holy Spirit. They do indeed give us what is our own, for the Inner Light and Spirit is already within us; with the light transmission and movements of the Holy Spirit, we become aware of the Holy Light and Spirit. In effect, they awaken the Inner Light and Spirit of Christ, Messiah within us and call out our holy soul: who and what we already are in the Messiah and Holy One.

These holy and righteous ones reflect ourselves to us, our true being in the Pleroma of Light. What they give to us is not theirs—it is ours. They do not give from themselves; they give from the Messiah and the Eternal One. As the Mother Spirit gives birth to the Sun of God in us, they are midwives: it is the Holy One, Holy Shekinah who has conceived, gestated, and now gives birth to us as we are in the Pleroma.

This is the way of imparting all blessings and empowerments, calling out of what is within us, giving to us what is our own from the Holy One, in the Holy One. Unless it is in us, there can be no blessing or empowerment. Blessings and empowerments are the increase of good in a person—their talents, abilities, and innate faculties—not the giving of something a person does not have within them. Otherwise, blessings and empowerments would not be possible. In truth, when apostles, prophets, and tzaddikim initiate, bless, or empower, they are not the ones initiating, blessing, or empowering—it is the Holy One and Shekinah, the Holy Spirit who initiates, blesses, and empowers. What is given is not theirs—it is God's own.

The idea of us giving others what we have and wondering when they will come take what is their own occurs in twoness, not oneness, mistaking what and how it is given, as though there is a giver and receiver of such things other than the Holy One, Holy Shekinah. This is a common misunderstanding among novice initiates early in the journey. Likewise, one might think that the messengers can take back what was given, what in fact the Holy One, Holy Shekinah, has given. The messengers cannot, nor would they want to. The only thing they may remove is their angel, their direct presence with a person in order to let a person go their way if that person strays too far and wishes to depart from them. To do so honors that person's free will and choices, lovingly letting them go their way. So, whatever has been received is yours from the Holy One and cannot be taken away, though it is possible for you to disregard or discard it. Amen.

Verse 89

Yeshua said, "Why do you wash the outside of the cup? Don't you understand that the one who made the inside also made the outside?"

You want to clean the inside and the outside of the cup. You and your life are the dwelling of the Holy One. If the Messiah and Holy Spirit are to indwell you, you need to be pure and holy, clean and clear. In Genesis, it is said that a river flows out of Eden to water the garden, and the Kabbalah teaches that the river is light, the everflow of the divine attributes emerging from Wisdom-Hokmah, watering the garden of Malkut-Kingdom, the Holy Shekinah, the Divine Presence. That river of light is called the river of truth. You want to bathe in the river of truth daily and wash the inside and outside to be clean. Invoke the Name of God and pray and meditate every day. Be inward and commune with Christ, Messiah in you, open to the Holy Light and Spirit, the spiritual power that flows from the Names of God, the divine attributes—Sefirot—and let it flow through and clean you, change you, and make you like itself, like Christ and God, the Messiah and Holy One.

There is morning prayer, afternoon prayer, and evening prayer. In the morning is the invocation of the Holy One, Holy Shekinah into you and all your actions, all that will transpire in the day ahead. When beginning the new day, give praise and thanksgiving for the ongoing creation and revelation, for being renewed in the Holy One, reborn in the Holy Shekinah, Holy Spirit. Invoke the blessings of the Holy One, influxes of the divine attributes, and pray for what you and others need from the Eternal One. And beyond speaking, listen for the word, the guidance of the Lord within you—Adonai, Hayyah Yeshua—of what you are to do and what is to come, listening to the still small voice, the speaking silence, the One who makes the inside and outside. This is a way with morning prayers, which correspond with Mercy-Hesed, for all is new: You, your life, are new, renewed from the Holy One, Holy Shekinah.

Afternoon prayer and meditation are not as long or deep as in the morning. At this time, turn inward and go to the Lord within you: invoke the Name of the Lord, inquire of the Lord and see how you are doing, noting what is going well and not so well. Give praise and thanks for all the good, the blessings, and the good company of the powers of heaven and Holy Shekinah with you, and for Christ, Messiah indwelling you. Seek to mend anything that needs mending; seek guidance and redirection from the Lord, the Spirit, if you have fallen into negativity and error or have not done so well in some situation. It is a time to restore your true intention—to be in the love and the light—and to clarify your walk in the Lord, with the Lord, from the Lord, to the Lord, and for the Lord—Adonai, Yeshua, Yahweh. Afternoon prayers correspond with Severity-Gevurah because it is a time of discernment of what is good and true versus what is not, and the restoration of your true intention, the correction of your aim to be fully in the Holy One, Holy Shekinah.

At the conclusion of each day is evening prayer, invoking the Names of God, reflecting upon the day, and integrating what has happened, bringing it all into the Inner Light and Spirit with praise and thanks to the Eternal One. It is a time to go deep within and commune, just being in the Holy One, Holy Shekinah, in intimate nearness or oneness, aware that you live, move, and have your being in the Holy One in you, aware that you have neither been nor cannot ever be separate or apart from the Holy One. As with morning prayer, this is a time of seeking revelations of secrets, words of the Lord, and unveilings, self-disclosures of the Holy One and Holy Shekinah in your heart. A time of reintegration, revelation, and deep abiding in the Holy One, evening prayers correspond with Beauty-Tiferet, or Compassion-Rehamim.

We invoke often, pray and pray and pray, meditate deep, and seek to abide in inward communion. We pray without ceasing, being inward, living from within, making the outside like the inside, aligned and in harmony with the Holy One who makes the inside and outside. If we have faith and if we have love, we will invoke, pray, meditate, and worship the Holy One in spirit and truth. What sort of lover does not want time with their beloved, that they may love and be loved by them, sharing in intimate communion? It is the same with remembering and keeping the Holy Shabbat.

Bathe in the river of truth daily and be in the truth, be in the light, be in the love—be in the Holy One and remember the truth of the Absolute Oneness of the Eternal One, the Supreme. The Eternal is One—Yahweh Achad—there is no other, nothing else. The Holy One is in you, in all people, creatures, and things; you, all people, creatures, and things are in the Holy One. All emanates from the Holy One, and all returns to the Holy One; there is no other, there is nothing else. All that arises, appears, and transpires inward and outward is all the dance of the Holy Shekinah, the manifestation of the presence and power of the Eternal One. There is no other, there is the Holy One, Holy Shekinah, alone. Soak in these living and radiant waters of truth every day and invoke the Name often to remember and be in the truth, righteousness, light, love, and peace. Seek to walk in a sacred manner in your life, in the beauty and holiness of the Messiah and Eternal One.

Do not be idle-headed and mindless—instead be mindful and alert. You want the presence of awareness. You want to be awake and want to keep awake. You do not want your heart and mind occupied with inane, random, and meaningless thoughts anymore, let alone a mind filled with negative, dark thoughts, imaginations, and emotions that give way to wrong speech and wrong action. That is not you or who you are, nor is it the Way of faithful or spiritual people, let alone a divine-human, Christ, Messiah. You want to clean the inside and outside. You want to bathe in the river of truth, not the ramblings of the father of lies. You want to strive with the Holy Spirit to change and change and change, so that more and more you resemble Christ, Messiah—a human being of light—who more and more is revealed and appears as you. Immerse yourself fully in these living waters every day, all day long. Be in the love and the light, and you will be united and filled, no longer in separation and lack. Having received the Holy Light and Spirit, the Inner Light and Spirit in you is awakened—you already are, so keep awake! Amen.

Verse 90

Yeshua said, "Come to me, for my yoke is easy and my mastery gentle, and you will find rest for yourselves."

Although this saying appears in canonical gospels, this particular translation is somewhat awkward.

Essentially, this is a teaching of bringing your troubles, burdens, and everything to the Lord—Adonai, Hayyah Yeshua. In the Divine Life, you want to invoke the Lord, the Spirit, in all your affairs and activities and pray that the Lord, the Spirit, takes them up, moves with, in, and through you to accomplish good for yourself and those with whom you meet and interact in life. Whatever is happening or about to happen, you want to offer to the Lord, uplift in the Lord. The same is true for afterwards: give praise and thanks to the Lord for what has happened and been made manifest through the Spirit. Do this with all things, even if only with a simple, momentary, conscious intention to be from inwardness, from the Lord, the Spirit, to be in the love, to be in the light, even in seemingly small and insignificant matters.

The truth is that except when the Inner Light and Spirit reveals to us and gives us some sense of feeling, intuition, or foresight, we often neither know what is significant nor when the Spirit will move in a powerful way between us and others. We must therefore invoke, invite, and welcome the Holy Shekinah, Holy Spirit, into everything and all our doings, and be ready for the coming of the Lord in openness and sensitivity to the Spirit, the fiery intelligence in us. We need to let the Spirit lead us, move with, in, and through us in everything that we are doing, everywhere we go, with whomever we are present in the Lord, the Spirit.

In all that you do, you want to serve the kingdom of heaven. You want to serve the Lord and be from the Lord, to the Lord, and for the Lord to do what is good and true. You want to live according to your faith, love, and knowledge of the Holy One, Holy Shekinah in everything. If there is any-where in your life this does not seem possible, it is likely not good for you and would be better to leave behind and no longer engage in.

There is, of course, something deeper: If you must be the doer, then serve the Lord in your doing. Seek guidance from the Lord, the Spirit as to what is to be done; seek awareness of how and when you are to do it. But remember, as has already been shared, our ultimate intention is to rest in the Lord, to pass away in the Inner Light and Spirit. When we merge with the Lord, the Spirit, aware of the Holy One in all and all in the Holy One, regardless of outward appearances or manifestation of the Holy Shekinah, the Divine Presence, we are no longer the doer—the Lord, the Spirit does through us.

Having received the Holy Light and Spirit with Christ, Messiah being revealed in you, know that whenever there is a call or need at any time and place with anyone, as the Holy One, Holy Shekinah wills, any power of the Holy Spirit may be manifest with you. There is a great Living Presence and Power in you—the presence and power of the Most High—such that there can be prophecy and revelation, healings and the working of won-ders, all as the Spirit moves with, in, and through you.

In faith and love with inward cleaving, anything can happen anytime, anywhere with anyone: Anything is possible in the Messiah and Holy One. Who knows what the Holy One intends to do with you and through you? Be ready and willing! Amen.

Verse 91

They said to him, "Tell us who you are so that we may believe in you." He said to them, "You examine the face of heaven and earth but you have not come to know the face of the one who is in your presence, and you do not know how to examine this moment."

On one hand, this may be understood to be speaking of Yeshua Messiah. This could also be true in an encounter with any living apostle, prophet, or tzaddik when they engage with people and speak with power, with the Holy Spirit. Many might struggle with them as messengers, as holy women or men, or being aware of the Divine Presence with them, or the radiance of the Divine Presence. On the other hand, "You examine the face of heaven and earth" can be taken to mean others are looking for their Lord outside, not knowing or understanding that they need to be inward to seek and find the Lord within themselves.

These two interpretations are interconnected; they are one and the same. However, true recognition of messengers, tzaddikim, and the Divine Presence with them—let alone greater revelations of that Living Presence and its radiance and power—require some degree of inwardness, openness, and sensitivity to the Holy Light and Spirit, along with some sense or feeling of the Inner Light and Spirit, the indwelling presence and power of the Holy One within oneself. To believe in living messengers, tzaddikim, or divine-humans, you have to believe and have faith that the presence and power of the Divine can indeed be manifest through and as them, including yourself. The call of deeper inwardness is why souls seek a living teacher and guide, why they become disciples, companions, or followers of messengers, tzaddikim, and seek out mystical and gnostic communities of whatever faith or wisdom tradition resonates within themselves. They have faith or a sense that actual realization or enlightenment or direct experience of heaven and God is possible. They've likely had some hint of the possibility, glimpses, or tastes of this for themselves, along with intuitions of experiences that they may not have had as of yet. Because of this feeling, they have some sense of the Holy Shekinah, Divine Presence with a holy woman or man. Provided they have the faith of an open heart and mind, seekers who draw near and learn inward cleaving—how to go deeper within to find and know the Lord, the Inner Light and Spirit within themselves—may see, hear, feel, or sense the holiness, beauty, and radiance in another and therefore in themselves.

These moments of divine destiny, meeting a living messenger or tzaddik and entering into a sacred friendship with them, are what greater inwardness is all about: knowledge of the Divine in others as in oneself, the realization of that divinity within you as with them, your coming into being as a divine-human, or Christed one. But this recognition is realized according to your own call and anointing, your own way and works, and the divine action given to you in this life—you as who and what you are in the Holy One, Holy Shekinah, and who and what they are as a unique individual. In this regard, while you may share in the same Divine Presence, the same Holy Light and Spirit, as you come into being you will resemble another. Even if you share something of the same anointing and call or even the same works and mission, you will have your own way. As you both are, you will not resemble another. God does not repeat Godself in creation and revelation. But in self-realization, each is unique and individual, as is the manifestation of the Holy One, Holy Shekinah, the Messiah through themselves and as themselves.

The gnostic path and its community are all about living ones coming into being as living ones, which happens when living, anointed ones engage with one another in divine actions and spiritual works together. With devotions and worship of the Divine in spirit and truth, living ones are revelations and realizations of the enlightened and divine being, the Holy One. Amen.

Verse 92

Yeshua said, "Seek and you will find. In the past I did not tell you about the things you asked me. Now I am willing to tell you, but you do not seek them."

First are outer teachings—the outer gospel—then inner teachings, and the secret. At the outset, messengers, tzaddikim will not share the inner and secret teachings. They cannot. Even if they do, at the outset we cannot hear them. We do not really understand where they are coming from or the true and deeper meaning of their words, teachings, and revelations. While we are inward to some extent, we remain outward and tend to engage with them outward to outward, not inward to inward. Although they speak from inwardness to inwardness, we tend to hear in outwardness and so hear outer teachings when they speak with us, hearing through the many filters of our unenlightened mentalities, preconceptions, preconditions, and expectations.

To listen and hear the inner and the secret teachings, our inward communion needs to deepen and expand to give way to deeper spiritual and mystical experiences that open us to greater influxes of the Holy Light and Spirit. It is through deeper, mystical experiences of Christ and God, the Messiah and Holy One, that we come to the inner and secret. Because we have entered a shared experience of the Inner Light and Spirit, we hear the teachings and revelations of our holy tzaddik in a new light and a whole different context than before. Just as we inquire of the mysteries from our tzaddik and from more experienced, seasoned sisters and brothers in gnostic community, in the same way we seek and find our Lord within us as we invoke, pray, meditate, contemplate, and seek revelations of the secret mysteries from the Lord, the Spirit. Regarding inner teachings and the secret, tzaddikim tend to speak to those who know already, those who already have some experiential insight and understanding they then play upon as they share something more in the Spirit, along with corresponding light power.

There is an open secret to understand, however. Even in what sounds like the most simple and straightforward teachings for beginners, inner teachings are being given—the secret is there for those with understanding! If we are inward and deep within, we will see if we look, hear if we listen, and find the most awesome and wonderful revelations and illuminations in our hearts and minds. Indeed, from the Holy One and Messiah in them, in the love, in the light, it is all there. The Lord will be speaking to us in the flesh, and the Lord will be hearing in our flesh! Hallelu Yah! Praise the Lord!

It needs to be said that when you seek the revelation of secret mysteries from your holy tzaddik and the Lord within you, you need to learn how to wait patiently on the Spirit of the Lord—Ruach Yahweh—until it is time, all in due season. In this, you will learn how to inquire in a spacious, playful, loving way, free from vital demands and lust for answers; you will become willing to wait until it is time. God wills to reveal Godself, to reveal and give knowledge of the secret mysteries to you.

Understand that there is a time and place for the revelations of the inner and secret things. It needs to be in the power of the moment, and the Holy Shekinah, Holy Spirit needs to be moving in that way. The intention among mystics and gnostics is that inquiries and responses come from inwardness, from the Lord, the Spirit, not so much our ordinary intellect and reason. The truth is that the ordinary state of mind or surface consciousness is too dense and dull to comprehend the mysteries. When the Spirit is speaking in revelation, the ordinary mind weighs us down and can actually bring down the energy in an environment of sacred discourse. We want to listen and hear in faith and love with inward cleaving. Being uplifted into higher, more expanded states of mental consciousness, perhaps through grace, the supramental will flow through us. Amen.

Verse 93

"Do not give what is holy to dogs. They might throw it upon the manure pile. Do not throw pearls before swine. They might ... it ..."

The final line of the saying is fragmentary but basically echoes the same teaching that appears in canonical gospels, where it is said: "Do not throw your pearls before swine or they will trample them under their feet" (Matthew 7:6). We may naturally assume words to this effect were originally part of this saying.

This teaching is straightforward and obvious, though very harsh. There is no point in speaking about matters of faith and spirituality with people who are unfaithful and unspiritual, with no interest or desire in them let alone about what is holy, such as our mystical experiences and revelations of the secret mysteries of God in us. While we are to be in the love and be kind with all people, acting with compassion, we should neither impose our faith on them nor speak of such things with them but instead keep it to ourselves.

Truly, to speak of such things or speak the word of God with power requires a listener to have some desire to hear it. That desire needs to be in and from the Spirit, with the Spirit leading and inspiring us to share and speak of the kingdom of heaven and God.

The terms "pigs" and "beasts of the field" refer to those living in bestial nature; they are the mixed multitude bound up in the ways of unenlightened society, who aren't faithful, let alone spiritual. Generally speaking, it is the luminous among the faithful and the spiritual with whom mystics and gnostics will share teachings and the word of the Lord with power. In scripture, dogs are often parallel with sorcerers, soothsaying psychics, and false prophets. These are people who are entangled with the impure and dark forces of the Other Side, the archonic and demonic, who, in giving strange and false teachings, lead many into greater ignorance, error, and bondage, they who pervert true spiritual teachings, revelations, and secret wisdom to serve their own ends. We merely need to consider the gross perversions of the Holy Kabbalah in the new-age movement and modern occultism, ceremonial magic, and much of so-called Western esotericism. They are neither teachings of faith, love, and devotion nor the result of actual spiritual or supernal realization. Except for those individuals who come to see the error of their ways and actively leave them behind in search of true knowledge of God the True Light, it is very unwise to give teachings and initiation to those involved in such falsehood.

It is not a pleasant saying, but it is very true. We need to take this guardianship to heart and bear in mind the times we live in; misinformation, deception, and conspiracy theories abound and are becoming the norm, accepted by too many. God help us, and God have mercy! Amen.

Verse 94

Yeshua said, "One who seeks will find. For one who knocks, it will be opened."

If we seek we will find, certainly so! If we invoke, pray, and meditate on a regular basis in an inward communion, Christ, Messiah will be revealed in us, and the Inner Light and Spirit will be known to us. As we progress with the Spirit in a spiritual and supernal realization, the inner and secret teachings of the gospel will be disclosed to us. Perhaps in being inward, invoking, praying, and meditating, spiritual influxes might come very soon; perhaps right away or in a few days. But more often, influxes come with time: weeks, months, and even years. If you go seeking the Lord within you, you need to be willing to wait upon the Spirit of the Lord; as the second saying of Thomas teaches, continue seeking until you find. Do not give up—keep at it, and if possible, get involved in an anointed community to be in the Divine Presence with others, receive a true spiritual education of teachings and practices, and receive guidance and support in your spiritual life and practice.

At the same time, remember what was taught earlier in this gospel: You need to learn to pray in oneness, not twoness, and be deeply inward as is the Way of the gnostic path. You need to invoke, pray, and meditate in faith and love. With your mind, heart, and life, you need to cleave to the Holy One and seek knowledge of the Holy One, Holy Shekinah, through direct spiritual and mystical experience inside and outside. As the Apostle James teaches, if there is doubt or doublemindedness, we cannot expect to receive anything from heaven and God. But if there is faith and cleaving free of doubt, we will receive all that we ask for and more. Things we do not know to ask for but that the Holy One intends for us will be our own.

Something to know about light transmission and the passing of the Spirit: To experience this and integrate what you have received, you must be inward and invoke, pray and meditate daily. You need to cultivate a life of true prayer and meditation, an actual spiritual life and practice. Otherwise, though you may be blessed to experience something of the light transmission in glimpses or tastes as it were, you will neither receive nor integrate what you receive, if you remain in separation and lack. Likewise, though you may be blessed to find a tzaddik, there will be little they can do to help you if you are not helping yourself, seeking until you find, engaging in devotions daily, and keeping Shabbat. An actual spiritual or supernal realization requires an actual spiritual life and practice, not just thinking and talking about it, but being and acting in spirituality, faith, and love, co-laboring with the Holy Spirit for greater and greater self-transformation and self-realization in the Sun of God.

Remember: Devotions themselves are realization. Good works themselves are realization. The spiritual life and practice itself is realization. If you are faithful and keep at it, your realization will unfold and manifest in your experience.

There is no goal but the path; take the goal as the path. This is a teaching of the gnostic path. Realization, enlightenment, is living the Life Divine itself. Taking the goal as the path is invocation, prayer, meditation; it is living in oneness, unity, and fullness and not twoness, separation, and lack. At the outset, this is done in faith. But with time and experience, this is done in awareness, knowledge.

Until there is seeking and finding, there are two, not One. Seek, never doubting that you will find. Know that the one who is seeking is the one who is sought. Amen.

Verse 95

Yeshua said, "If you have money, do not lend it at interest, but give
it to someone from whom you will not get it back."

We have spoken of the mentality of business in unenlightened society:
Taking for oneself more than one gives is the direct expression and mentality of the evil inclination—*sitra ahara*—the desire to receive for oneself
alone, often at the expense of others. By its nature, it is bestial and violent.
Mahatma Gandhi observed that poverty is the worst form of violence and
he was right. Poverty is the price of doing business in unenlightened society, the product of lust and greed in gross materialism and consumerism in
which a relative few become extremely wealthy and powerful, while vast
numbers of people live in or near poverty. Unenlightened business is completely wicked, a great evil in the world that causes immeasurable sorrow
and suffering for billions of people in every generation.

In this verse, Yeshua is saying do not be like the worldly business person—be and do the opposite and seek to give as much as you receive. If
you are willing, seek to give more than you receive: seek to give your all to
the Divine Life.

Yeshua is talking about being the light and love in a most straightforward and practical way. Consider an ordinary life example: If a person had
extra money and a loved one needed a loan, they would not charge them
interest, would they? Likewise, if seeing someone in desperate need who
would not be able to pay anything back, many good-hearted people who
have extra money would give the needed funds, wouldn't they? Yeshua
is teaching that this way of tending to the needs of others by ordinary,
good-hearted people is the baseline or minimum among truly faithful and
spiritual people. When we go beyond, and are in the love and the light,
quite naturally such loving kindness and charity will expand beyond the
minimum.

Recall earlier in the Gospel of Thomas that Yeshua taught his disciples that giving charity as a religious obligation or to appear as good and righteous in the eyes of others—that is, in twoness, not love or oneness—could cause them spiritual harm. Here, however, he is calling for charity in love, in oneness, from unity and fullness, no giver, no receiver, all in the Holy One, Holy Shekinah. If you know the Lord within you, that God is in you and all people and you are called from the Lord, the Spirit to love someone and give them what they need, it will be loving God and giving to God: God giving to God, neither giver nor receiver. Moreover, all that you are and all that you have are from God; when you give, it is in truth God who is giving through you. Often what is given to us is for others. It is not our own, but belongs to God. In this play of giving and receiving, the more one gives, the more one receives. You will discover a perpetual, continual flow of true abundance and good fortune—there is always enough. God provides!

Being in the love and the light, this is what we experience in giving and self-offering on all levels—material, psychic, and spiritual. In the love, it is all an offering to the Holy One, loving the Holy One.

How can we finite, mortal, earthly beings love and cleave to the Infinite and Eternal One? In that we are all emanations of the Holy and Eternal One—One from One—it is through loving one another, as Adonai Yeshua taught us to do and be with one another. As Spirit-filled people, this is our noble ideal for which we strive. It is our inmost heart's desire, our holy intention to engage in a total and complete self-offering to the Holy One, Holy Shekinah, passing away in the Holy One, returning to be One.

When you give yourself completely to God, God gives Godself completely to you. The Sun of God, the fullness of the Holy Light and Spirit, is realized in you and revealed through you! Amen.

Verse 96

Yeshua said, "The Father's kingdom is like a woman who took a little yeast, hid it in dough, and made large loaves of bread. Whoever has ears should hear."

In the gnostic teachings of our tradition and our Christian Kabbalah, God the Father corresponds with the transcendent and hidden aspects of the Divine, while God the Mother corresponds with the immanent and revealed aspects of the Divine. The Father and Mother are the Holy One—One Divinity—not two, not as a god and goddess. As much as we speak of the Holy One as Father and Son, so we speak of the Holy One as Mother and Daughter. What is revealed and known of the Father is the Mother and the Son and Daughter—Bridegroom and Holy Bride. So it is said in our oral tradition, it is your mother who shows you the face of your father and reveals who your father is. Without her, there is no knowing your father. Yeshua speaking here of the kingdom of heaven as a woman brings this to mind among Sophian Gnostics, very much so!

It is through the Mother, the immanent presence and power of God, that creation and revelation happens. Being immanent, involved, the Mother corresponds with God in all things. As has been shared previously, there is a holy spark of the Infinite Light within all things; the very existence of all things, their power, is a manifestation of the Mother Spirit, the Holy Spirit, hidden in them. So it may be said that this is the yeast within creatures and creation as the dough. Yeast, of course, is what makes dough rise and expand. In a similar way, the holy spark and the power of the Spirit imbued within all things and all creatures throughout creation is a drive or the impulse for the emergence and evolution of life toward greater self-awareness and intelligence. At first, the holy spark is a completely unconsciousness impulse. Then it becomes manifest in various gradations of semiconsciousness, more or less, until it becomes fully aware, able to consciously strive to evolve into the highest of life: divine or enlightened being, conscious union with the Eternal One, conscious reintegration with the Infinite Light.

So while it may be said that there is a revelation of the kingdom of heaven from above, in fact the reality and experience of the kingdom of heaven is that it emerges from within creatures and creation, in self-aware and intelligent life—human beings. This is the truth, reality of Christ, Messiah, the Divine Human. There is, indeed, an experience of the reception of the Holy Light and Spirit that awakens the Inner Light and Spirit, revealing Christ, Messiah in us, the kingdom of heaven within and all around us. But then Christ, Messiah—the kingdom of heaven—rises up and emerges, expands, from within us, that star of heaven shining within us, the full power of the Holy Spirit being manifest with, in, and through us.

This is the emergence of a new humanity that is something more than spiritual humanity—it is a humanity that is supernal and divine, so that not only are we to strive with the Spirit to be Christlike but to become Christ, Messiah—divine-humans. Yeshua Messiah was the firstborn of this new evolution into the Life Divine: With Mirya the Magdala, he opened the Way for us to come into being as supernal and divine humans. Yeshua Messiah, Mirya the Magdala, and those resurrected and ascended with them correspond with the highest of life that worlds of creation seek to reach.

When speaking of creation in our gnostic lineage and tradition, it is not an event of the past, but is understood to be ongoing, a creative evolution guided by a divine fiery intelligence, the Holy Spirit. Innate to creative evolution is the ongoing revelation, realization, and embodiment of the Divine, the Eternal One, the Infinite Light. The very nature of the second coming of Christ, Messiah in glory is this revelation and realization happening with, in, and through many souls, many people. Amen.

Verse 97

> Yeshua said, "The Father's kingdom is like a woman who was carrying a jar of meal. While she was walking along a distant road, the handle broke and meal spilled behind her along the road. She did not know it. She noticed no problem. When she reached her house, she put the jar down and found it empty."

This is quite the curious metaphor of the kingdom of heaven following the previous one; here, the woman is unaware and in the end has nothing, quite the contrast to the abundance of large loaves of sweet bread. Yet as pointed out, creative evolution begins in a subconscious way like ordinary dreams and emerges from a state of unconscious union from primordial and universal ignorance that is in effect, not union but unconscious oblivion. Consider how long it was from the Big Bang to now until the stars, galaxies, and planets were formed. Among these planets, how long was it before life emerged, let alone self-aware, intelligent life?

First were all manner of cosmic forces generating our sun and planets. From Earth's evolution emerged life in mineral, vegetable, animal, and more or less intelligent, human forms. As humans further evolved in self-awareness, they were able to receive revelations of the Holy One, remember their origin, and realize a conscious union with their source: Primordial and Supernal Being, the Infinite Light, Radiant Nothingness. Indeed, how long has humanity still remained unconscious or at best semiconscious? Yet, Christ, Messiah has come, appeared in this world, and is emerging from it and thus in other worlds of this universe as well. Christ, Messiah has emerged, is emerging, and will emerge in this world and other worlds, existing before, simultaneously with, and long after the world of this universe.

Among the various gnostic scriptures suggesting this mystery is one called *Pistis Sophia*, or "Faith-Wisdom." This gospel tells a story of the fall and redemption of Sophia, the divine personification of the outermost emanation of the True Light, the daughter of the Virgin of Light. She was unaware of the True Light in herself and adored that Absolute Light from afar, as though she was separate from it and lacking. From her light power reflected in the surface of the primordial waters, a chief archon—the demiurge, half-maker—came to life, a distortion of Pistis Sophia's reflection from below the surface of those waters.

Mimicking the Pleroma of Light beyond, the demiurge emanated and created other archons, all of which were like itself, impure and dark manifestations of her power. As the story goes, they were jealous of her love for the True Light and wanted her for themselves to have a greater existence with greater dominion and power. As she was unaware in separation and lack, the demiurge and archons devised a scheme to trick Pistis Sophia to descend into the impure darkness of matter and realms outside of the Pleroma: they made a false copy of the True Light below, and when she was deceived by the false light and descended to join with it, the demiurge and archons accosted her, bound her to their dominion, and stole her light power for themselves.

The story of this woman with a jar of meal is a simpler presentation of the same great mystery of how power of the True Divine becomes bound up in impure, lesser divinities and spiritual forces, even in the creatures and forces of creation. It is completely parallel with the story of Pistis Sophia and was likely an early form of this teaching among original Christians.

Following the story of Pistis Sophia's fall in ignorance and her bondage is the story of her redemption. She begins to awaken, remember herself, and seek her salvation—her return to the Pleroma of Light, unification with her divine consort, whom she did not know before—the Christ. She engages in thirteen cycles of repentance, turning, returning, going within herself and invoking the presence and power of the Christ to bring about her liberation, to redeem herself. In fruition she is unified with Christ, realizes herself inseparable with the True Light, and so is united and filled, exalted beyond her former station with all of her light power restored to her. She is made manifest in the full glory and power of the Infinite and Eternal One.

Pistis Sophia corresponds with the feminine aspect of the One Soul asleep and dreaming, while Christ corresponds with the masculine aspect that remains ever awake, who has never slept. As such, she represents all living spirits and souls bound up in the matrix of creation and the impure and dark spiritual forces within and behind, even the gilgulim—the potentially endless rounds of reincarnation.

Her story is our story. She is the pure emanation of the True Light, inseparable from Christ—the Anointing—so are we, so is our soul. Like her, as we repent, return, reintegrate, and come to know the presence and power of Christ in us—the Holy Light and Spirit—so are we redeemed, united, and filled, resurrected and ascended with Christ—enlightened and liberated.

As we go inward, deep within, ingathered in the love and light of Christ and God, progressively we take back our light power, the sparks of our soul from the archonic and demonic forces of the unenlightened societies of this world, to whom we have given our light power in ignorance, in the illusion of separation and lack. We restore that light to the Eternal One and reintegrate those sparks with the Infinite Light. We experience an Integral Self-realization in Christ, Messiah, the realization of the Divine Self, the Divine I Am, inseparable from the Eternal One, the Endless Light. This is true salvation as experienced and known among Gnostic Christians. Amen.

Verse 98

Yeshua said, "That Father's kingdom is like a person who wanted to put someone powerful to death. While at home, he thrust his sword into a wall to find out whether his hand would go in. Then he killed the powerful person."

Although there are numerous interpretations of this saying, there is one that is most useful in our contemplations, one the Spirit leads me to share.

As we know, first there was the giving of the law with Moses, then supernal grace through Yeshua. From the first testament—Torah—to the second testament—Gospel—it is all one progressive revelation of the Holy One, Holy Shekinah, not two different gods as some ignorant, dualistic gnostic schools would propose. The apparent distinction and difference between the first and second testaments or cycles of revelation is in the collective consciousness of humankind and the level of realization in those receiving the revelation of the Eternal One—Yahweh. The distinction and difference are not in the Eternal One but in people: states of soul, consciousness, and mind.

Generally speaking, until Yohanan and Yeshua appeared, all revelations occurred in mental consciousness as spiritual realization—that is, in separation and dualism more or less. This is the giving of the law with no means of removing sin, or the cessation of karma, in a play of cause and effect. With Yohanan and Yeshua was the emergence of supramental, supernal realization in oneness, conscious union, nonduality, no longer an experience of the Holy One in separation and judgment. As souls enter this realization of oneness, it is in complete mercy, compassion, forgiveness, the cessation of karma—grace. A soul who surrenders feeling apparently separate from the Holy One passes away and returns to be One. They are no longer two, no longer other than the Holy One, Holy Shekinah.

However, the giving of the law was integral to the coming of Christ, Messiah, facilitating an evolution of the collective consciousness toward the awareness and realization of the single Supreme Being—the Eternal One, primordial and supernal—within all spiritual forces, behind all that arises, appears, and transpires in creation. While growing in states of nearness, a collective desire stirred for knowledge of the Supreme, opening to greater states of oneness, even conscious union. These evolutions generated the conditions for the emergence of Christ, Messiah within humanity, within human consciousness. This process reflects from the start how self-awareness and intelligent life emerged: revelations of enlightenment or God began to facilitate and drive an evolution in which humans progressively became more and more aware and intelligent as conscious agents in their evolution, intending and choosing far greater divine and supernal possibilities.

While many apostles and disciples who were with Yeshua and Mirya experienced supernal realization and were truly gnostic, there were many who remained in a spiritual realization, including some of the apostles and prophets who were among the original followers of the Way. The first coming of Christ, Messiah was the initial emergence, the dawn of supramental, supernal consciousness—Christ or God Consciousness—that was fully divine and fully human, a new divine and supernal humanity. Quite naturally, while the Supernal Light and Eternal Spirit was seeded in the spiritual ones who would eventually bear its fruit, many were not ready for the evolutionary leap, neither willing nor able to complete the passing away and great transformation that happens in supernal realization.

In this world, in any given generation, this will always be true to some degree. There are many different levels of psychic and spiritual development and evolution in humankind. Souls are at different points in their journey of coming into being.

On account of many remaining in the spiritual realization, as has become very self-evident, much of Christianity fell back into bondage under the law with all manner of religious rules and regulations in fear of God's judgment rather than God's love, complete grace, and supernal mercy. But today we are living in the second coming of Christ, Messiah in glory, in a cloud of witnesses with his angels. Parallel with the cycles of the end times is a greater movement of supernal realization underway. With Moses and Yeshua, there was a single, central voice of a prophet or apostle. In these times, there are many diverse voices and messengers who are not centralized in the same way in the first coming of Christ, Messiah, not at all! In grace and compassion, the Holy One, Holy Shekinah is reaching out through many messengers to ingather many more souls in these very challenging times.

There have been, are now, and will be many messengers of the supernal realization, many souls taken up with them through grace into the supramental, supernal consciousness—Messianic Consciousness. This is happening among various people of the faiths and wisdom traditions of this world and in various appearances and forms, but all reveal the same Supernal Truth and Light. There is a third testament—a new gospel—being revealed among us that goes beyond the second testament, the Gospel, just as the second testament went beyond the first, the Torah. Just as the Eternal One is the same within and behind the first and second testaments, so is the Eternal One, Eternal Messiah the same within and behind the second and third testaments; however, the third is a greater progress of the ongoing revelation and realization of the Divine.

As the first coming was a revelation of God as the Father and Son, so now in the second coming is a revelation of God as the Mother and Daughter. Because there are many voices and messengers in the second coming, the third testament is a weave of testaments, each holding the entirety of the word of the Eternal Messiah, Eternal One spoken in supernal grace and supernal love, each in the symbolic and mystical language of the messenger and their people, resonant with those souls that they are to ingather. As with us in a language of Christian Gnostics, Christian Kabbalah, so with other tongues speaking of this realization of unity and fullness—oneness, conscious union, the Non-Dual Truth.

It could be said that the first coming was the trying of the hand and the second coming is the actual striking of the blow completing this divine action, revelation, and realization of the True Divine, True Enlightenment, in the world. Amen.

Verse 99

The disciples said to him, "Your brothers and mother are stand-ing outside." He said to them, "Those here who do the will of my Father are my brothers and my mother. They will enter my Father's kingdom."

This is the way it is with apostles, prophets, tzaddikim: their people, their community is their enlightened family, those who live in the light and the love and so are sons and daughters of light, sons and daughters of God, the family of God. If there are earthly relatives who are ingathered, as some of Yeshua's were, then they are part of their heavenly family; if not, they are not. Their entire focus is upon the Holy One, Holy Shekinah and their people who are given to them to gather in. Nothing else in the world is their business or concern, nothing at all!

It is just as true of the messengers as it is of every woman or man reborn from above, from the Pleroma of Light and the Holy One, Holy Shekinah. As Adonai Yeshua taught in John, what is born of the flesh is flesh, but what is born of living water and the Spirit is spiritual, and more so is supernal and divine. They are sons and daughters of light ordained in a royal priesthood, having been born of a royal family and being of royal blood: sons and daughters of God in the family of God. They are a holy and chosen people not of this world or the flesh but of the kingdom of heaven—the Pleroma of Light. Therefore, they walk in a sacred manner, in the beauty and holiness of the Christ Presence, the Shekinah of Messiah— the Shekinah of the Eternal One.

Receiving the Holy Light and Spirit, you are in the family of God. If you are outside, come inside; be inward and open to the Holy Light and Spirit to be reborn from above and within. Be united and filled, be ingathered into anointed community—the family of God. Anyone who truly desires it, and has faith and love, and invokes can receive the Holy Light and Spirit.

Anyone who seeks will find, anyone who knocks will be let inside, ingathered. This supernal grace is present for everybody and anybody who wants it. No one is excluded except those who exclude themselves. No one is left outside except those who choose to live outside, unwilling to go inside. As Yeshua teaches in the Secret Book of James, you need to acquire grace for yourselves: Open to the Holy Light and Spirit, abide in inward communion, and live in the love and the light. Be the love, be the light.

There are no rules or regulations to follow; just be inside, living in the love and the light. You either are or you are not. Living in the love, living in the light, fulfills all commandments of the law in their spiritual and supernal essence. All knowledge, understanding, and wisdom; all righteousness and truth; all divine attributes, powers, actions are in the light and love of Messiah—everything good and true.

Just be in the love and the light. Be and do what is good and true: Do not do what you hate. Follow your heart, and the Lord, the Spirit dwelling in it, and therefore in the family of God, the True Light.

As we know, Mother Miriam and Yeshua's brothers and sisters were in his enlightened family, the Holy Mother sharing in the very same supernal realization. They were free to come, go, and draw near as they wished with no obstruction, but Yeshua chose to give this teaching: In the anointed community, enlightened family—the Family of God—all are equal as they are in the Messiah and Eternal One. If there is a distinction or difference from one to another, it is the extent to which they are in the light and love, and thus are being and doing the will of the Eternal One. Amen.

Verse 100

They showed him a gold coin and said to him, "Caesar's people demand taxes from us." He said to them, "Give Caesar the things that are Caesar's, give God the things that are God's, and give me what is mine."

The heads of state, governments of nations, and their militaries, establishments, and hierarchies stratifying regional and local communities are all expressions of archonic influences and forces in the world. Likewise, large corporations, industries, influential secular and religious institutions of the world, and the wealthy, powerful, and famous are all archonic, generally speaking. Virtually all centers of power in the unenlightened society tend to be archonic. It is not as simple as speaking of archons as dark and evil, though they can be. Rather, they are impure and admixed powers that serve their own self-interests. At times and in some circumstances, they can be aligned and in harmony with the Divine but at others, they can be aligned with demonic forces and the satan, opposed to the Divine. Most often, archons are engaged in *both* what is good and true, as well as what is evil and false.

Looking into gnostic scriptures, you will find that they speak more about the archonic than the demonic and evil. When we consider the archonic influences within the world and the unenlightened people structuring its societies, it is archonic forces that pose the greatest temptations and barriers to souls seeking enlightenment or return to God. While dark and hostile forces—the demonic—also assault and prevent many from becoming enlightened and liberated, it is the archons more than the demons—spiritual forces of impurity bound up in the ignorance, separation, and lack—that keep souls in ignorance and bondage. While seeming good and true, many souls get caught up in archonic influences, unaware of what entangles them and ignorant to what they are doing. On the other hand, the outright demonic and evil, which is more obvious in its opposition to enlightenment and the Divine, is typically not so attractive to people. Being mad beyond belief, demons take perverse delight in the complete corruption, death, and destruction of anything and everything. In order to preserve their own dominions, archons tend to rise against demonic forces to subjugate and vanquish them. In this regard, you may note that Yeshua says nothing about giving way to demons; if demonic forces were given what is their own, it would be subjugation—binding and banishing—and destruction.

There is no living in this world separate and apart from unenlightened society and archons. As it is, this is an archonic realm. To acquire what is essential and necessary for life in this world, we must interact with archonic powers and realms; there is no avoiding it. We are to give archons what is their own: the flesh and its toils along with the most essential necessities that existence demands. But our soul belongs to God and is to be returned to God, ingathered to God. As Yeshua lives in us, as Christ, Messiah indwells us, so does our person and life belong to the Messiah. We are given to the Messiah and Holy Spirit to live and to be revealed, realized, and made manifest through us.

As is the Way of the messengers—apostles, prophets, tzaddikim—we are to give to each what is their own and receive what is our own, from the Holy One, the Messiah, and even the archons. So too is it with all people and creatures we encounter and interact with in life: we are to give what is good to give. To each we are to give what is their own, praying for their pacification and enrichment, their happiness and satisfaction, and their ultimate fulfillment—their eventual enlightenment and liberation. This is being in the light and the love with all in heaven and on earth. Amen.

Verse 101

Yeshua said, "Those who do not hate their father and mother as I do cannot be my disciples, and those who do not love their father and mother as I do cannot be my disciples. For my mother … but my true mother gave me life."

When you turn to the Eternal One and go inside, deep within, you turn away from creatures and creation. You have no desire for them nor do you cleave to them; you desire the Eternal One, only the Eternal One, and you cleave to the Eternal One, the Messiah within you, and no other, nothing else in heaven or on earth. When you are deep within, in the Eternal One, Eternal Now, you are no longer in space-time, you no longer see creatures and creation, you only see the Holy One, you only listen to the Holy One. You do not see or hear anyone else, only the image of the Holy One, only the voice of the Holy One, and you feel the living presence of the Holy One—Shekinah—in all people, all creatures, all things.

Your earthly father and mother are nothing. Your Father and Mother is the Holy One, Holy Shekinah, and the same is true with all your relations and all people and creatures—they are nothing. There is the Holy One and the Holy One alone—no you or them, only the Eternal Messiah, the Eternal One appearing, speaking, and touching you with the Living Presence, Living Spirit. The Living Presence touches the Living Presence in the "not-you," the Shekinah of the Messiah, the Shekinah of the Eternal One.

In the Messiah, the Holy One, you have nothing to do with things outward or outside, only inward, inside. There is nothing outward to cleave to, nothing real apart from what is inward, so you cleave to what is inward, inside you, all people, creatures, and things. You cleave to the Messiah and Holy One, having faith and love, aware there is nothing else that is real, no other Reality other than the Pleroma of Light—Infinite Light, Endless Love. So there is love for the Holy One, the Holy One in all, the All-In-All.

What else can I say? What else matters? What else is there to talk about? There is nothing else, nothing at all!

This is the truth known in the heart of your soul, your holy soul—*neshamah*—whether you are aware of it or not. Your holy soul in you knows this truth. If you go deep within, not outward, into the heart of your soul, into your holy soul, into yourself—the Messiah and Holy One—you will know and understand that in yourself as yourself, in others as themselves, you will have discovered the Holy One—the secret. If and when the secret is known inward, realized inward, the inside and outside will join as one, all in the Holy One, the Holy One in all.

Now you know God in everyone and everything. You know everyone and everything as it is in God. It is all seen in its inwardness, no longer in outwardness. In everyone you see the face and image of God, you hear the voice of God, and feel the living presence of God. Just as God is being revealed to you inside, in the heart of your soul, so it is outside, in everyone and everything, in all that is happening moment to moment. Revelation and realization are happening all the time, everywhere. God is giving Godself to you all the time, in everything. You see, hear, and feel this; with awareness, you see creatures and creation, the outward and outside. As you are aware of people, creatures, things as they are in God and God in them, so are you also aware of them as they are in themselves, the outwardness, the outside. There is love, compassion, forgiveness, and kindness.

Because you know the truth, you know that many are as yet caught up in ignorance, separation, and lack, bound up on the outside in outwardness, unable and unwilling to be inward. They know neither themselves, nor the Holy One, Holy Shekinah. They know neither themselves nor what they are doing; they are not being themselves. Knowing this, have mercy for them instead of judgment. Have compassion and an open heart, so that you may forgive them, and be kind. You hold all in your heart, in the Holy One, Holy Shekinah and desire true good for them: deliverance, healing, and their salvation, realization, enlightenment, and liberation. Invoke and pray and meditate on behalf of all as you do for yourself. You know in the Holy One that they are you and you are they. You give to each what is good to give, what is their own. You give to each whatever good they desire and are willing to receive, loving them as you can, having mercy and compassion for them. You are in the light and the love, being light and love.

As you might imagine, it is the same with angels, archons, and demons: All are known first in inwardness then in outwardness. Seeing, hearing, and feeling in this inward way, you, your soul, is immune to the influences of the archonic forces and the assaults of demonic forces—you are free of them! You only listen to the voice of the Holy One, Messiah, Holy Spirit and know that they are nothing, separate and apart in themselves from the Holy One, Holy Shekinah.

Deeply inward, you are inseparable from the Holy One, Holy Shekinah. You are lacking nothing, nothing at all! Go look and see, listen and hear, and feel. Seek and you will find! Amen.

Verse 102

Yeshua said, "Shame on the Pharisees. They are like a dog sleeping in the cattle manger. [They] do not eat or let the cattle eat."

Sadducees and Pharisees were the Jewish religious authorities of the day, but the same is true of most religious authorities and scholars in any age and religious faith. They teach man-made doctrines, performing religious rites and rituals of those doctrines. Never having been in inwardness, they remain in outwardness and discourage others from being insiders or being inward. If a person is outward and speaking or preaching to outwardness in others, what is spoken are their words, speculations, and opinions, not a speaking of the Holy Spirit or the word of God with power. This is the great difficulty in much of organized religion. Very often those preaching and teaching have little, if any, direct experience of what is being spoken about; there is no inwardness, no reception of the Holy Light and Spirit, and no experience of the revelation and realization of enlightenment or the Divine. Many religious leaders do not even believe true mystical experience is possible or believe it is valid when it happens, let alone the gnostic experience of full enlightenment or conscious union with the Divine. And yet, ironically, deep mystical and gnostic experience was at the heart of the scriptures from which they preach and teach, all of them arising from revelations and realizations of enlightenment, of the Divine.

All these outward religious authorities have is the scriptures outside with little or no direct experience of what the scriptures are speaking about inside. This is very unfortunate, very sad. Many are well-meaning but have no understanding of how to enter into the direct experience of revelation and realization. Without revelation, they are unable to teach, guide, or help facilitate the realization of others or themselves.

In Messiah Yeshua and the Holy Bride, the Magdala, we are called to the way of the apostles and prophets: We are called to a mystical spirituality of direct experience, revelation, and realization in Christ, Messiah—the Sun of God—the light, the love. Messengers are appearing in the world today to remind us who we truly are in Christ, Messiah, bearing light transmission and the Holy Spirit so that the inner Christ, Messiah may be revealed and realized though us and as us. And yes, in the current outpouring of the Supernal Light and Eternal Spirit, the anointing of the Holy Light and Spirit can also come upon religious leaders of true faith who are in the outer and unspiritual church, so that they too may come into being as a messenger. Likewise, the outpouring of the Spirit comes upon people of faith and love who, in those congregations, have a natural, inward cleaving so that they become insiders, being ingathered by the Spirit. Supernal grace abounds!

This is why in Thomas as well as canonical gospels, Yeshua often rebukes and denounces religious authorities and institutions. He had no intention of creating a new religion or religious doctrine for that matter; he wanted to initiate a spiritual movement. He shared spiritual teachings born of revelation and realization and shared an initiation—light transmission and passing of the Holy Spirit—so that people could have a spirituality of direct experience and knowledge of heaven and God. He revealed the Inner Light and Spirit—the holy soul—within people, revealing who and what they are in the Eternal One and Shekinah. He taught his people, disciples, and followers how to abide in direct, inward communion with the Holy One, Holy Shekinah just as the apostles and prophets did before them. He taught a mystical and gnostic spirituality.

Where religion climaxes and ends, mysticism and gnosticism begin. By nature, the birth of a mystic—let alone the emergence of a gnostic—carries people beyond religion and religious doctrines into an experience of actual revelation and realization of the Divine in true knowledge of the Divine with understanding and wisdom. In truth, this was the good news, the gospel, that Yeshua preached. Those who believed, had faith, and drew near he initiated, blessed, and empowered, imparting the Holy Light and Spirit. He taught them how to abide inward in communion with Christ, Messiah in their hearts, the Holy One, Holy Shekinah inside them and outside them, all in the Holy One. Once established in an inward communion, there is no need for a religious doctrine: We have the indwelling Messiah and Holy Spirit—the Spirit of Truth—as our teacher and guide as we are guided by the light and love of Christ, Messiah.

This is the Way of true anointed community—gnostic community. Amen.

Verse 103

Yeshua said, "Blessings on you if you know where the robbers will enter so you can wake up, rouse your estate, and arm yourself before they break in."

Passages like this, parallel with teachings in the Gospel of Philip, make clear that there are powers or psychic and spiritual forces that are opposed to the kingdom of heaven—Pleroma of Light. These powers neither want souls to enter the kingdom nor to be enlightened and liberated. These archonic and demonic kinds of spiritual forces want to keep souls in bondage to their dominions, steal the light power and life force from souls for themselves. Spiritually and energetically, they in effect feed off of souls.

As the Apostle Paul taught, our struggle in this world is not against flesh and blood but archonic and demonic spiritual forces established in celestial places: astral and spiritual realms of the inner dimensions. Just as Christ, Messiah appears through us, the Holy Light and Spirit embodied in us and the powers of heaven manifest through us, so do archonic and demonic powers manifest their influence and intentions through people of the unenlightened society.

Made in the image and likeness of God—Elohim—the very nature of human beings and their souls is to be conduits, channels, vehicles for the actualization and realization of spiritual forces. If not in the love and the light, then in the impurity, darkness, and fire. Rather than the Holy Shekinah, Holy Spirit and powers of heaven, people manifest archonic and demonic forces of the Other Side in the world.

Because of the influence and power of these deceptive, impure, and dark forces, as Philip points out, good and evil become sorely confused in the hearts and minds of many in the unenlightened society. Often, good is called evil and evil is called good; people often enact wickedness and evil, believing it to be good and righteous. Consider the plight of fundamentalism in religion and all the great and unimaginable evil, sorrow, and suffering it has manifested in the world over the ages. It is the most glaring example of all, for in the name of God, what can only be called works of satan or the antichrist have been and are being done. It is not in the love or light of the Eternal One; it is the complete opposite. The same is true in many other ways in the world and unenlightened society: What is normalized and called good is actually various degrees of impurity, darkness, and evil.

We face a great problem in this world. Quite frankly, to seek enlightenment, return to God, and reintegrate with the Infinite Light is something like swimming upstream against powerful currents of psychic and spiritual forces with strong predators along the way. According to gnostic teachings and the Holy Kabbalah, if souls do not become realized and liberated from this downward, backward pull in life, they will encounter it in the afterlife as well; they will be unable to ascend or pass into the Pleroma of Light and reintegrate with the Eternal One—the Infinite Light, Radiant Nothingness.

Philip also teaches that those who put on the perfect light can neither be seen by these forces nor be touched, restrained, attacked, or harmed in any way. As they are resurrected and ascended in this life, so they will be in the afterlife. The perfect light is said to be with those who are in the bridal chamber, those who in love pass away and merge with the Sun of the Eternal One whom we call Christ, Messiah. The term "bridal chamber" implies a space of love and being in the love, the light: in the fullness of union, so in the perfect light, the Pleroma of Light—reintegrated with the Infinite Light.

As the saying goes, love conquers all; in this verse of Thomas, waking up is being in the love and the light. In the light, there are no shades and shadows, nothing else but the infinite and all-pervading radiance of the Eternal One. Rousing your estate and being armed is staying in the love, growing and maturing in love and thus in spiritual and supernal radiance, awareness, intelligence. In this supernal light and love of Christ, Messiah is everything—all the divine attributes, powers, actions—so that you are armed, having all stations and states of soul to engage in a conscious response to whatever is happening, not only for yourself but others as well.

You will be able to engage in divine interventions and works of spiritual assistance, uplifting others in ascension with you.

As you come into being, it is also necessary to cultivate mindfulness and be on guard against negativity, sin, and error, certainly so! There is a need for self-awareness and self-reflection, as well as knowledge of your vulnerabilities and weaknesses—the points of entrance whereby archons influence and demons assault—so as not to give in to them. Negativity and wickedness are what people entertain, cherish, and cleave to in their hearts and minds which links them with spiritual forces of the Other Side. Rather than the Holy Light, Spirit and powers of heaven, negative hearts and minds become conduits, channels, vehicles, through which archonic and demonic forces manifest, binding them to their dominions and realities.

Pay attention to what you entertain and hold in your heart and mind. If you have vulnerabilities, know how to respond with invocation, prayer, and meditation to overcome them when they arise. Restore yourself to inwardness, the inward communion in the Inner Light and Spirit.

You want to stay in the love. If you find you are not in the love, return to being in the love. You want to clean the inside and outside and keep it clean. You want to bathe in the river of truth daily, and on the Holy Shabbat soak yourself in it: your soul, mind, heart, and life in the truth of oneness, unity, and fullness in the Holy One, Holy Shekinah. In so doing, you will seal the points of entrance and close the inroads to the impure and dark spiritual forces from outside. You will have the blessing Yeshua speaks of in this saying. Amen.

Verse 104

They said to him, "Come let us pray today and fast." Yeshua said to them, "What sin have I committed or how have I been undone? When the bridegroom leaves the bridal chamber, then let the people fast and pray."

As has been shared, devotions are not for the Eternal One—they are for us so that we are in the love, in the light, in balance and harmony, in resonance with the Holy One, Holy Shekinah, unified with the Messiah in us. If in supernal realization, unified with the Messiah in the Eternal One and the Holy Shekinah, the Divine Presence is manifesting through us as us. There is no need of outward devotions except on behalf of others, when an outward manifestation of invocation and prayer serves as a vehicle to bless and uplift those around us or as a means of light transmission and passing of the Spirit. In truth, in supernal realization, there is no need of any outward devotion at all, no thought and thinking, words, or outward gestures. But in conscious union with the Messiah in the Holy One, Holy Shekinah, everything is accomplished through silent volition, simple conscious intention held in the heart of the soul. In the dance of the Holy Shekinah, in various movements of the Holy Spirit, in anointed community and with people, there will be outward manifestations of devotions: invocation and prayer, sacred discourse, sacred ceremony, gestures, laying on of hands, glancing, intently gazing, the use of sound-vibration, all in the Holy One, all the manifestation of the Holy Shekinah.

In this regard, as it is recounted in the Gospel of John, we may recall Yeshua Messiah and his prayer before calling Lazarus out of the tomb. At the outset of the invocation, he states that there was no need for him to invoke and pray because his intention was known to and in the Holy One. He states instead that his prayer was for the sake of the people, to reveal to them what was happening, to uplift and unite them with that divine action, that movement of the Spirit of Messiah. This was true of Messiah Yeshua and Mirya the Magdala, so it is also true of the gnostic apostles after them who embody the supernal realization, the fullness of the Holy Light and Spirit—Shekinah of Messiah.

On account of this, full supernal realization has been called no more devotion, no more practice. When there is invocation or prayer, the Holy One invokes the Holy One, the Holy One prays to the Holy One; there is no one other than the Holy One, Holy Shekinah.

Aside from gnostic apostles or prophets, some sisters and brothers who reach supernal realization have other messianic works and missions or are called to be concealed tzaddikim. As we mature in our spiritual realization and the Spirit more and more takes up action with, in, and through us, we may glimpse or taste something of this, touching something of the supernal. The presence and power of the Holy One and Messiah is supernal; while the Holy Shekinah, Holy Spirit can manifest in various spiritual gradations, she is supernal. The Supernal Light and Spirit is within and behind all our experiences in Christ, Messiah; the very nature of our holy soul—*neshamah*—is supernal. As our faith, love, and inward cleaving deepen, we will naturally and spontaneously experience times of deep ingathering, being elevated into the supernal and tasting the experience of passing away, merging with Messiah, the Shekinah, the Spirit, without having engaged in any effort or devotion. In those movements of the Spirit we will find that through simple conscious intention, there are powerful manifestations of the Spirit and powers of heaven not just moving through us but manifesting *as* us.

Likewise, during ingathered communion and Spirit-filled worship, at times we experience elevation into supernal stations and states of soul, reaching but not reaching, touching but not touching, as it is called in the Kabbalah. When this happens, there is an experience of passing away, merging with the Messiah in the Holy One, Holy Shekinah: an experience the reality of supernal being and consciousness, the Divine Presence manifesting as us. As the Living Presence intends, so it comes to pass with us. When this happens, these experiences are empowerments from the Messiah and Holy Spirit for our eventual supernal realization, showing us, as it were, the inmost space of the bridal chamber and the fullness of the light and love of Messiah.

The very way of gnostic devotions in the straight path lends itself to this. As has been shared, we seek to invoke, pray, and meditate in oneness, unity, and fullness. We seek to live from an inward communion, being deeply inward, and thus living from the Lord, to the Lord, and for the Lord. We seek to see, hear, and feel with the Spirit, to smell, taste, and touch with the Spirit and thus in our lives be in the Lord, the Spirit. Engaging in a worship of the Holy One in spirit and truth in this way, through grace, the power of the Holy One, the Holy Spirit, we will touch supernal stations and states of soul. We may experience supernal realization, actually reaching those stations and states to abide in them. The supernal realization may happen in the midst of this life or in our experience of dying and death, passing beyond, going *beyond* beyond. Hallelu Yah! Praise the Lord! Amen.

Verse 105

Yeshua said, "Whoever knows the Father and the Mother will be called the child of a whore."

On the surface, perhaps this is a most shocking and perplexing statement, but there is deep wisdom in it, alluding to secret mysteries of the Messiah and Holy One. For Sophian Gnostics who are passionate devotees of the Divine and Sacred Feminine, as well as Divine and Sacred Masculine, this statement make us smile and laugh. It's so true!

If you speak with most religious faithful of the three branches of Abrahamic Faith—Judaism, Christianity, and Islam—to speak of God as the Mother or refer to God in feminine terms ("she," "her," and "hers"), is considered very strange. It is a cause of agitation that may be proclaimed heretical, even blasphemous. To them, God is male, masculine only and can only be referred to in masculine terms—not female, feminine. With the exception of more liberal or progressive sects among them as well as some mystics and gnostics of these faiths, the leadership is patriarchal, and women are excluded from spiritual leadership. According to most religious faithful, anyone who speaks of God as Father and as Mother might very well be called children of a whore, judged to be apart from the true God, outside the faith. However, that is really none of our concern, for we are blessed to know the Eternal One as Father and Mother and beyond: the Infinite One—Ain Sof—or God beyond God—beyond names, personifications, attributes, and the entire play of creation and revelation—completely transcendent, the Primordial One.

When we speak of God giving Godself to us, understand that this is the Mother, the Motherhood of God, through whom the Son and Daughter are birthed, emanate, and appear within the matrix of creation, itself the Mother—Imma. Though indeed ever virgin, being within and appearing as all, being their very existence, their life and power, their good and evil and admixture alike, Mother is a whore giving herself to anyone and everyone, giving herself to all, being in all, being all, however they manifest! They are all her children; they have come from within her and she is in them. Their substance is her Substance. Their spirit is her Spirit. Whether known or unknown, realized or unrealized, they are all her children. She is with them and she loves them, whether they are ingathered to her or remove themselves from her. God never removes Godself from you, or anyone, though you, others, can, in effect, in your relative experience, remove yourself from God and so from yourself.

Here is the wild thing about God: Reality as It Is, this great dance of beauty and danger, beauty and horror, is God as God Is. God is being revealed and realized through it all. God the Mother loves all her children, all that emanates from herself. All that is in her is herself; whether or not they know her and love her or realize who and what they are, she loves them as they are—she loves you just as you are! And so she loves everybody, everything. From the outside, the love of the Mother is incomprehensible. The love of God is immeasurable. So it is taught in John that God so loved the world. God gave the world the Christ, Messiah the anointing with the Holy Light and Spirit. Take note: It does not say God loves some of the world or just the righteous in it—*all* the world. This is the Mother, the Motherhood of God, loving all her children, such as only the Mother can and does. Hallelu Imma! Praise Mother! Praise God—El, Elohim!

Because she, wisdom—*Hokmah-Sophia*—opens herself to anyone and everyone who desires her, she is called a whore. So here with the Mother, who gives herself to all, she who loves all most dearly and withholds herself from no one, not even those of the Other Side.

When we speak of being in the love, *this* is the love. It is a wild, immeasurable passionate love, the crazy wisdom of the Mother, who will do anything for her children. She gives herself completely to them to ensure they mature and come into being, resembling her, being as her image, having her radiant and holy face, her eyes, her ears, her heart, her everything. She refuses no child who comes to her seeking her embrace, love, light, or life power, which is endless light, and life forever after. As much as her children give themselves to her, she gives herself to them; she gives them what is their own—herself—as much as they can take, all as is good for each and everyone. If they go away from her, desiring to remove themselves from her, not wanting to know and love her, in love she will hide herself from them, though never departing from them. She waits patiently for their return and their coming into true being because they are hers and she is theirs. She is them and they are her. The time will come when they know and love her and live only in her, as none other than her, Mother God—*Imma Elohim*.

Be in the Mother, in the love and the light, and you will have all of the other attributes. They are all her and she is them: the Holy Shekinah in the Infinite and Eternal One, Holy Shekinah in creation, you, and me. Being in the Mother, in the love and the light, so you will know the Father and know the image of No-Thingness hidden within the Infinite Light: the truth, reality, of all as Radiant Nothingness, the delight of the Holy Mother, the play of her Son and Daughter, the ever-becoming of all her children within her, she within them.

She is the All-Inclusive One, she excludes no one.

If you will be in the love, in the light, return to her so that you might be reborn as yourself—as you are in her and none other than her—she will unveil herself and disclose herself to you as she is in herself, the Father, and as she is in all of her images and forms, the Mother: the great matrix of radiance, the Pleroma of Light, above and below, inside and outside. Do you see? Do you feel the love? I pray that you do!

She will not exclude you. If you go to her, she will receive you. If you seek her love, she will give it to you. You, me, try as we might, we cannot love in this way, but she can and she will. She will fill our hearts and souls with her love. She will give us her heart and soul. She will give us what is our own so that we can love, be her love, her light, her everything, all that she is. She will make us all mothers of one another and of the Lord himself!

If we love as the Mother loves, we will rightly be called children of a whore, loving all, giving ourselves to all as our Mother does without reservation or exception. Amen.

Verse 106

Yeshua said, "When you make two into one, you will become human children. When you say, 'Mountain, move,' the mountain will move."

Previously, faith was spoken of as the power to move mountains. Indeed, complete and perfect faith free from doubt and double mindedness makes two into one: One mind, one heart united, one single intention-desire from the depths of the soul. But understand that here, it is faith joined with love that Yeshua is speaking about, for it is love that unites, brings union, oneness. When one has faith and love and is in the love, such is true and perfect faith.

Here we may take note: Yeshua does not say you will invoke and pray about it; just intend and speak it, and what is intended and spoken will come to pass. This is speaking from supernal realization, being elevated by the Holy Spirit into supernal stations and states through faith, love, and inward cleaving. Love cleaves and unites. In the love-play with the Holy One and Shekinah in the bridal chamber of your heart, there is spontaneous passing away, merging with the Holy One, Holy Shekinah. When you love and pass away in love, your intention-desire becomes the intention-desire of the Holy One and the intention-desire of the Holy One becomes your own. The full force of the presence and power of the Holy One—the Holy Shekinah—moves through you and manifests as you in that moment.

Consider the things done by Moses and the great prophets such as Elijah and Elisha, who raised the dead. Then consider the even more gracious and wonderful things done by Messiah Yeshua and Mirya the Magdala and apostles and prophets after them. The Master is telling you the secret of how such things and more can be done. Remember in the Gospel of John that he said to his disciples and thus to us, "You will do greater things than you have seen me do" (John 14:12). Surely Adonai Yeshua did not lie, did he? In faith, in love, greater things are possible for me, for you, for all of us—certainly so!

Though we may appear as a human in human form, until we cultivate the qualities of a human being—the divine attributes and manifestation of God's image and likeness in us and our way in life—from a spiritual and more so a gnostic perspective, we are not true and authentic human beings—human children. Our supernal and heavenly soul—*neshamah*—needs to be unified with our intelligence and vital soul—*ruach* and *nefesh*—into one integral soul and self. Who we are in the Holy One, Holy Shekinah, needs to unite with who we are in ourselves—our person and life—to be realized and embodied. The soul we are—the divine attributes, powers, actions from which our soul is woven—is all spiritual and supernal potentials, possibilities that need to be actualized and realized, embodied. So, while incarnate in human form, being created in the image and likeness of God—Elohim—there is the potential for all people to be and become a true human being and more so, enlightened or divine humans. But we must strive with the Spirit to actualize and realize our human and divine potential. We must choose to be and do the divine attributes and actions, therefore being and becoming who and what we most truly are: Christ, Messiah—One Anointed.

From a gnostic perspective, the intention of the first and second coming of Christ, Messiah is the manifestation of the anointing from the Eternal One, the imparting of the Holy Light and Spirit through which our true human and divine potential is awakened, activated, and may be actualized, realized, embodied, and incarnate. In our experiences of light transmission and powerful movements of the Holy Spirit, Christ, Messiah is being revealed to us; Christ, Messiah is being revealed in and through us, such that in the second coming, Christ, Messiah appears as us, as our person and life. As Yeshua was the Son of Man—Son of Adam, the Human One—so are we to be and become true sons and daughters of the Human

One—to realize our innate unity with the One Soul. Likewise, as Yeshua was the Son of God, so we are to be and become true sons and daughters of God—to realize our innate unity with the Eternal One.

He was and is the firstborn of this family of God; receiving the Holy Light and Spirit, being reborn from above, so are we born into this family of God: the Mother, the Virgin of Light, gives birth to us as to our Lord and Savior.

The presence and power of the Holy One we beheld in our Elder Brother and Elder Sister—Yeshua and Mirya—is also to be revealed and realized in us. Amen.

Verse 107

Yeshua said, "The kingdom of heaven is like a shepherd who had a hundred sheep. One of them, the largest, went astray. He left the ninety-nine and looked for the one until he found it. After so much trouble, he said to the sheep, 'I love you more than the ninety-nine.'"

This saying, which also appears in canonical gospels, has deep meaning in gnostic teachings and the Christian Kabbalah. It conveys secret mysteries of Christ, Messiah, mysteries of the Divine Incarnation.

As has been shared, there are ten principal light emanations—Sefirot, divine attributes—from the Infinite Light. Within each of them are another ten, called the interiors of the emanations of Light that correspond with light realms, light worlds, realities of the Pleroma of Light, into which souls can reach, the full array of stations and states of souls that can be realized and embodied. According to the Holy Kabbalah, the Spirit and Soul of the Messiah emanates from the inmost interior of the very first emanation—Keter of Keter, Crown of Crown—encompassing them all, the realization of them all.

In the *Pistis Sophia*, essential insight is given to the incarnation of Christ, Messiah. When Yeshua was raised from the dead and ascended through all the heavens into the heaven of heavens—the Pleroma of Light—he returned and appeared to his close disciples on the Mount of Olives in full glory. In that revelation, he tells them that he left behind his three light vestures when incarnating and that through his self-offering in the resurrection and ascension, he took them up again, fully restored to him. They had to be left behind because the material world could not endure the full presence and power of the Pleroma of Light and the Eternal One in him, the fullness of the primordial and supernal Christ, or universal Messiah. When he appeared to the disciples in full glory—astral, spiritual, and supernal—the earth and its heavens were so agitated and shaken that the disciples realized that if the revelation of his full glory continued right then and there, it would induce the end of days. Overwhelmed by the full array of the light transmission underway, they pleaded with him to put Yeshua back on, his outer worldly appearance.

A soul entering into the inmost supernal realization and reaching into the primordial as Yeshua Messiah did in the resurrection and ascension can only flash forth for a short duration, unable to remain very long in this world because it would not be able to withstand the full force of that Divine Presence. So, in the resurrection and ascension, Yeshua would appear and disappear, come and go from his disciples for forty days or so, and did not remain with them while he revealed the inner and secret gospel: secret mysteries of creation, the eternal realm, of Christ and God, the Messiah and Eternal One.

To appear in this world, to bring the anointing of the Holy Light and Spirit to humankind, and to ingather souls from among humankind, he left the ninety-nine behind—the array of all of the divine entities, powers, worlds of supernal, spiritual and astral light—to gather that one sheep in a severe restriction of the radiance of the Infinite One that is the Christ, Messiah. The restriction is his incarnation. Incarnate as a human being, he then engaged the divine action of the full actualization and realization of that Light-presence and Light-power, revealing and bringing it forth from within humanity and thus bringing salvation, true knowledge of God—God beyond God.

What was revealed through Adonai Yeshua was the truth, the reality of the soul within us all, the inmost aspect of which reaches into that space from which the Spirit and Soul of the Messiah emanates. Your person and life as well as mine, this incarnation of our souls, amounts to 1 percent of yourself and myself. Within and beyond this name, form, and personal history is the remaining 99 percent of yourself and myself. Yeshua Messiah was not, in truth, who and what he appeared to be on the outside, but neither are we. Veiled behind his appearance were realities far more than finite, mortal intellect and reason can fathom or imagine. The same is true of you and me. He came as a holy apostle and prophet and made a holy sacrifice of himself to reveal this to us, to ingather the 1 percent into the 99. The incarnation in which a soul enters into this supernal realization is indeed as wondrous as the emergence of another holy and enlightened one in the world, in the universe—the appearance of a great star of heaven within the Pleroma. In this, perhaps, you may recall the Great Vision of Melchizedek of which we spoke earlier, generating a threefold body of enlightenment—the three light vestures of truth, glory, and manifestation.

You may also realize why we need to be inward, deep within and no longer cling to name, form, personal history, and the little self or ego associated with it. Instead, cleave to the inner Christ, Messiah and your Divine Self, Divine I Am. Truly, this appearance of you and me in this world and incarnation is the least and smallest part of you and me. The greater truth and reality of yourself and myself is within, behind, and beyond it. Amen.

Verse 108

Yeshua said, "Whoever drinks from my mouth will become like me. I myself will become that person and hidden things will be revealed to that one."

To drink from the mouth is most intimate, like kissing. In Philip there is a delightful passage that speaks of Mirya the Magdala as the inmost disciple of Yeshua and his spiritual consort. The male disciples inquire why he kisses her on the mouth more than them. He responds by turning the question on them: "Why don't I kiss you as often as I kiss her?" Clearly they were not inquiring about physical intimacy but instead a spiritual intimacy through which light and knowledge of secret mysteries is communicated. In this regard, we may recall an occasion Thomas got intoxicated drinking from the mouth of Adonai Yeshua, who transmitted to Thomas in private in that elevated state. Yeshua communicated three secrets to Thomas that the other disciples were not able to hear. If we consider this saying, we may recall Thomas being called the twin of Yeshua, not only resembling him but appearing as though born of the same spiritual womb.

To receive in this way from a gnostic apostle or gnostic master happens through being inward, deep within, and abiding in an inward communion, being intimate with the Inner Light and Spirit within oneself. We ourselves need to be inwardly joined with Christ, Messiah to receive the light and knowledge communicated by the Holy Spirit through a living apostle and prophet. If deeply inward, the light power being transmitted will be received and there may be a soul-to-soul, heart-to-heart, or mind-to-mind transmission of knowledge, such that the knowledge and understanding comes from within ourselves: thunderous insights and illuminations arise far beyond whatever outward words are spoken. It is like in that moment, the holy tzaddik becomes us, we become them, and hidden things that cannot be communicated with words are revealed and known. Aside from these exchanges with living messengers, this verse speaks of ingathered, deep inward communion, being in the love and the light wherein we pass away, merge with the Sun of God in ourselves, and become Christ, Messiah as that Divine Presence appears as us and becomes manifest through us in that moment.

Yeshua speaks with straightforward clarity on the mystery of the bridal chamber and being wed to Christ, Messiah—the Sun of God. We are unified with Christ in us, with Christ in all, with Christ ever beyond. Quite naturally there will be knowledge, understanding, and wisdom of secret mysteries, most holy secrets of the Eternal One—the Infinite Light, Radiant Nothingness.

This is the most holy mystery among gnostics—the mystery of the bridal chamber—that we celebrate with an outward feast of bread and wine. We call it a wedding feast. Our communion, however, is dependent upon nothing outward at all; it is inward, in Christ, Messiah in us—the Holy Light and Spirit. We abide in unity and fullness, a most intimate communion in Christ, Messiah within our heart and soul—the bridal chamber. If and when we take up and consecrate bread and wine, it is from within, from the Lord, the Spirit. Just as it is not women and men who speak the inner and secret teachings and revelations but the Spirit who speaks through us with the power that delivers, heals, and enlightens, so it is not women and men who imbue the Holy Light and Fire into the bread and wine but the Messiah and Holy Spirit who consecrates.

When we come together for ingathered communion, there isn't always a call or need for bread and wine. But when there is, we celebrate the outward feast joined to the inward delight of the love and light within us shining. In this, understand that ours is not a feast of bread and wine in remembrance of Yeshua as though he has gone away and we are awaiting his return—not in the least! It is a feast and celebration of knowing Hayyah Yeshua within us and being united with the Messiah in the Eternal One in this world and the World-That-Is-Coming. Amen.

Verse 109

Yeshua said, "The kingdom of heaven is like a person who had a treasure hidden in his field. He did not know it, and when he died he left it to his son. The son did not know about it. He took the field and sold it. The buyer was plowing and found the treasure, and he began to lend money at interest to whomever he wished."

The kingdom of heaven is inside you, me, all of us, but the majority of us do not know it. Among those who believe it is within them, many have not glimpsed or tasted it as yet, let alone discovered how to enter and abide so as to realize it. For many of us, the realization of the kingdom of heaven inside and outside is a work in progress. Whether realized or unrealized, it is within us and is a present reality deep within. It is important that we believe this, having faith that we seek until we find. If we do not, the kingdom of God cannot be found or realized, and we may die before realizing our innate unity with the Messiah in the Eternal One.

Apparently, the man and his son in this verse did not plough the field. You may recall from Genesis that the Human One was put in the garden of Eden to till the soil and tend the garden. In the Holy Kabbalah, the supernal garden and the kingdom of heaven are synonymous: tilling and tending the garden is turning to the Lord, going inward to seek and find the Lord in invocation of the Names of God in prayer and deep meditation, contemplation, and cultivation of the attributes of a true human—the Messiah—of the Holy One, Holy Shekinah.

The garden is a garden of souls. Its flowers and fruits are souls blooming and fulfilling their messianic works and missions, their divine purpose and destiny. In order to bloom or be actualized and realized, you must go within and know how to abide in an ingathered communion, rest in the Lord, and live from within—from the Lord, to the Lord, and for the Lord. When souls bloom, they release their fragrance while realizing something of their essence, delighting the Holy One, Holy Shekinah and attracting the powers of heaven, the saints and angels into their communion. Something of the Messiah, the Holy One and Shekinah is being revealed and realized through them: the kingdom of heaven is being manifest on earth as it is in heaven.

The holy soul—*neshamah*—is the kingdom, the reality of heaven and God; your holy soul, and my holy soul, is the kingdom of God. Christ, Messiah is the kingdom of heaven and God. It is far beyond, far more awesome and wonderful than some glowing, gated community in the sky filled with big fancy houses, as some in ignorance might conceive of heaven. Truly, it is an unimaginable supernal reality, an experience of unfathomable peace and joy—pure delight, immeasurable bliss—such that the mortal, finite heart and mind cannot comprehend it. Souls must be uplifted into higher stations and states by the Holy Spirit, deeply ingathered by the Spirit, and the Spirit must reveal the kingdom of God to them. For our part, we need to engage in an active and dynamic surrender, collaborating with the Spirit to create the conditions necessary for her full divine action. As we are inward, we invoke, pray, meditate, and commune, seeking to live according to our faith, love, and knowledge of Christ and God while its revelation and realization happens with, in, and through us.

We seek to see, hear, and feel with the Spirit, to smell, taste, and touch with the Spirit, to listen only to the voice of the Lord, the Spirit, and follow the Lord, the Spirit—no other, only the Holy One, Holy Shekinah.

Truly, being in the love and the light and striving to love and have mercy, compassion, and forgiveness, you will be in the garden, in the kingdom. You will enter it right here, right now! Being in the garden, being in the kingdom, being in Messiah is the blooming of your soul, the release of that most wonderful and delightful celestial and supernal fragrance: the expansion of your communion, your soul in the Eternal One—the Infinite Light.

The kingdom of God is the experience of being united and filled, lacking nothing, so that indeed you have plenty of abundant good, light power, and love to give to whomever you wish and engage in your messianic works as a co-redeemer with Christ, Messiah—forgiving, relieving suffering, healing, and uplifting in the resurrection and ascension, ingathering into the Pleroma of Light. Loaning at interest here means bearing good fruits and glorifying the Holy One, Holy Shekinah through facilitating the realization and enlightenment of others in your life—letting the light of the Sun of God shine from within you. Amen.

Verse 110

Yeshua said, "You who have found the world and become wealthy, renounce the world."

If you want to experience realization and enlightenment or acquire true knowledge of God—gnosis, *da'at*—you will need to do whatever it takes. You will need passion for the spiritual life as well as practice, in addition to a true desire to give yourself and your life completely to God, seeking God and God alone. You need to go inward, deep within and be in the Inner Light and Spirit, be in the Messiah, be in the Holy One, Holy Shekinah. Be in the Messiah and Holy Spirit, the Holy One and Holy Shekinah, all the time in everything, not just at the times of your daily devotions or when you are with your holy tzaddik, when gathered with brothers and sisters in anointed community, or on Shabbat. You want to be with the Messiah and Holy One inside and outside, abiding in communion: seeing, hearing, feeling the Holy One in all and all in the Holy One, being in the love and so being in the light. If there is anything inward or outward that comes between you and the Messiah or causes you to turn away from the Holy One in any direction out of the light and love and into the darkness and fire, you need to renounce it. You need to look only to the face and image of the Holy One, hear only the voice of the Holy One, accept only what is in and from the Holy One, Holy Shekinah, and nothing else.

If something is not in the light and the love, as a daughter or son of light and member of the family of God, you have nothing to do with it—it has nothing to do with you!

Striving with the Holy Spirit to cultivate the qualities of the Messiah, the Holy One requires that you remove all unnecessary qualities not in the Messiah, not in the Holy One: anything not in the light and love in thought, speech, action, or activity in life. Anything that takes you from being inward into outwardness or impairs your communion and removes you from the Messiah, the Holy One must be removed and renounced from your life.

Quite naturally, being open and sensitive to the Holy Spirit and being of the enlightened family—anointed community—we renounce the ways of the unenlightened society. There is much in the unenlightened society we cannot be part of or involve ourselves in because the Lord, the Spirit leads us another way; we see it is not in the light and love—it is the opposite.

Among mystics and gnostics, there is no rule but the love, the light, and the truth revealed to each of us, the guidance of the Holy Spirit—the Spirit of Truth. We are not bound to a religious law, its man-made doctrines, or its rites and rituals. But we are in grace, in the love, and so in the light. We can see for ourselves what is good and true. Doing what is good and true, we acquire grace for ourselves. We acquire true knowledge of God.

What is good and true for one individual is not necessarily good and true for another. Likewise, what is not good and true for one individual is neither necessarily good nor true for another. Equally, what may be good and true at one time or under certain circumstances, may not be at another time or in other circumstances. Each of us has our own strengths and weakness, our own talents and abilities in ourselves and in the Spirit; we each have our own works and mission, our own way. We need to be inward, deep within, and live from inwardness, from inward communion and be guided by the love and by the Spirit. We need to be open and honest with ourselves, our tzaddik, our sisters and brothers, and the Messiah, the Holy One so that we have no denial whenever we may be in error. We do not cling to what is not ours, what is not in the light and love of the Messiah, the Holy One.

You are the Way. Who you truly are inward, in the Messiah, the Holy One is the Way for you. Invoke often and pray and pray and pray, asking the Messiah, the Holy One to remove your unnecessary human qualities and replace them with divine attributes, powers, actions. Ask the Messiah, the Holy One to reveal to you your way and to lead you in your way of the realization and embodiment of your holy soul—your Divine Self, the Divine I Am. Pray for all the divine attributes you need to do your work and accomplish your mission and to make the outside like the inside and so return to be One—One from One, in the Real.

Seek from the Messiah and the Eternal One what is your own, all that is in Messiah, the Holy One, Holy Shekinah. Amen.

Verse 111

Yeshua said, "The heavens and earth will roll up in your presence, and you who live from the Living One will not see death." Doesn't Yeshua say this? Whoever has found oneself, of that person the world is not worthy.

Now that we may have some intuitive sense and insight into the secret meaning of these sayings, this verse returns us to the first saying of the gospel as we near its end, bringing us full circle. The secret, of course, is Hayyah Yeshua—the Living One—within you and me, within all people, all creatures, all things. The secret is being inward, deep inward, abiding in an inward communion, merging with the Inner Light and Spirit, and living from the Inner Light and Spirit—Christ, Messiah in us. In this is our realization, our enlightenment and liberation, true knowledge of God: God beyond doctrine, God beyond God.

I will share with you an open secret: the gnostic—the knower of God—has renounced the heavens and earth: God and God alone is their Reality. They know and have realized that the Only Reality is the Eternal One, Eternal Messiah, that in truth there is no other, nothing else. The Holy One, the Messiah is the light and life of all things in the heavens and on earth, and in all realms and worlds of creation: Nothing exists separate or apart from the Holy One. The seven heavens, the earth, and all of the various worlds, realities, of the great matrix of creation—material, astral, and spiritual—serve as vehicles for this realization, but the source of it all is the Eternal One, the Eternal Messiah, the true kingdom of heaven—the Pleroma of Light, the Infinite Light.

Though this kingdom of heaven is inside you and outside you, it is through the inside, being deep inside, that you discover and enter into the kingdom of God. If not realized inside, then it will not be realized outside.

If it is not realized in this world and this life, it will not be realized in dying, death, and the afterlife.

When your soul departs the body and you go beyond, all that you have and are on the outside falls away and is rolled up; what you are left with is what is inside of you, in your heart and mind and soul. In the afterlife states, what is inside you becomes your reality: If it is love and light, that is your reality; if it is darkness and fire, that is your reality. Whatever is held inside and cleaved to is what arises as the realities in-between, creating your afterlife experience and shaping the next incarnation. Having lived only on the outside, when souls depart the body, generally speaking, the world for them passes away. For the soul, the end of days has come; when going into brilliant light, most souls are overwhelmed and fall unconscious. Falling unconscious is tasting or seeing death. Just as many souls go to sleep at night and pass into dreamless sleep and unconsciousness to arise from it into ordinary dreams, unaware of being asleep and dreaming, so do many souls fall into unconsciousness when they pass beyond. They arise at the outset of afterlife states, having forgotten they are dead and are now in the afterlife. Of course, the experience of death and the afterlife is far more intense and vivid than our dreams; the Kabbalah teaches it is sixty times more powerful. Many souls get caught up in the Midst—various impure and dark realms—unable to ascend into the seven heavens, let alone pass into the Pleroma of Light. They are driven into material incarnation again out of desire or fear.

However, those who have lived a life in true faith and love, who have been inward from even a spiritual realization may receive assistance and interventions from tzaddikim, angels, and Christ, Messiah to awaken swiftly in the afterlife and ascend to the corresponding heavenly realms. Having lived fully and deeply within from the Inner Light and Spirit and reached an inmost spiritual or supernal realization, they might not fall unconscious at all but instead maintain a presence of awareness passing beyond, ascending into the heaven of heavens. They pass into the Pleroma of Light or experience full reintegration with the Infinite Light.

In this, perhaps, you will realize that you have a very precious opportunity in this life's climax with death, when your soul passes beyond. In this very life you can realize the true kingdom of heaven inside and outside. You can realize the divine, bornless nature of your soul, consciousness, mind—the Living One, the Eternal One—and so be in that Pleroma of Light when you depart the body, free of the necessity of physical, material incarnation—the gilgulim.

Do you recall what Yeshua taught in this gospel of the choosing of souls one out of a thousand, two out of ten thousand? Of souls reaching a spiritual realization and souls reaching a supernal realization, being made a single one? This is the supernal grace, mercy, compassion, and forgiveness of the Infinite and Eternal One in Christ, Messiah. In fruition, all who have believed and lived in true faith, who love with inward cleaving will be ingathered into the Pleroma of Light.

Receiving the Holy Light and Spirit, being inward, and living from within, knowing the Sun of God in you, living in the light, living in the love, it will thus come to pass with you: you will arise as a star of heaven when you pass beyond! Hallelu Yah! Praise the Lord! Amen.

Verse 112

Yeshua said, "Shame on the flesh that is dependent upon the soul. Shame on the soul dependent upon the flesh."

Truly so, it is a shame! What a dreadful, horrible condition of immeasurable sorrow and suffering. While there is no such thing as eternal damnation as taught by those who are ignorant of the truth of the Messiah and Eternal One who are ignorant of Reality as It Is, the bondage to the gilgulim—potentially endless rounds of birth, life, aging, illness, and death in ignorance, separation, and lack—is nevertheless a great and terrible sorrow and suffering.

While the Eternal One damns nothing for all time, afterlife experiences of heaven and hells, realms of fierce spirits and hungry ghosts, archonic realms and various other astral and spiritual worlds or realities in-between unconsciously compel souls to transmigrate from incarnation to incarnation. It is a shame! In the light and love of the Holy One, beholding literally countless living spirits and souls caught in this suffering, lost in this aimless wandering, in need of salvation, enlightenment, and liberation is a vision of great sorrow. When one knows how near the kingdom of heaven is to souls, knowing the Holy One is nearer to souls than they are to themselves, and when one can see, hear, and feel souls in the Holy One and the Holy One in souls but are unable and unwilling to hear the word of the Christ, Messiah or believe, go inward, and know heaven and the Holy One within themselves—all of this pains the heart of love and compassion terribly.

There is something that needs to be said: If we have been blessed in this life to come to faith in enlightenment or God and have been blessed to encounter one of the living, inner spiritual and mystical traditions of one of the world's great faiths or wisdom traditions that bears the light transmission and passing of the Spirit, we definitely want to take advantage of it. We want to seek teachings and initiation with zeal, a spiritual education on how to be inward and seek, find, and realize the Inner Light and Spirit, the Lord within us. We have a precious opportunity, with no time to waste on vain entertainments, things nonessential to life, or religious doctrines or strange and false teachings that do not reveal a way to actual self-realization or enlightenment—true salvation.

If we do not accept this blessing and do not make the most of this precious opportunity in this life, there is no guarantee it will be present for us in our next incarnation, or that our next incarnation will be as auspicious as this one is. If we do not let the Truth and Light take root, it could be many lives before the opportunity presents itself again. In a manner of speaking, if we turn away, it could be a long time before the thought and desire to return and reintegrate with the Infinite Light arises again. Such is the play of the law, karma—cause and effect—apart from grace, apart from an active labor to seek and find and so be in grace.

On the other hand, if we take up the opportunity of this life and actively labor to seek and find and let the Truth and Light take root—regardless of how far we progress in our realization—light power and positive karma will be generated, as will soul bonds with tzaddikim and angels. There will be grace for us. If we are not ingathered into the Pleroma of Light when we depart this body, we will encounter a holy tzaddik, anointed community, and light transmission again in our next life. In three to seven lives, we will experience full enlightenment and liberation, having been set upon the gnostic path in one of its many forms.

They who seek first the kingdom of enlightenment and its righteousness are wise, aware that everything else that they need will be given to them. All that is their own and all that they need in the Holy One, Holy Shekinah, will be theirs. Amen.

Verse 113

His disciples said to him, "When will the kingdom come?" Yeshua said, "It will not come because you are waiting for it. No one will announce, 'Look, here it is,' or 'Look, there it is.' The kingdom of heaven is spread out upon the earth and people do not see it."

There is an open secret to be shared. Present inside and outside of us, here and now on earth and in these bodies and all the various material, astral, spiritual, and supernal dimensions, realms, worlds, realities in them—exist in the same space at the same time. As such, the true kingdom of heaven—the Pleroma of Light within the supernal dimension—is inside and outside of us and is indeed spread out upon the earth, but most people do not see it. To those living outside, in outwardness, it cannot be seen.

The kingdom of heaven is inside of everything, within and behind everything that appears, and so is outside as well as inside of us. But we need to be deeply inward to be aware of it within us, within all people, creatures, and things to see, hear, feel, know, and be in the Pleroma of Light. When we become aware of it inside of us, we are aware of it inside all things and come to see that it is spread out upon the earth.

We see, hear, and feel this truth, this reality, in moments of light transmission, when the Holy Spirit moves with us and uplifts us into higher stations and states of soul or more expanded states of mental and supramental consciousness. Then we see, hear, and feel with the Spirit and perceive realities of the astral, spiritual, and supernal dimensions within and around us. We glimpse, taste, the reality of the kingdom of heaven—Pleroma of Light—and know it to be true, real. In this, perhaps, you may understand that in truth, in reality, heaven and earth are not two, but one!

Now truly, the second coming of Christ, Messiah in glory—the coming of the kingdom—will not happen because you wait for it. If you wait for it but do not seek and find it now in this life, it will not happen for you in this life nor in the afterlife. As taught at the outset, you must seek and continue seeking until you find. You need to go within, deep inward, and find the kingdom, find the Lord within the heart of your soul, your inner being. You need to be willing to be troubled, willing to change and change and change until you are in the image and likeness of Christ, Messiah until the inside and outside are joined as one. Then you will rule over all—you will live in the kingdom of heaven, in the Messiah and Holy One, Holy Shekinah.

What are you waiting for? Why wait? Why waste any time? You and I are not getting any younger. This time is precious, there is no time to waste! Look outside and see what is happening in the world around you. The time is short. This is why I am writing to you, speaking to you from inside to inside, from my heart to your heart, from my soul to your soul in the Holy One, Holy Shekinah. I want you to know the Inner Light and Spirit; the inner Christ, Messiah; the Sun of God in you! I want you to be inward, deep inward, to be in the light, to be in the love, to be in the kingdom of heaven here and now and when you pass beyond. I want you to have true knowledge of God—the Eternal One, the Infinite Light.

All of this is within you as it is within everyone. This holy gospel gives you the keys to the kingdom inside and outside, to the knowledge of the Sun of God in you, to the knowledge of yourself as a star of heaven: Yourself as you are in Messiah, as you are in the Holy One, Holy Shekinah. Amen.

Verse 114

Peter said to them, "Mirya should leave us. Females are not worthy of life." Yeshua said, "Look, I shall guide her to make her male, so she too may become a living spirit resembling you males. For every female who makes herself male will enter the kingdom of heaven."

In the Messiah and Eternal One, male, female, man, woman—there is no difference. One race or another, one ethnic group or another—there is no difference. One sexual orientation or another—there is no difference. That is all outside. Inside all people is Christ, Messiah—the Inner Light and Spirit. When realized, they are all the same in essence, a unique and special star of heaven in the image and likeness of the Sun of God—Son of Infinite Light, the Supreme.

In the Holy Kabbalah, female indicates receiving and male indicates giving. In this regard, first we are all female; we all need to receive the Holy Light and Spirit. We are as brides to the Sun of God in us. In the mystery of the bridal chamber, passing away in the love, the light, merging with the Sun of God, we become female and male in one body of light. There is a free flow of the Holy Light and Spirit with, in, and through us. Receiving and giving are joined as one holy intention and desire in the Messiah, the Eternal One.

As it is the same with women and men alike, so it is true in anointed community. Women and men are equals. Women are also among the messengers—gnostic apostles, prophets, tzaddikim—who serve as teachers and guides. In this saying, Yeshua speaks a prophecy of Mirya: She would also come into being as a messenger, a holy apostle, bearing light transmission and able to impart the Holy Spirit. In fact, according to our gospel, she is the first gnostic apostle, sharing in the same supernal realization and embodying the fullness of the Holy Light and Spirit as Yeshua did. She was therefore the apostle of the apostles—the Holy Mother of Apostles.

The gnostic story of the fall and redemption of Sophia-Wisdom plays itself out in the story of Mirya the Magdala, where in a period of exile she endured outside the Holy Land. Upon returning and being redeemed, she became the inmost disciple of Yeshua and his spiritual consort. As his inmost disciple, she drew out teachings from him that no one else could, intimate secrets of heaven, the Messiah, the Eternal One, and the Infinite Light. Because she drew them out, everyone present was able to hear and receive them. As his spiritual consort, she embodied the Spirit and Soul of the Messiah in a woman's form as he did in a man's form, so that the fullness of the Holy Light and Spirit would spread to all humanity. She was a co-preacher and teacher with him. She was a co-redeemer, opening the Way for those who would follow. Though completely interconnected, their divine actions were different. He was the Messiah and she was the Magdala.

His mission was that of the firstborn, the sacrifice of himself to reveal the resurrection and ascension, the rising of the Sun of God in full glory and power. She was his supernal soulmate and perfect twin, able to receive the full force of the influx of that glory and power, the fullness of the Supernal Light and Eternal Spirit. Her mission was to receive that full force of the supernal influx so that it would radiate out through her to all who believed and desired to receive it.

Mirya the Magdala was uplifted with Yeshua Messiah in ascension, but while it was given to him to pass into full reintegration with the Infinite Light, she spoke her holy word, a promise to return in woman's form in every generation until the end of days, when all is accomplished—the fruition of the second coming of Christ, Messiah. He ascended and she returned.

In the upper room at Pentecost, that great supernal influx flowed through her to all gathered with her and the Holy Mother, anointing some holy apostles with spiritual realization and other holy apostles with supernal realization. That same Holy Light and Spirit continued passing to all believers and followers gathered outside. In this way, as with all holy vessels of light and mysteries of the Holy One, the Holy Shekinah generated the first anointed community of interior and exterior light.

There is a teaching in our tradition: He is the light, she is the love. Be in the love, be in the light, and you will be perfect, complete in the Human One of Light: female and male in one Body of Light.

That Mirya embodied the supernal realization and fullness of the Holy Light and Spirit as Yeshua did is important. It is an essential message of the Holy Gospel. Through her, we know that we also are to strive to embody the full presence and power of Christ, Messiah, the fullness of the Holy Light and Spirit. We are to let that light shine and the Spirit pass through us to others, just as she did with him: the gnostic understanding of the Holy Gospel.

My love to you in the Messiah and the Magdala! Amen.

Glossary

Adam Elyon: Supernal Human; the Human One of Light; the One Soul awakened, realized; the One Soul inseparable from the Eternal God—Yahweh Elohim; the Soul of the Messiah; Soul of God.

Adam Kadmon: Primordial Human; the Human One in pre-eternity; primordial enlightenment, the bornless nature; the One Soul inseparable from the Infinite—Ain Sof; Soul of the Messiah, Soul of God.

Adam Rishon: First Human; the One Soul as unrealized spiritual and supernal potential; the aspects of the One Soul asleep and dreaming, and awakening, being realized, through all living spirits and souls.

Adonai: Lord, specifically "my Lord."

Ain: Nothingness, a term for the Supreme, or the Infinite One, the nameless and unknowable, the Concealed of the Concealed, God beyond God.

Ain Sof: Infinite One, One-Without-End; Godhead; God as God is in Godself; the hidden source of all.

Ain Sof Or: Infinite Light, Radiant Nothingness, radiance of the Infinite One.

Archon: Ruler; impure, undivine forces within and behind the centers of power and great institutions of the unenlightened society, to include large religious institutions.

Asiyah: Universe of making, action; material dimension, universe, world; physical, material creation.

Atzilut: Universe of nearness, emanation, everflow; supernal dimension, universe; Pleroma of Light; eternal realm; Universe of the Sefirot.

Beriyah: Universe of creation; spiritual dimension universe; reality of the inner heavens; reality of holy souls and archangels.

Binah: Understanding; third Sefirah; also called Holy Shekinah, interior Shekinah.

Bridal Chamber: Place of intimate communion and union with Christ and God; the heart, the heart of the soul.

Da'at: Knowledge; Union; what is revealed of the inmost, concealed Sefirah, Keter; holds the place of Keter at each level of the Tree of Life because Keter never appears but is concealed, hidden.

Demiurge: Half-Maker; personification of universal ignorance, the comic ego; self-willed triple power; glowing husk—*klippah nogah*; false religious concepts of God; source of false prophecy or the corruption of revelation.

Ehyeh: I Am, I Shall Be; the inmost Essential Name of the Eternal One.

Elohim: A feminine noun with a masculine plural connoting God as male and female—Father and Mother but as One God; connotes the immanent presence and power of God, God in creation; One become countless Many, but all being One; the All-Powerful One, or the Holy One manifest through the vast array of Holy Sefirot.

Gevurah: Severity, Judgment; fifth Sefirah.

Gilgulim: The transmigration of souls; reincarnation of souls; potentially endless rounds of birth, life, aging, illness, and death; the bondage of souls, but also the vehicle of their realization.

Gnosis: True knowledge of Christ and God; enlightenment; spiritual or supernal realization; knowledge of the Divine through direct spiritual and mystical experience; experiential knowledge of the Divine.

Gnostic: A knower of God; realized soul; enlightened one.

Gnosticism: Way of the knowers of God; way of self-realization or enlightenment.

Hayyah: Light power, life force of the soul.

Hesed: Love, Mercy, Loving-Kindness; fourth Sefirah.

Hod: Glory, Splendor, Radiance, Surrender, Submission; eighth Sefirah.

Hokmah: Wisdom; second Sefirah.

Keter: Crown; first Sefirah.

Kingdom of Heaven: Pleroma of Light; enlightenment; reality of the Messiah; reality of Atzilut; eternal realm; heaven of heavens; eighth heaven.

Klippot or Klippah (singular): Husks, shells of impurity or darkness; outsiders; impure or dark manifestations of divine powers; archonic and demonic forces; the Other Side.

Light Transmission: Initiation; an actual energetic transmission that passes between people in anointed community; the transmission of the spiritual or supernal power of an apostle, prophet, or the tzaddik's realization or gnosis; a spiritual empowerment; and actual passing of the Holy Light of the risen and ascended Christ, Messiah.

Malkut: Sovereignty, Kingdom; tenth and final Sefirah; also called Holy Shekinah, exterior Shekinah.

Mirya Magdala: Aramaic for Mary Magdalene; Tower of the Flock; Holy Bride; Apostle of Apostles; Mother of Apostles; the appearance of Christ, Messiah in woman's form; Holy Daughter of God.

Nefesh: Vital soul.

Nefesh Behamit: Bestial soul; vital soul in the unenlightened condition.

Nefesh Elokit: Godly soul; vital soul redeemed, realized, integrated with inner aspects of the soul.

Neshamot or Neshamah (singular): Holy soul, heavenly and supernal soul, divine nature; soul associated with the Divine Self; who and what the soul is in the Eternal One.

Netzach: Victory, Divine Dominion, Eternity; seventh Sefirah.

Olamot or Olam (singular): Dimensions, universes, worlds; different levels of the manifestation of the Sefirot.

One Soul: Adam, Human One; Soul from which all living spirits and souls emanate; contains all creatures, all creation, from beginning to end.

Pleroma of Light: See entries *Atzilut* and *Kingdom of Heaven.*

Ruach: Spirit, human intelligence, divine intelligence.

Ruach Elohim: Spirit of God; outer aspect of the Holy Spirit; Holy Spirit in creatures and creation.

Ruach Yahweh: Spirit of the Eternal One—Yahweh; inner aspect of the Holy Spirit; Holy Spirit in Heaven; Spirit of the Messiah.

Satan: Adversary, opponent, enemy; the evil one; spirit of the Other Side; the force of darkness and evil; shadow of the demiurge.

Sefirot: Emanations of the Infinite Light; divine attributes, powers, actions; stations and states of the soul; light realms, realities, of the Pleroma; Names of God; personifications of God; Sefirah, singular; Sefirot, plural.

Seth Gadol: A name of the Messiah in the Holy Kabbalah; Second Adam; playing upon Seth as the image and likeness of Adam, the One Soul; Seth is spelled with *Shin* and *Tau,* the last two letters of the Hebrew *Alef-Bet. Shin* is fire or light and *Tau* is the cross, together connoting the cross of light, or light transmission in Christian Kabbalah; Supernal Humanity; Divine Humanity; Son of the Human One—Son of Man.

Shaddai: Almighty; also Many-Breasted One.

Shekinah: Divine Presence; Presence and Power of the Eternal One; the feminine aspect of the Holy One; Mother, Daughter, Bride.

Sophia: Personification of the wisdom of God.

Tiferet: Beauty, Harmony; sixth Sefirah; also called Rehamim, Compassion.

True Gnosis: Supernal realization, knowledge of Christ and God through conscious union, oneness; the state of Christ or God consciousness; God knowing God.

Tzaddikim or Tzaddik (singular): Righteous One; a realized individual, a true teacher and guide.

Wedding Feast: The holy feast of bread and wine among gnostics; celebration of the mystery of the bridal chamber—our unity with Christ in God, unity and fullness.

Yahweh: That Which Was, Is, and forever Shall Be; Eternal One; All-Inclusive Name; Explicit Name; Great Name of God; the LORD; this word is a verb, not a noun—God as a movement.

Yechidah: Divine spark, unique essence, inmost aspect of the soul.

Yahweh Elohim: Eternal God; Complete Name of God; see *Yahweh* and *Elohim.*

Yeshua: Aramaic for Jesus; in Hebrew, *Yoshua,* "Yahweh delivers."

Yesod: Foundation; ninth Sefirah; also called Righteous One, Holy Tzaddik.

Yetzirah: Universe of formation; astral dimension, universe; outer heavens; reality of human spirits and orders of angels, the lesser angels.